Kinsey

OTHER NEWMARKET PRESS BOOKS BY BILL CONDON

Gods and Monsters: The Shooting Script
Chicago: The Movie and Lyrics

Kinsey

Public and Private

Introduction by Jonathan Gathorne-Hardy

A Brief History of Alfred Kinsey by Linda Wolfe

Final Shooting Script by Bill Condon

A Newmarket Pictorial Moviebook

Newmarket Press • New York

Copyright © 2004 by Twentieth Century Fox

Introduction by Jonathan Gathorne-Hardy © 2004 by Jonathan Gathorne-Hardy
A Brief History of Alfred Kinsey © 2004 by Linda Wolfe
A Conversation with Bill Condon © 2004 by Rob Feld

Acknowledgment of permission to use copyrighted material is listed
in the acknowledgments on page 349.

This book is published in the United States of America.

First Edition

1 2 3 4 5 6 7 8 9 10

Library of Congress Cataloging-in-Publication Data available upon request

ISBN 1-55704-647-6

Designer: Charles Kreloff
Editorial Consultants: Christopher Measom, Steven Jacobson
Creative Consultants: Breena Camden, Healey Young, Megan Colligan
Photo Editor of Movie Stills: Paula Davidson
Photographer of Movie Stills: Ken Regan/Camera 5

QUANTITY PURCHASES

Companies, professional groups, clubs, and other organizations may qualify
for special terms when ordering quantities of this title. For information, write Special Sales
Department, Newmarket Press, 18 East 48th Street, New York, NY 10017;
call (212) 832-3575; fax (212) 832-3629; or e-mail mailbox@newmarketpress.com.

www.newmarketpress.com

Manufactured in the United States of America

Contents

Part One

Kinsey: His Life and Legacy

Introduction

Kinsey—The Man and the Film

By Jonathan Gathorne-Hardy

I FIRST READ KINSEY'S *Sexual Behavior in the Human Male* in 1949. I was sixteen. My father, who was a doctor, had bought it when it came out. To me, electrified, it read as a work of erotic revelation. It seemed quite clear, for instance, that I should be allowed to sleep with my sixteen-year-old girlfriend—almost impossible in middle-class, late 1940s Britain. This frustration continued till I was twenty. I think it was this initial fascination that really led me to agree when my publisher suggested I write Kinsey's biography. In June 1995 I arrived in Bloomington, Indiana, therefore, very curious. I knew already that all biographies are, to some extent, autobiographies. Would I have anything in common with Alfred Kinsey? I discovered, not much—but what we did share was crucial.

Kinsey's own sexual frustration, agonizing to a highly sexed man, continued till he was twenty-seven, when he finally, and with considerable difficulty made love to his wife, Clara Kinsey—Mac. His anger at his frustration, his bewilderment at his ignorance about sexual matters, made him determined that others, especially his students (as ignorant and often as frustrated as him) shouldn't suffer like him—these were two of the main motives behind his later work. (Later, because in fact he spent the first years of his working life as a successful, indeed acclaimed entomologist—much longer than he spent doing sex research.)

But behind this early sexual suppression lay the formidable figure of his bullying, Methodist father and his harsh, puritanical regime. As I read Kinsey's letters and talked to those who had known him, to his family, to those he had sex with, I uncovered a more and more complex figure. He fought free of his father, yet he himself was often aggressive and could be a bully. He was extremely intelligent and extremely impatient with those less intelligent—often to the irritation of the faculty at Indiana University. He was secretive, ruthless in achieving his ends. Even though inherently a very moral man, he was sometimes prepared to side-step conventional morality in pursuit of his sex histories (he once, for example, decided not to do anything about a prostitute who told him she'd knifed her unfaithful pimp/husband. To betray confidences would end them). From the start, again long before his sex research, he was an obsessive work-alcoholic (as was his younger brother, oddly enough).

At the same time, he was sensitive, extremely musical (nearly a concert pianist). In their house, it was Kinsey who did the flowers (he grew two hundred varieties of iris); he was a slapdash cook, a father who, though strict, not only loved his children but bathed them, washed their diapers, fed them when small, and read to them at night—all not usual for fathers in the 1920s and 1930s. He was bisexual, fell in love with at least one man, yet continued to love his wife till he died, as she him—though the dynamics in a marriage are always opaque to those on the outside (and often to those inside).

And Kinsey had a compassionate heart. He used to come back, his cheeks wet with tears, after hearing about some sexual, or just life, catastrophe. The files at the Kinsey Institute in Bloomington are full of letters of great kindness—offering advice, sympathy and, to the poor, quite often sending money, which was clearly not expected back.

When Gail Mutrux asked me if my biography of Kinsey could be used as research material for the film she was planning, my first thought, therefore, was—how on earth could you tell the story, with any degree of accuracy and fullness, of this complicated, contradictory, driven, often difficult, yet also often moving man? I imagined that Bill Condon would take some key incidents, or even a single one, and concoct a film. This in fact is what had happened with my last biography, of the British writer Gerald Brenan.

But I realized as soon as I began to receive the scripts, which were sent to me for my comments, that Condon was planning something far more ambitious and far more difficult—an accurate, complete but also dramatic bio-pic, a full film biography. And as I read the scripts, I realized he was succeeding—and this was confirmed when I finally saw the film. He has indeed succeeded. This is so seldom achieved, it is worth seeing why and how.

There are two strokes of genius: One we see, or hear in fact without at first seeing, in the first moments of the film; the second is in the casting. All sex surveys and studies of sexual behavior depend on people telling everything and telling the truth. No matter how probing your questions or how representative and large your sample, if this doesn't happen you might as well give up. Kinsey was an interviewer of genius and the instrument he evolved to obtain the truth was the most subtle, most searching and by far the most effective that had ever been used before, or has ever been used since. It took over a year to learn how to use it. It is the reason, in my view, why Kinsey's research far surpasses, in accuracy and depth, anything that has come since.

Kinsey hadn't the remotest interest in drama, but it was the power of his interviewing technique that Condon spotted and, by focusing on it, gave himself one of the most intense and dramatic forms of dialogue in theatrical history—that of question and answer. It was first discovered—or invented—by Plato two and a half thousand years ago and used for his dialogues with Socrates. It has remained popular ever since, culminating in today's courtroom scenes in plays and films. It is how Condon's film begins and, running like a thread right through it, allows him to demonstrate with both economy and vividness Kinsey's rigor as a scientist, his relationship with his team, some of his childhood, and the character of his father, and then to follow Kinsey out across America, to every corner, in his heroic voyage to uncover sexual behavior.

The second stroke of genius, the casting, centers on Liam Neeson. He was an inspired choice. This is not just because he is a very good actor indeed, but also because he has something you can't simulate. Jack Tebbel, very close to the research, said this about Kinsey to me: "You felt, you could actually *feel*, here was someone outstanding. He emanated power. The only other person I met, who seemed at first mild, but radiated power and strength in the same way was Einstein." It is this power you feel coming off the screen from Neeson's Kinsey.

Laura Linney, as his wife Mac, was another inspired choice. She is, quite simply, brilliant. And here Condon penetrates that opaqueness I said surrounded every marriage. That between the film Kinsey and film Mac is sometimes humorous, often moving, from their first difficulties, both virgins, making love (one reason was the exceptional largeness of Kinsey's penis), to her hurt when with great honesty he explains his bisexuality, to his final appeal for, and expression of, love at the end just before he dies. A biographer isn't allowed to penetrate the opaqueness, but a creative screenwriter is so allowed—and I think it must have been something like this.

The last casting stroke of genius is Peter Sarsgaard as Clyde Martin. And here another aspect of Condon's writing/directing becomes evident—compression. In the film, Martin seduces Kinsey. I rather doubt this happened—though it is conceivable. I suspect, though actually unusual, it was the other way about. But it allows Condon to illustrate an unsuspected side of Kinsey—his sexual diffidence, his sensitivity to rejection. He found it difficult to make the first advance. Yet the kernel of this moment in the film is completely accurate—Martin was one of the great loves of his life (the other was Mac).

Diffident—but also extremely bold. The film shirks nothing—not just his bisexuality, but his experiments with pain and pleasure, his encouraging of very free sexual behaviors between his team and their wives, in which he and Mac joined in, his less than ideal treatment of his son, Bruce. And by the sort of elision and compression demonstrated by the character of Sarsgaard's Martin (wonderfully acted incidentally), Condon is able to do what I had imagined impossible, to cover Kinsey's whole life—his childhood, his rows with his father, his twenty years of obsessive and painstaking science with gall wasps. And this enables the film, like Kinsey's life, to take on an epic quality—the humble beginnings, fighting for acceptance in a disapproved of and pioneering field, years of intolerably hard work, triumph, and then, with the furious popular reception and popular rejection of his female volume, the collapse of his funding and the plunge into despair. Kinsey died thinking he had failed.

It remains only to ask: What had he achieved and does this (and therefore a film about him) have any relevance to day?

Kinsey has been credited (or blamed) for more or less single-handedly bringing about the "sexual revolution" of the 1960s and 1970s, that great movement of increased tolerance towards personal, noninvasive sexual behavior. He himself would not have agreed. He felt that by far the greatest engine of social change in this regard was the Second World War and its aftermath. Besides, his work was not about changing anything but rather about seeking knowledge—he simply wanted to find out about *what had already happened*, how people were actually behaving. Nevertheless, works that describe and crystallize social change as it is happening are indeed very influential in speeding it along—I think of Betty Friedan writing in 1963 and the movement toward feminism and female liberation, or of Rousseau in the eighteenth century. In this respect, Kinsey had enormous effect—especially as regards homosexuals.

As to relevance—it seems to me that he and therefore this film have more relevance today than at any time since the 1950s. Now, as then, conservative and religious repressive forces are in the ascendant. Once again, vigorous and unpleasant attempts are being made to regulate personal and private sexual lives in an illiberal way—especially of gays. Kinsey is significant again as a symbol of common sense and tolerance.

And the film, with its emphasis on his careful science, implicitly refutes scurrilous attacks still being made on him. It has been suggested, for example, that he deliberately weighted his findings to exaggerate the figures for homosexuality. This is demonstrable nonsense—and in my biography (*Kinsey: Sex the Measure of All Things*, Indiana University Press, paperback $18), I demonstrate it. Or the accusation that he encouraged pedophiles. Why should he do this? He wanted to find out what people actually did—not encourage them to do anything in particular. He interviewed pedophiles in pursuit of this, but to accuse him of "encouraging" them is as ludicrous as saying those investigating HIV are "encouraging" AIDS.

Finally, Kinsey is relevant to us in the most direct way possible. Almost at the end of the film comes one of its most moving moments, when Kinsey in his last interview—Condon again employing the question-answer dialogue as effortlessly and effectively as Plato—learns how he helped a guilty, desperate and despairing woman, marvelously played by Lynn Redgrave, move in middle age into a happy and successful relationship with another woman. *Of course,* he hadn't failed. There are as many people with sexual problems now as there were then—and Kinsey and this film, by reviving his stance of tolerance, can still help them.

A Brief
History of
Alfred Kinsey

by Linda Wolfe

Alfred Kinsey: A Pioneer

ALFRED C. KINSEY was one of the most important—and controversial—figures of the twentieth century. Scientist, taxonomist, and author of two groundbreaking books, the 1948 *Sexual Behavior in the Human Male*, later dubbed "The Kinsey Report," and the 1953 *Sexual Behavior in the Human Female*, Kinsey in his own day was revered by millions, reviled by some. What's particularly fascinating about him, however, is that in recent years, as more and more details about Kinsey's life and work have surfaced, he's become an even more polarizing figure. The movie *Kinsey* is an attempt to see the man whole, to remind people of his remarkable achievements while refusing to shy away from the unusual activities that he and his famous Institute for Sex Research kept hidden from the public.

The achievements are in the end the reason Kinsey's name has lasted.

And those achievements were far from minor. Kinsey changed the national conversation, set us to talking about a sub-

Alfred Kinsey photographed in 1950 by portrait, fashion and erotic photographer George Platt Lynes.

ject Americans never discussed publicly, and only rarely discussed privately: sexual behavior. It is difficult to imagine, in today's climate of sexual openness, how extraordinary that feat was. But America in the 1930s and 1940s, when Kinsey first began studying sexual behavior, was a different world.

It was a world in which homosexuality and adultery were viewed as criminal. In which masturbation was seen as a cause of mental illness, premarital sex was considered immoral, and common sexual practices like fellatio and cunnilingus were deemed perverted.

Moreover, it was a world in which there were no hints that sex played a central role in life. There were no explicit depictions of sex in the movies. Hollywood's filmmakers, observing a strict self-censorship code, avoided not only the suggestion that married men or women engaged in sex outside their marriages, but even that they engaged in sex *within* their marriages—they never showed married couples sleeping in anything but separate beds. Nor were there allusions to sex in the sweetly romantic songs played on the radio, nor late-night comedians delivering double entendre jokes on the infant TV, no magazines showing nude women or men, no words like penis, vagina, sexual intercourse— not to mention their more colorful vernacular terms—used in the pages of newspapers or popular books.

Indeed, there was no hint at all that when it came to sex, American society was anything but ignorant, and obedient to the strictest of moral and religious prohibitions. But in reality, many Americans were busily ignoring the sexual rules. Secretly and often with a searing amount of guilt, they were pursuing the very activities that religious and moral authorities proscribed—and a great many others to boot.

Kinsey, who began collecting what he called "sexual histories" in 1938 and eventually obtained and analyzed thousands of them, was determined to throw light on the hidden actualities of American sexual behavior. His detailed books about how we as a people went about sex were not the first to talk openly about sex-

A typical family scene, c. 1950.

ual behavior. After the Revolutionary War, a popular book, *Aristotle's Master-Piece Completed,* written by an anonymous physician, provided information on how to accomplish reproduction and advised husbands to stimulate their wives during intercourse—but gave few details as to how to go about this. After the Civil War, marital guides became a staple of publishing, although they still tended to be quite vague in their advice. In the early years of the twentieth century a few doctor-composed sex manuals—still written, ostensibly, only for the married—got down to specifics. Most famous was Theodor van de Velde's *Ideal Marriage—Its Physiology, and Technique,* published in 1930, which detailed foreplay, erotic parts of the body, and ten—count 'em—intercourse positions. By then a few sexologists, most notably the reform-minded British writer Henry Havelock Ellis, had begun

Let's Look at the Data

Alfred Kinsey's legacy is three-fold. He was the first sex scientist to talk about sex dispassionately and nonjudgmentally. Second, Kinsey was an observer and a describer rather than a theorist—prior to Kinsey, professionals engaged in theorizing without any data. And third, Kinsey came in when everybody was running about panicking and said, "Calm down. Lets just look around and see if there's really a fire. Let's not panic, let's look at the data." This was the first time anyone had done that.

Aristotle's Master-Piece, *a Revolutionary War–era sex manual.*

The study on female sexuality was extremely controversial because our society wanted to look at women as mothers, housewives and caretakers, not as sexual beings, and Kinsey exploded that myth. Kinsey's influence on the general population is still happening today. It cannot be overestimated, particularly for women, because before Kinsey, female sexuality was not talked about. It was seen as problematic and something that needed to be suppressed, and of course, it wasn't understood. Nobody knew anything about female sexuality, although researchers—mostly male—were only too happy to tell us about it. Again, Kinsey said, "Let's look at the data. That's how we'll find what people actually do and how they feel about it." His data showed that women were self-pleasuring, they were having sex with men, they were having sex with women, they had sexual feelings and thoughts, and you couldn't ignore it.

I teach undergraduates and I talk to women in their teens and twenties every week, and sometimes I think we haven't moved forward at all. On the other hand, there's been a tremendous change because even my eighteen- and nineteen-year-olds from very sexually repressive backgrounds have much more information about sexuality than women did before. Some of it is wrong, but they have knowledge, particularly about things like the clitoris. In the fifties, nobody knew anything about the clitoris. Women thought they were just a giant, walking vagina. Girls now know that they're not and that they have other options. As a sexologist, there isn't a day that goes by that I don't refer to Kinsey's body of data. It's that helpful and important to our field. So I live with him every day.

—Janice M. Epp, Ph.D., Dean of Students at
The Institute for Advanced Study of Human
Sexuality in San Francisco, November 2003

analyzing the physiology of sex and somewhat haphazardly collecting and publishing data on sexual habits, primarily the sex habits of women. Most of the authors relied on very small samples, although in 1931, one prominent gynecologist, Robert Latou Dickinson, published a book that contained the rudimentary sex histories of five-thousand female patients.

A blizzard of subsequent investigations of American sexual behavior eventually tempered some of his findings. But in their day Kinsey's studies were the boldest and the most widely disseminated, exploding on the national consciousness like the atomic bomb that had made its first appearance just a few years earlier and producing, just as that bomb did, widespread and stunning fallout. Indeed, so influential were the books that arguably, when it comes to sex, we are what we are today because of Alfred C. Kinsey.

A Religious Boyhood

At first glance it seems unlikely that, given his childhood, he would grow up to become a pioneer of sex research. Born in 1894, he was raised in Hoboken, New Jersey, by a passive mother and a tyrannical, repressive father, a Sunday school teacher obsessed with religion and cleanliness. Kinsey had a brother and sister, and their father, who never addressed the subject of sex directly, nevertheless managed to communicate to them that touching their private parts was sinful, that even nocturnal emissions were shameful, and that they were to avoid close contact with the opposite sex. To adult eyes, little Alfred seemed thoroughly dutiful to his father's dictums. He was a good little boy who regularly accompanied his father to church services, sometimes several a day on Sundays, who concentrated on his homework during the week and at school was so standoffish with other children that he was known as a loner. He was also a sickly child, suffering before

he was ten years old three major illnesses, first, a case of rickets that left him with a lifelong curvature of the spine, next, rheumatic fever, and finally, typhoid—the last two diseases forcing him to spend months in bed and isolating him even further from friendships. But he did occasionally have contact with other children. And on at least one occasion he had, while playing, a memorable and probably formative sexual experience, one he was eventually to spell out to an associate. When he was about nine years old, he and a group of playmates went down to the basement of the Kinsey home, where they examined one another's genitalia and poked straws into various apertures.

When he was ten, his family moved to South Orange, New Jersey, where Kinsey, now recovered from his illnesses, finished grade school. There, unable or unwilling to engage in competitive sports, he was the frequent butt of bullying by tougher boys. But shortly he discovered an athletic activity at which he could excel. Advised by a doctor to get more fresh air, he took up hiking, exploring the woods and marshes and rolling hills that surrounded his town, walking for miles, collecting weeds and wildflowers and leaves and pressing them in a book his father gave him.

Collecting was a passion with him, as it is with many young boys. He'd been taught to play the piano and appreciate classical music, and in addition to his flora collection, he collected—sometimes scrimping and denying himself other boyhood treats—orchestral recordings. But collecting also had a compulsive aspect for Kinsey. Jonathan Gathorne-Hardy, author of the biography of *Kinsey: Sex the Measure of All Things,* says, "When Kinsey collected he *collected.* Intrigued by a puzzling (and unknown) aspect of male masturbation, which was most easily recorded on film, most researchers would have been content with fifty, perhaps, or a hundred examples. Kinsey had well over a thousand—possibly as many as two thousand—filmed sequences of different men masturbating to orgasm." The biographer concludes, "There is a suggestion here of comforting and reassuring oneself, like eat-

Above: Kinsey (standing, second from left) with his eighth grade class in 1908.

Below: Kinsey's great aunt Lizzie's home in Broadway, New Jersey, was a Kinsey family vacation spot.

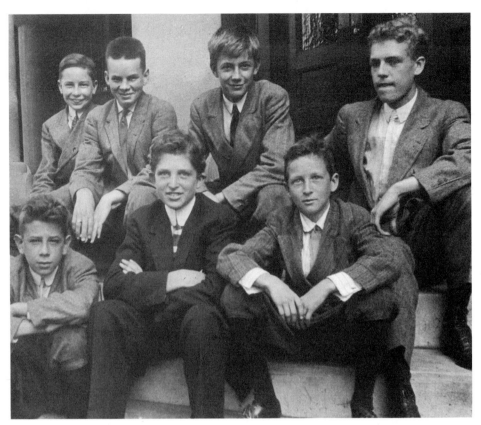

Kinsey (top right) sits with boys from his Sunday school class, c. 1910.

ing," and speculates that for the lonely boy, "Pressed leaves and butterflies took the place of friendship," thus setting the stage for his adult drive to amass more and more of whatever it was he set out to collect.

There are other ways in which one can read the man in the life of the boy. Take his fascination with biology, which began early in high school when he came under the influence of a dedicated high school biology teacher. He not only studied with her but joined her after-school biology club, learning on field trips how to observe and understand the habits of birds and insects. He would go on observational field trips the rest of his life, although eventually his quarry would be human beings.

Then there are his formidable abilities as a speaker and his

Variation and Expression

Kinsey enlightened the world. Before his work, general thought was that a lot of people weren't sexual or didn't have varied sexual behaviors. It really validated the fact that people are sexual beings and he pointed out an important concept: there's enormous variation in sexual attraction and expression and that variation itself doesn't need to be labeled as normal or pathological but simply as a variation.

If we look back at the attitudes of sexuality a lot was inherited from Victorian England and was dominated by a Judeo Christian ethic. Sexuality was only for procreation. Kinsey's information helped people feel more comfortable about sexuality.

He broke ground and opened the door for other people to do research studies. That said, sex research in America today has a lot of growth yet to do. There are people doing sex research but certainly not as much in other kinds of human behavior. There is political opposition, and it's very difficult to get funding for sex research unless it deals with risky types of behavior.

The kind of work that I'm doing at the Kinsey Institute involves a look at an aspect of risk behavior that hasn't been investigated much: dealing with the errors and problems that people have using condoms. We're finding that these problems are leaving people vulnerable to unintended pregnancies and sexually transmitted infections. This is the type of information that we should be stressing in both school and in public health areas.

—William Yarber, Professor of Applied Health Science
at Indiana University, and Professor of Gender Studies and a
senior research fellow to The Kinsey Institute, November 2003

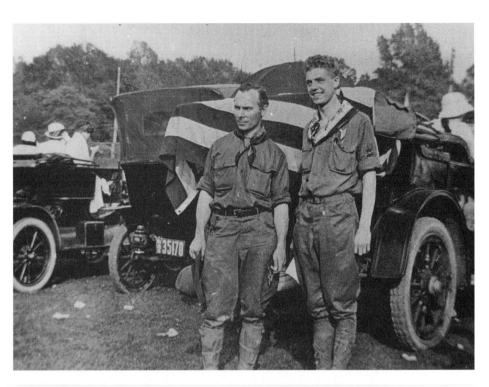

extraordinary powers of persuasion. That too began when he was young. At the insistence of his evangelical father, Kinsey learned to preach and by the time he was sixteen, regularly delivered the Word of God to his father's Sunday school students. He was always to be a preacher—although in time he would preach not religion but sexual liberation.

But perhaps the most powerful predictor of the man Alfred Kinsey was to become came from his adolescent experiences in the Boy Scouts of America. Scouting was in its early days largely a Christian movement. Prayers opened every meeting, prayers sent the children home. Kinsey's father saw the scouts as an organization that would further his son's religiosity. He also saw it, as did many Americans of the time, as a means of toughening up a boy.

Kinsey Sr., and even Kinsey himself, may have felt the young high school student needed to be more manly. Not popular with the boys at his school—"We thought he was a sissy guy," one of his classmates recollected, "feminine-like, like a girl"—Kinsey flung himself into scouting. He wore his uniform constantly, passed in record speed and with flying colors all the required tests in knot tying, fire starting, woodland crafts, first aid, and in short order found himself leading camping trips, teaching younger scouts, just as he himself had been taught, the skills needed when observing birds and flowers and wildlife.

He also attempted to tutor his tenderfoots about sex, or at least to answer, as best he was able, their questions about the subject. Many boys—Kinsey among them—were troubled because they masturbated. "Pity the boy who has wrong ideas" about his sexual fluid, cautioned the 1914 *Boy Scouts Handbook*. "Any habit which a boy has that causes this fluid to be discharged from the body tends to weaken his strength, to make him less able to resist disease, and often unfortunately fastens upon him habits which in later life can be broken only with great difficulty." Convinced that this was so, and himself suffering from great guilt about what was then known as "self-abuse," Kinsey advised his

Eagle Scout Kinsey (above, right) in 1913, and (below) the following year in South Orange, New Jersey.

Above: Kinsey and his boy's club.

Right: Kinsey when he was a counselor at Camp Wyanoke, New Hampshire.

younger charges to pray for God's help in resisting the urge to masturbate—an early effort at sexual counseling that is re-created in the movie *Kinsey* in a scene drawn from Kinsey's own sexual history.

His advice didn't keep his juniors from masturbating. Nor was he able to give up the practice himself. But his scouting days brought about one important change in the teenager. Idolized by the younger boys and reveling in their regard, he at last learned how to have friends—at least friends younger than himself. He would never lose his delight in having such friends. For the rest of his life he would find playing tutor to the young or the uninformed his preferred role. It was why he became a teacher—one

A New Life

I don't think I ever really knew the impact Kinsey had until I took a group of graduate students to Sweden around 1980. We used to spend the summer in Sweden—which was very far ahead of us in terms of sexuality at that time—and hire people to come in and talk to us about their lives.

That summer we asked an elderly Swedish man who was gay to talk about his homosexuality and gay life in Sweden because in 1980 American students did not know anything about gay life. So, he came in and told an amazing story reflecting on the power of Kinsey's work. Raised in rural Sweden, he first had sex in a barn when he was a teenager—the mother of a friend seduced him. He didn't care for it. Six months later she seduced him again with the same results. He went his whole life feeling he was different, but not knowing why and never discussing it with anyone.

Then Kinsey's book came out and he read everything, including this thing about men who are attracted to men. The following year, when he was fifty-two, he had a job in Korea, where he was approached by a young man who asked if he would like a woman. "No," he answered. So the young entrepreneur countered with, "How about a man?" And this 70-some-odd-year-old Swede told my students, "I thought back to what I read in Kinsey and I said, 'okay'." And he had sex with a man for the first time at fifty-two—the first time he ever had a fulfilling sexual orgasm. He thanked Kinsey for giving him this new life—a sexual life. Think about how many people in the world were affected like that.

Kinsey made sexuality a science. He gave us the right to study it as we would anything else that was important to humanity. And I don't think it's so much Kinsey's work that is controversial as the topic of sexuality itself. That has always been taboo. An orgasm is a very powerful physical expression and if you don't know that it's just a physiological experience, it's very scary.

Talking about sex was radical. Asking them about their sexual behavior was *very* radical.

There are still problems around funding talks about sexuality to adolescents. This whole idea of abstinence education where you can talk about not having sex but you can't talk about the consequences of having sex—that's insane.

Kinsey was way ahead of his time.

—Professor Ronald Moglia, New York University's Department of
Applied Psychology in the Steinhardt School of Education, November 2003

of his daughters said that he was happiest when imparting knowledge—and interestingly, when he started his researches into sex, he invariably surrounded himself with colleagues younger than himself.

If scouting provided Kinsey with his first social success, scholarship was to provide him with even greater rewards. For years he had been an industrious, indefatigable student, and in his senior year of high school, he reaped the rewards of his labor. "Alfred is our staid and steadfast student," said the inscription under his photograph in his senior yearbook. "Dignity, learning, and ability are all written upon his unruffled brow." More importantly, his academic excellence had garnered him if not popularity at least a goodly amount of admiration. He was voted his class's "Brightest" and "Most Respected" boy, and his official "Class Prophecy" predicted he would become a world-class scientist— "a second Darwin."

A second Darwin. After his graduation, those words must have reverberated through Kinsey's brain, fueling dreams of a career in biology. But first there was the summer to get through. As usual, he went as a counselor to a Boy Scout camp. But this summer, something unusual happened. He became infatuated with one of his campers, a handsome intense fifteen-year-old. He and the object of his affections wrote to each other frequently once camp was over and curiously Kinsey, who threw away nearly all the letters he received during his adolescence, saved this boy's letters his entire life. He also threw away the minutes of the numerous boyhood scout meetings he attended. But he saved one set of minutes, one that reported that "After repeating the Lord's Prayer," fifteen scouts "passed their tenderfoot." The fifteen are named, and one of the names is that of the boy to whom Kinsey had been so drawn. Years later he would point to his attraction to this camper as a crucial incident in his life—his first inkling that he had homosexual longings.

In the fall Kinsey set off for college. But it was not to study biology. It was to study engineering.

The subject was forced on him by his father. Kinsey Sr. was the head of a nonacademic department at a prominent, nearby school, The Stevens Institute of Technology. But he'd yearned for a better station in life, longed to be an engineer like the more eminent members of the faculty. Now, he expected young Alfred to fulfill his own lost dreams. Over his son's objections, and despite his stated preference for biology, he insisted the teenager study engineering and do so at the very place at which he worked, Stevens. Kinsey gave in.

Two years later, however, he decided to resist his father. He'd been bored and frustrated at Stevens and even, for the first time in his life, getting poor grades. Defiantly, he told Alfred Sr. that now that he was twenty years old, he was going to fashion his own future. Become a biologist.

It was not an easy thing to do battle with Kinsey Sr. "Grandfather Kinsey was a hard man," a nephew of Kinsey's would one day say. He was also immensely controlling. Kinsey *must* go to Stevens, he insisted, *must* become an engineer. If he didn't, he threatened, he would cease supporting him financially. But young Alfred, as not just this incident but many from his later life would show, was just as stubborn as his father. He resisted the older man for weeks, and the two of them engaged in fierce, furious verbal fights and scorching displays of temper.

It was the younger Kinsey who won. One day he simply upped and left home—with no support from his family except for a new suit, worth twenty-five dollars. Bowdoin College in Maine had offered him a scholarship, and he felt certain he could work and earn the rest of the money he needed.

It was the beginning of the end of his domination by his father. Not once in the future would he ever again defer to the man or court his approval. Nor would he ever gain insight into his father's demons. In the movie *Kinsey*, director and scriptwriter Bill Condon, imagines a touching and reconciliatory scene between Kinsey and his father, an encounter set in the family home at the time of the death of Kinsey's mother.

Above: Alfred Kinsey (center) with (from left to right) his mother Sarah Ann, his brother Robert, his sister Mildred and his father Alfred Seguine Kinsey in 1917.

Below: Three generations of Kinsey men: Alfred C., his infant son Donald, and his father Alfred S. in 1922.

Talking Ethics

Dr. Kinsey changed the dialogue about sexuality in America, breaking the centuries-old silence about sexuality. By getting America to talk about these issues, he changed the way we think about them.

Kinsey said, "America, you are having more sex than you knew, with more variety. Talking about this is a good thing." Kinsey helped start a new national conversation on sex. The last fifty years have shaped the current dialogue in America. Our sexual understandings have changed dramatically: the Pill, the women's movement, new understandings of sexual orientation and gender identity, new medications and so on have changed the way people act and think about sexuality. The dialogue that Kinsey helped start needs to continue because we are still the most culturally confused society in the world on these issues.

It is natural for people think about sex, but it's talking about sex that enables us to make healthy decisions. As a minister, I try to help people talk ethically about their sexuality and to remember that it is a life-giving and life-fulfilling gift from God. We owe young people an opportunity, with adult guidance and adult supervision, to have full access to good information.

—The Reverend Debra W. Haffner, director of the Religious Institute on Sexual Morality, Justice and Healing, an ecumenical interfaith organization of religious leaders committed to sexual health, education, and justice, November 2003

Saying Isn't Doing

Kinsey changed the way people and researchers look at sex. He made us realize that sexual behavior, or sex, is no different than any other behavior; it has a great deal of variety. He also showed us that there's a big difference in what people say and what they do. And that is a great thing to know about.

Most people thought that males just needed one switch to be turned on. Of course that's a lie, but at least that was the mythology. Women, on the other hand, were supposed to be very reserved and virginal until marriage. What he showed, however, is that women's sexual behavior was quite varied. There were women who were not virgins when they got married, there were women who liked sex, there were women who masturbated and there were women who did many things, which, quote, "proper" women at the time were not supposed to do.

This is still a field today that many people don't think we ought to study scientifically. Yet, what was one of the biggest sellers last year, pharmaceutically? Viagra. What does that tell you about public need? Are people interested in sex? Of course. Kinsey took it out of the bathroom and brought it into the living room.

—Milton Diamond, University of Hawaii School of Medicine, November 2003

Nevertheless, while at Bowdoin, Kinsey continued the strict religious observance Kinsey Sr. had imbued in him. He prayed and attended church regularly, and went on working for Christian organizations, the Boy Scouts still, and also the YMCA, the Young Men's Christian Association. In his role as counselor to youths in those groups, he continued to provide superficial guidance about sex, on occasion revealing in the process that his own guilt over masturbation had continued.

In a few years he would he give up his faith, indeed develop a loathing for religion. "The whole army of religion," he would one day tell a friend, "is our central enemy." But if he freed himself from his father's religiosity, he would never be altogether free of the man. His personality—he was often autocratic and argumentative—resembled his father's. Some of his obsessions—he was fiercely insistent on personal cleanliness—were the same as his father's. And his reaction against paternal control shaped the rest of his life. It extended in some respects, writes Gathorne-Hardy, "to a reaction against all authority," making him into a man who "liked to shock," who "enjoyed knocking people off balance."

Kinsey's career at Bowdoin was a sterling one. He distinguished himself, won the admiration of his professors, and was accepted for graduate school at Harvard. There, yearning for recognition, he buried himself in his work, studying entomology and concentrating his research efforts on a particular bug, the gall wasp.

Tall now, and handsome, with a gleaming shock of yellow hair, a sunny smile, and a twinkle in his eyes, he attracted the attention of female students and university office workers. But he kept them at a distance, not once inviting any of them out on a date.

He wasn't much interested in extracurricular activities, either. "Recreational pursuits had little claim on Kinsey," notes James Jones in his biography, *Alfred C. Kinsey: A Public/Private Life*. "Complete relaxation...was something I never knew him to achieve," wrote Edgar Anderson, a fellow graduate student.

On a gall wasp trip to Mexico in 1935, Kinsey stands bare-chested, center.

Anderson was one of Kinsey's only friends during those Harvard years. The budding young scientist was still very much a loner. But as always, he enjoyed going on field trips, and Anderson, who went with him on one, was awed by his woodland skills. Kinsey "built the smallest cooking fire I had ever seen," Anderson recalled, and "In less time than it takes to be served in a restaurant, we had a pleasant meal and no scar was left on the landscape." Moreover, Kinsey extinguished every last spark of coal, buried the cooking cans under a rock, and carefully collected and folded up all their paper refuse.

His meticulousness, apparent in everything he did, combined with his intense dedication to his studies, paid off. In 1920 he was offered an assistant professorship in the Zoology Department of Indiana University in Bloomington, Indiana, heart of the Midwest.

Coming of Age in Bloomington

Bloomington was a very small town in those days, a community of 13,000 people, a rural place still ringed by pastureland and virgin forests. The university, too, was small, with a mere 2,300 or so undergraduates and only a few departments offering graduate courses. Kinsey, with his Harvard training, envisioned becoming a permanent and prominent member of the faculty, for most of his colleagues were low-level scientists. He also dreamed of changing his life, of finally being more socially active than he'd been in the past. But the friends he made were, it turned out, casual, his relationships superficial and built around his same old hobbies of camping and nature walks.

That changed, however, when a young graduate student, Clara McMillen, set her cap for him. A plain-faced woman, Clara was small-boned, boyish-looking and very athletic. She was also a brilliant student, highly serious about her studies, and determined to pursue the shy new professor of zoology—he was winsome, had an endearing smile, and besides, he was one of the only unattached males in the department. On a departmental picnic Clara tried to attract Kinsey's attention by deliberating tripping and plunging down a hillside. Later that afternoon, when it came time to eat, she chose to sit beside him.

The two soon began dating—if dating can be the word for the series of tests Kinsey put her through, arduous hikes, expeditions and camping trips on which he invariably invited not just Mac but other people as well. Even the presents he bought for her were hardly the stuff of intimacy—among his gifts to her that first year were a knife, a compass, and a pair of hiking boots.

But he had been smitten. Clara McMillen—he'd called her Mac by then—he told an associate years later, was the first person with whom he ever fell in love. She was also, it would turn out, to be a member of a very small company, for he was to fall in love only two more times in his life. His other two loves were men.

Alfred Kinsey and Clara "Mac" McMillen's wedding, June 1921.

In June 1921 Mac and Kinsey got married. They were both virgins. They remained virginal throughout their honeymoon—a strenuous hiking expedition through the White Mountains of New Hampshire—and for several months after that, months during which they worked as camp counselors at a rugged girls' camp in Vermont. They tried to have intercourse. But Kinsey was unable to penetrate Mac's vagina. Their mutual lack of experi-

The Kinsey Mission

The Kinsey Institute has three aspects to its mission: to promote scientific research in the areas of human sexuality, to archive and collect materials related to sexuality for interdisciplinary scholarship in human sexuality, and to educate professionals in the fields that use sexuality or have to integrate sexuality into their work. Kinsey believed that if you presented scientific information to people about problems that were facing society, that it could really transform how society dealt with issues related to sexuality. He tried to apply the same rigorous science he used to study gall wasps to the study of human sexuality. He wanted do it in a dispassionate, scientific way. That said, I think he was a passionate man with respect to the rights and treatment of humans in relation to sexuality.

His detailed methodology, focusing on so many aspects of what people could do behaviorally, was new and he wanted to get a large sample because he believed in numbers. He felt if you knew a lot about a lot of people, then you'd know something about society in general. There are no other studies with those numbers and that kind of detailed interviewing. Of course we have to look at that work in terms of the science of the day. They didn't have the kind of techniques we have now for sampling, and people are much more open to this kind of scientific research now. But Kinsey was remarkable at getting people to open up and he was very good at detecting lies, so that work stands as setting up the field for a more scientific approach to the study of sexuality. Those volumes still serve as wonderful texts for how to take a sex history. In fact many of the questions that Kinsey raised remain unanswered.

I often think about how sexuality and particularly Kinsey's work still spark so much controversy. It reflects an anxiety that if we talk about sexuality, if we share information, somehow that will erode the sexual mores of society. I think the majority actually are quite open to information and want young people to learn about sexuality.

Things have changed, but so has our society. Gender dynamics have changed tremendously. There are more women in the workplace and this influences how people conduct their personal lives; their pair-bonding lives, their family lives, and their sexual lives. Two of the biggest changes since Kinsey's studies are the age people get married and the number of partners they have before marriage. But this was a trend that was already starting. Kinsey's documentation is what made people a little bit anxious.

I see Kinsey as a very brave person because he undertook the scientific study of sexuality despite what he knew would be difficult times getting it accepted. When the female volume came out he was criticized for trying to undermine the American family.

The fact that it emerged from the heartland helped people accept it as a reflection of what people across the country were doing. Kinsey also got to do some of his work while the focus of the media was on the war and not on what he was doing. So he got to quietly do his work until there was enough of it to be published.

—Stephanie A. Sanders, Associate Director of The Kinsey Institute for Research in Sex, Gender, and Reproduction and Associate Professor of Gender Studies at Indiana University, November 2003

ence, her apprehensiveness, and his hesitancy, Kinsey later told a friend, all played a role in frustrating their efforts.

In the fall, back in Bloomington, they sought advice from a local doctor. He examined Mac, reported that she had an overly thick hymen, and performed a minor—and not uncommon—surgical procedure to make penetration possible.

In years to come Kinsey would decry the sexual ignorance and inhibitions that society imposed on young people while simultaneously expecting them to overcome their training the moment they got married. "There is no magic in the marriage ceremony which can accomplish this," he would write, and as a result, "a very high proportion of females [and] a considerable number of males" suffered sexual frustrations that could take years to overcome.

In his own case, Kinsey overcame his ignorance and inhibitions by studying sex manuals, approaching the task with the same doggedness he'd applied to his academic studies. The results were, as they always were when he gave himself over to learning, superb. He and Mac tried out many new sexual positions and activities, and he was delighted by Mac's responsiveness—so delighted that one day he boasted about it to a graduate student. In six years' time, he and Mac had four children. They bought a car, decorated and furnished a house, and to all outward appearances appeared to be just like all their neighbors, a staid and conventional couple.

But they weren't. For Kinsey was in love again. The new object of his affections was a young man, a graduate student of his named Ralph Voris. Kinsey and Voris shared a fascination with insects and a love of the outdoors and they frequently went on field trips together. Later, when Voris received his graduate degree from Indiana and began teaching at a distant university, he and Kinsey stayed in close touch with one another by mail. A historian who read the letters they exchanged termed their correspondence "intimate and tender." Other writers have disputed that characterization, finding the letters more chatty than tender, more jokey than intimate.

"Mac" (short for McMillen, Kinsey's endearment) and "Prok" (a contraction of Professor and Kinsey given to Dr. Kinsey by his graduate students) on a hike.

Whatever the nature of their correspondence, Kinsey was eventually to call Voris his "second great love." And it's likely that Voris was his first homosexual partner.

In time he would have many more. Ultimately he would have so many that on a famous scale he devised to chart sexual orientation, he would rank himself a "3," a rating indicating an individual with approximately equal heterosexual and homosexual experience and preference.

Kinsey studied gall wasps throughout the 1920s, trekking all over the country and down into Central America to collect speci-

Kinsey (center) with two graduate students on a gall wasp expedition.

A Little of This,
A Little of That

When the Kinsey reports were published, they were a PR bombshell. They really took sexuality out of the closet in more ways than one. Homosexuality was particularly provocative to a country that didn't want to hear the words "homosexuality," "masturbation," or even the word "sex" really. It was the only quantitative data we'd ever had of any large and diverse population. So it was a huge thing.

Female sexuality, per se, has had a somewhat more discreet presentation, because if you go there you get issues. He did take on, for example, the whole idea of the clitoral and vaginal orgasm long before Masters and Johnson created a stir. Kinsey was taking on this idea of Freudian psychology and the kind of orgasm that mattered. He re-brought the clitoris into its proper spotlight, if you will. Homosexual data, premarital sex, which wasn't supposed to be happening; there were a lot of shockers.

The most important thing that Kinsey did was take homosexuality out of the deviance category and put it into the sexual continuum category. You know, some people do a little of this and some people do a little of that and what's the big deal? But the idea that a third of men—look to your left, look to your right—could've touched each other past the age of infancy or childhood, was profoundly disturbing to people.

His idea of looking at what we all do gives us a sense of where we fit in to some larger firmament. It gives us more information about ourselves. We can know about sex like we can know about any other part of our health.

Kinsey's wife accepted him, she understood his sexuality, his peccadilloes, his multiple attractions and she believed in him and what he did. She was so grateful for those of us who were carrying on his work. Considering the attacks he got, if he hadn't had someone like her along side him and behind him, it just would've been impossible.

His work is controversial because his methods have lots of problems. On the other hand, lots of it has been replicated by more carefully done studies, and he's been given more credibility than not. We went into the private lives of people. People are nutty about sex when it comes out in the public. People don't want to hear about sexuality. They get really upset about it. I've done a lot of research on a lot of topics and people are very willing to talk about themselves, but when it comes into a public forum, they've been taught for so long that sex is dirty or taboo, that sex becomes stigmatized and there's this kind of proactive anger about seeing it discussed in public.

Kinsey's a real person and when you become famous at the level that Kinsey becomes famous, you become a target. Like all men and women, we have our foibles and we have our strengths and we have to be looked as a whole being.

—Pepper Schwartz, Professor of Sociology at the
University of Washington, November 2003

Above: Kinsey's gall wasp collection.

Below: From the mountains of Guatemala, the largest known gall.

mens, and in 1930 he published a massive book on the tiny bug, *The Gall Wasp Genus Cynips—A Study in the Origin of Species*, a work that established him as a major zoologist and taxonomist. He had learned more about gall wasps and collected more examples of their habits and variety than had any previous scholar. Subsequently, throughout the nineteen-thirties, he continued to research and write about gall wasps, but more and more he found himself fascinated by another matter—sex.

Sex had always interested him. And it had occurred to him that by using the same methods he had used with gall wasps, namely studying habits and individual variations, he might be able to make an important scientific contribution in yet another field, one that was exciting to him and largely neglected by other scientists.

He already had some scholarly material at hand. For years now, he had been counseling students who came to him with sex problems, just as in the past he'd counseled Boy Scouts—albeit now with his inhibitions overcome and a lot of experience under his belt, so to speak. Through his counseling, he'd informally garnered a good deal of sexual information, and he'd subsequently devised a more formal means of learning about sexual habits, a questionnaire about sex that he distributed among his graduate students and at fraternity houses.

In 1938 he approached the president of his university, Herman Wells, and suggested he teach a course that would prepare students for marriage by addressing sexual issues frankly and with precise detail.

Wells liked the idea—sex hygiene courses were being taught at many universities—and in 1938 Kinsey began a series of biology lectures in a course the university called a marriage course: to enroll, students had to prove they were married or engaged to be married. Using words that most of his listeners had never heard spoken, and illustrating his words with dramatic slides, he covered topics like petting, contraception, fantasies, techniques of intercourse. "The vagina must be spread open as the erect male organ

Physiology or Love

Intercourse consists of a series of physiological reactions which are as mechanical as the blinking of an eyelid. The ultimate outcome may be, of course, significant in the propagation of the species. Emotional acceptance of this series of physiological events may be what you recognize as love. It may provide the inspiration for the writing of the poet, the philosopher, of all of mankind, but fundamentally, at base, the first part of the story is a story of mechanical responses which are as inevitable when the stimuli are provided as any other ordinary reflex of any other part of the body. The stimuli which provide for this which we call an erotic response, a sexual response, are called erotic stimuli commemorating the name of the Greek god of love. The stimuli are fundamentally motion, contact, a rise in temperature, and various other such stimuli. In the case of the insects it is fundamentally a contact response which brings the genitalia of the male and female into union where they may effect fertilization. Such insects as the big moths respond to odor. The female may be detected at several miles and the males will work their ways against the wind until they locate her. This reaction to the odor you may not care to call a sexual response, but you will see that it is just as much a sexual contact as is any other contact.

In the human erotic response is stimulated by physical contact chiefly. That reaction to that contact leads to a pressing together of physical structures. It is the same sort of response that leads the speaker to lean against the table, the same sort of pressure against an object. We have a technical name for such a response, but I want to emphasize that it is a physical response. This stimulation may be received through any of the touch organs of the body. There are three parts of the male and female body where those touch organs come closest to the surface and greatest response is achieved when it affects the lips, the female breasts, or the external genetalia of the male or female. Similar response may be effected by contact with still other parts of the body. This stimulus is carried to the central nervous system where the switchboard then sets to work the response which ultimately may lead to sexual intercourse and fertilization.

—Dr. A. C. Kinsey
excerpted from "Reproductive Anatomy and Physiology"
Marriage Course
Lecture VI
February 21, 1940

The original staff of The Institute for Sex Research, c. 1948, included Clyde Martin (front, far left), translator Hedwig Leser (seated next to Martin), Paul Gebhard (top center with the infamous moustache), Wardell Pomeroy, Dr. Kinsey (right rear), and librarian Jean Brown (front, right).

penetrates," he said in his lecture on erotic areas, while displaying a slide of a penis entering a vagina, "You will see that...the clitoris at this point is stimulated, thus providing the erotic stimulation necessary for the completion of the act on the part of the female."

His specificity and directness was stunning—altogether revolutionary for its time. He held his audiences rapt. And whenever he finished speaking, he implored everyone in the lecture hall to help him make his talks even more accurate and helpful by volunteering to fill out new, detailed questionnaires about their sexual knowledge, attitudes, fantasies, and behavior.

Most of his listeners, enormously grateful to their charismatic professor for his straightforward and permissive approach to sex, agreed to answer his questions.

The Institute Is Born

The Kinsey Report grew out of those student questionnaires. But Kinsey elaborated on his initial approach to obtaining information about sexuality by asking his questions in face-to-face interviews and entering the answers with a confidential coded system that allowed for statistical analysis—the soon-to-be celebrated Kinsey "sex histories." Obtaining research grants from the National Research Council and the Rockefeller Foundation, which provided the bulk of the money, he set up his own institute, the Institute for Sex Research, in Bloomington, and traveled all across the country to collect sexual histories, just as he'd traveled to collect gall wasps. He took histories from heterosexuals and homosexuals, from convicts and churchgoers, from prostitutes and businessmen, from psychiatrists and pimps, from whites and blacks, from graduate students, from elderly, from all manner of people.

His respondents were, of course, volunteers. One charge that has always been leveled against sex research is that it relies on volunteers—which of course it does, for who would answer intimate questions except volunteers—and that those who volunteer are less inhibited than those who decline to do so, therefore providing results that are not typical of society as a whole. Kinsey came up with a method that he felt obviated this basic flaw of sex research. Instead of seeking out only individual volunteers, he tried to get entire groups of people to give him their sex histories. His technique was to persuade a prominent member of, say, a fraternal organization, to exert his influence and get *all* the members of the organization to promise him their histories, in exchange for which he, Kinsey, would give the organization a free lecture about sexuality. His idea was that by using this technique he would be interviewing some people who would gladly have volunteered, others who would have been reluctant to do so, others who would surely have refused. It was a method that did in fact make his findings quite representative of society as a whole.

In pursuit of knowledge about sex Kinsey was indefatigable. Corresponding with art dealers all over the world, he assembled a vast collection of erotic photographs, paintings and sculpture, including precious antiquities from the Far East and Central America, and work by celebrated modern masters like Picasso, Matisse and Chagall. He lectured all over the country, going wherever he could be assured of ending up with sex histories, he penetrated little known homosexual communities in the Midwest and he traveled great distances to seek out various sexual oddities, like a farmer he was told had a penis that when flaccid was nearly a foot long. Once he even managed to arrange an interview and demonstration with a sixty-three-year-old man who claimed to be able to bring himself to orgasm in ten seconds, a scene the movie *Kinsey* replicates. The record-setter also claimed to have had homosexual sex with six hundred pre-adolescent males, heterosexual relations with two hundred pre-adolescent females, sexual intercourse with

Wardell Pomeroy, Paul Gebhard, Alfred Kinsey and Clyde Martin (from left to right) with manuscript pages from the female volume.

Two pieces from The
Kinsey Institute Art and
Artifact Collection:
Before, *an engraving by
William Hogarth, 1736
(above) and (below)*
Well—what the hell are
you staring at? *ink and
colored pencil, c. 1940.*

animals of many species and with countless adults of both sexes, including his grandparents and thirty-seven other members of his family. He had recorded all these encounters in a mammoth hand-written sex diary—a diary he gave to Kinsey, who in turn gave it to Mac to type up.

Kinsey was assisted in his research efforts not just by Mac but by three men who would be closely associated with his project, Wardell Pomeroy, Paul Gebhard and Clyde Martin. Pomeroy was a good-looking young psychologist who had been working for the Department of Public Welfare in South Bend, Indiana. Gebhard was an anthropologist who had done his graduate work at Harvard. Martin, who was actually the first member of Kinsey's team, had no professional credentials. He'd been an undergraduate at Indiana University when he crossed paths with Kinsey, who offered him a job first as a gardener, soon thereafter as his assistant.

Martin was an extremely handsome, amiable young man, and Kinsey fell in love with him. They became lovers, and although Kinsey had by this time had other male sex partners and in the future was to have a great many more, he never again fell in love. Martin, he claimed, was the third and final love of his life.

His first love, Mac, may not have known that what he felt toward Ralph Voris and Clyde Martin was love, but she had long known about her husband's extramarital homosexual activities. He had always been completely candid with her. In return, she had been uncommonly understanding and accepting.

Like him, in the early days of their marriage, she had read marriage manuals and nudist magazines and enthusiastically tried out a variety of sexual positions. Later, again like him, she had become something of a sex expert, someone to whom her neighbors turned when they had sexual questions. However, she was a much more domestic creature than Kinsey, content to stay at home during his long field trips, to manage their household and children, to cook and bake cookies for her husband's guests, and to pursue her own more modest interests; she had given up her graduate studies, but she started the Bloomington Girl

Scouts Day Camp and ran it for thirty-eight years. She adored her husband, and to all reports he returned that feeling, remaining devoted to Mac throughout their long marriage and continuing, no matter his other passionate attachments or casual sexual experiences, to maintain a sexual relationship with her.

Clyde Martin also adored Kinsey, adored and respected him. But Martin was not homosexual. He had sexual relations with Kinsey, but his preference was for sex with women. One day after he and Kinsey had become sex partners, he asked Kinsey—possibly as a way of deflecting his physical attentions—what his wife would say if he asked *her* to have sex with him. Kinsey was surprised that someone wanted to have sex with Mac. It hadn't occurred to him that others beside himself might find her desirable. But he found the idea intriguing. He passed Martin's request along to Mac, and she accepted Martin into her bed.

No one knows whether she did so because she felt neglected, because Kinsey persuaded her to, or because she shared his views about sexual experimentation. But whatever her reasons, she went along with the notion of having sex with her husband's partner, and eventually Kinsey urged all the men who worked closely with him to have sex with one another's wives.

Not all the wives were agreeable. One complained that Kinsey exerted "sickening pressure" on her, and made her feel as if her "husband's career at the Institute depended on it." In time, however, whatever their individual reservations, all the members of the team were participating in what later came to be called "open marriages," a development they kept secret for years.

There were other secrets. Hoping to be able to describe with precision the physiological changes that occurred in men and women both when they were aroused and when they climaxed, Kinsey became interested in recording sexual activities on film. He hired a talented commercial photographer to serve as his cameraman, turned one of his attic bedrooms into a film studio, and enlisted some of his staff and their wives to perform various sexual activities as the film rolled. Later he had a friend recruit perform-

Nothing New Under the Sun

Kinsey is really responsible for launching sex research and open talk about sex. He started the kind of openness that would have not been possible had he not asked the questions and done the research that he did. When you think about sex there are three names that came to mind. There's Kinsey who did the sex research and there's the team of Masters and Johnson who started the therapeutic techniques. Between those two entities, sex became an open subject gaining some validity and scientific basis. People didn't have to whisper about it quietly; they could talk about it as a body of respectable information.

A twentieth-century painting from India, artist unknown—one of more than 7,000 pieces from the Kinsey Collection.

Kinsey also served a purpose by popularizing the subject of women and sexuality here in America. Sex has been around for centuries and eastern countries like India and China—which honored women's sexuality in ancient times—have developed sex manuals for centuries. Kinsey exploded openness about sex for us in this country, and gave us license to talk about it.

He created a revolution in his time, which turned into an evolution. After Kinsey's work, things went into a dip, then there was the sexual revolution in the sixties with more openness, and then we went into a slump and now there's a bit of repression. Openess about sex is still evolving and Kinsey's groundwork is still having an impact.

Now we have two opposing energies going on. There are professionals in the field of sexual research and sexology who have really established their credibility who stand for keeping the openness alive, and then there is the opposite end of the continuum, with groups and organizations creating repression and trying to keep the subject of sex in the closet.

To this day there are critics of Kinsey's work. Many say his work was not scientific enough, that he came to conclusions that weren't accurate, or his samples of people were not representative. But one cannot criticize the fact that he made a tremendous courageous step toward openness about sex that exists to this day.

—Dr. Judy Kuriansky, Adjunct Professor of Psychology at
Columbia University Teachers College and the author of *Generation Sex*
and *The Complete Idiots Guide to Tantric Sex*

ers from a number of homosexual communities. These newcomers to the project were photographed masturbating, engaging in oral and anal sex, and employing violent sadomasochistic techniques. One observer Kinsey invited to witness several filmmaking sessions wrote afterwards that the team took notes while "Mrs. Kinsey—herself a true scientist as well—appeared in the attic and once in a while calmly changed the sheets on the workbench."

Kinsey's sexual demands on his staff, his filming of sexual activity, and his personal sexual habits would all one day come out into the open. But at the time he was pursuing his research, these matters were unknown to the public. This was fortunate, because there was enough in the research itself to cause shock and outrage. Kinsey's first big book detailing what he'd learned was about to appear and when it did, there would be shock and outrage aplenty.

Above, left:
Dr. Kinsey and
Clara, 1953.

Above, right: The
Kinsey family (from
left to right) Bruce
on the shoulders of a
family friend, Dr.
Kinsey, Anne, Joan
and Clara.

Below: Clara with a
Girl Scout Troop.

1948 at a Glance

- Gandhi is assassinated in New Delhi

- The Nation of Israel is born

- The Berlin Airlift begins

- Truman ends segregation in the U.S. Army

- Margaret Sanger founds Planned Parenthood

- Unemployment is 3.9%

- Cost of a first class stamp is 3¢

- The Hollywood Ten refuse to tell The House Un-American Activities Committee whether they are now or ever have been communists, and are jailed for contempt of Congress

- Cleveland defeats the Boston Braves in the World Series

- Columbia Records introduces the 33 1/3 LP replacing the 4 minute long 78

- *Miracle on 34th Street*, *Gentleman's Agreement* and *Song of the South* are up for Oscars

- *A Streetcar Named Desire* wins a Pulitzer Prize

- *Kiss Me Kate* opens on Broadway

- The "Big Bang" theory is introduced to explain the origins of the universe

- The Polaroid Land camera is invented

- D. W. Griffith, Babe Ruth and Orville Wright die

- Alfred C. Kinsey's *Sexual Behavior in the Human Male* is published

Fame and Furor: The Kinsey Books

Sexual Behavior in the Human Male hit the bookstores on January 6, 1948. There had been so much advance publicity about the book, so many interviews and articles, that by mid-January the book had sold 40,000 copies and by June, 150,000 copies—extraordinarily big sales in those days. Topping virtually all the bestseller lists of its time, the work was reprinted eight times in rapid succession, and translated into numerous foreign languages. It earned a huge amount of money for Kinsey's publisher, a scientific press, and for his Institute for Sex Research. However, best of all for Kinsey, perhaps, was that some reviewers compared him to Darwin. He had managed the rare feat of living up to a high school yearbook prophecy.

The book's findings, which were based on a sample of 5,300 men, blew the cover on American sexuality. Almost half of all the married men in the sample had had extramarital intercourse at some time in their lives, Kinsey reported. Premarital sex was even more common: sixty-seven percent of college-educated men had had sexual intercourse prior to marriage; men who hadn't gone to college were even more likely to have engaged in premarital sex. As to masturbation, it was so common—92 percent of those he'd interviewed had masturbated—that Kinsey went out of his way to explain the few who hadn't tried it. "There are some individuals who do not masturbate for the simple reason that they do not have sufficient sex drive to cause them to find any sort of outlet," he wrote. "There are some boys, particularly at lower social levels, who do not masturbate because they become involved in heterosexual coitus at such an early age that they have little need for other sources of outlet. There are some duller and slower reacting individuals who find it impossible to effect orgasm in masturbation..."

He also made a plea for putting an end to the notion that masturbation was harmful, and in it one can hear the boy he once

Cartoon from
The Kinsey Institute
archives, source
unknown.

was speaking through the man he had become. "Millions of boys have lived in continual mental conflict over this problem," he wrote. "For that matter, many a boy still does. Many boys pass through a periodic succession of attempts to stop the habit, inevitable failures in those attempts, consequent periods of remorse, the making of new resolutions—and a new start on the whole cycle. It is difficult to imagine anything better calculated to do permanent damage to the personality of an individual."

Many of Kinsey's findings startled his readers. Among the most jolting were that close to sixty percent of the sample had engaged in oral sex, thirty-seven percent had had at least one homosexual contact that resulted in orgasm, and a surprising seventeen percent of farm boys had had sexual relations with an animal. Still, despite their astonishment at the figures, a majority of Americans seemed to approve of the book—according to a

Practice, Practice, Practice

When I finished my residency in psychiatry in the sixties I was very interested in sexual dysfunction problems and transgender people. But there was no one in Southern California doing any work like that then, so I started my own practice and began treating those individuals. It was through my practice that I ultimately got connected with the Kinsey Institute.

I was selected to be on the Scientific Advisory board of the Institute because my partner and I had just published a book called *The Male Couple:* the study we had done interviewing male couples over a period of five years.

Kinsey was the first that had any credibility on the way homosexuality was viewed. He could say that homosexuality was just another aspect of sexuality, seen and found everywhere. When Kinsey's male volume came out, I was in high school getting ready to join the monastery, and masturbation was a major issue for me. I thought that I was the worst sinner in the world. Then I read in Kinsey's book that ninety-five percent of the males interviewed were masturbators—somebody told me years later that the other five percent were liars. Anyway, reading that book sparked a change in my attitude about my own sexuality and certainly got me very interested in his work.

In the late sixties or early seventies, I had the opportunity to work with Wardell Pomeroy learning about sexuality in a very important and creative way, talking to many of the scientists who had worked with Kinsey originally.

Kinsey opened the gate for us to move forward as gay men. His work before Stonewall—which is supposedly the marker for the beginning of the gay liberation movement—set the foundation. He wasn't out to start the new gay movement but he did because of his research.

The zero to six scale that Kinsey instituted has been added to in many ways by other researchers. His scale dealt only with behaviors—zero being a completely heterosexual and six being completely homosexual. We use it to measure fantasies as well. And if I find that someone has a large discrepancy between their behavior number and their fantasy number, that person is likely struggling in a very serious kind of clinical way. It's a very important scale that has held up over the years.

Beside opening doors he generated the spirit that got us into the gay movement that has developed since. He's almost like the father of the gay movement.

—David McWhirter, psychiatrist, physician and Associate Professor
of Psychiatry at the University of California, San Diego, November 2003

Gallup poll, three-quarters of the general public viewed the appearance of his work as "a good thing."

Theologians, as might be expected, did not. He was condemned by many priests and ministers. But their disdain did not trouble Kinsey. He had expected to enrage what we today call the Religious Right. He'd been contending with their strictures all his life. What did upset him, however, was that a number of important intellectuals and social scientists took issue with him. Typical were the words of America's greatest literary critic, Lionel Trilling, who wrote that The Kinsey Report was "full of assumption and conclusion; it makes very positive statements on highly debatable matters and it editorializes very freely," and of British anthropologist Geoffrey Gorer who declared that, "the sampling is so poor that the only reliable figures are those for college graduates in six of the northeastern states."

Kinsey was stung by the criticism of peers. He became angry and a little paranoid. He took to railing during his public lectures against those who objected to his work and he hinted to friends that he not only knew the sex histories of many of his critics but that their histories revealed that they had hidden sexual flaws and prejudices. He warned one close friend not to breathe a word about the Institute's collection of erotic material, saying it would be too difficult to explain its significance. He exploded at his team, venting his fury on them for small mistakes or misjudgments. Without a doubt, what lay behind his irritable behavior was the fact that he was terrified that scholarly criticism of his work would cool the enthusiasm of his funders and that he would lose his research grants. He didn't. Not then. But he was filled with trepidation.

Nevertheless, he basked in his success. He was a household name, now, not just known to millions of readers and legions of scientists, but an icon of popular culture. Cartoonists drew him. Comedians cracked endless jokes about his report. Singer Martha Raye made a record, *Ohh Dr. Kinsey!*, that sold half a million copies. He was invited to speak at prestigious universities and clubs, became a spokesman for the repeal of sex laws that deemed homosexuality and adultery jailable offenses, and began moving in elite metropolitan and artistic circles, meeting and dining with such literary luminaries as E. M. Forster, Gore Vidal, Christopher Isherwood and W. H. Auden.

The success was something of a strain on his family. His son, now a college student at Oberlin, was asked by a professor if he was related to the author of the famous sex report; the young man replied, "Never heard of him." One of his daughters told people her father was the owner of the Kinsey Whiskey company, not a sex researcher. But Mac was unfazed. When she was deluged for personal details by women's magazines, she told them she was just an ordinary American housewife, fond of knitting and baking, a stay-at-home mom whose husband went off to work every day, though to a sex research center not an office. She maintained this average-woman image even though Kinsey asked her to participate in his movie-making project and allow herself to be filmed stimulating herself to orgasm and having sex with Pomeroy.

"She was wonderfully cooperative," the cameraman said later. "Mac so deeply believed in the research Kinsey was doing," Gebhard explained, "I swear if he'd asked her to cut her wrists, she probably would have." Neither fame nor uncommon demands seemed to affect her devotion, and as Kinsey began working ever longer hours, she would make supper for him, phone him when it was ready, serve him the food, bid him goodbye when he returned to his office, then call him at 11:30 to remind him to come home to sleep—a reminder he sometimes ignored.

He was working 'round the clock now, as was his team, gathering histories and making statistical analyses for their second volume, *Sexual Behavior in the Human Female.* It was published in 1953 and, like the male volume, reported on many aspects of sex, including sexual development, fantasies, masturbation, premarital petting, marital and extramarital coitus. But the most monumental contribution in the book was in large part the result

Rockefeller Underwrites Study

Kinsey was one of the most significant figures of twentieth-century America. He set the basis for what became a sexual revolution in the United States. He wasn't a political person, he wasn't a public person, but his research was singularly important because of its challenge to most of the traditionalized ideas at the time. He was an egotistical man, a very domineering man and I think that probably is the kind of personality that it took.

His methodology has got to be seen through the perspective of his time. If he were doing research today, I don't think he could get it through a human use subject committee. It's a different methodology than we'd use today.

When the book came out in 1948 it was tremendously controversial. The controversy came because he undermined most of the assumptions about sex in America. There was this idea that people grew up, got married fairly young, had children, lived happily ever after and never did anything else. He found, however, that most of them masturbated and many experimented. Furthermore, he indicated that it didn't really matter what religious authorities said, people did things sexually, and his finding provoked an uproar from those who regarded themselves as a guardians of moral standards in America. He was undermining assumptions.

His women's book became even more controversial because he indicated that women enjoyed sex. That lead to a threat to cut off the tax privileges of the Rockefeller Foundation. So the Rockefeller Foundation, which had been active in sex research since the 1920s, closed down their sexual division and gave money to some of his greater religious critics. I don't blame them for saving themselves, but it's indicative of just how controversial he was.

—Vern L. Bullough, Ph.D., D.Sci., R.N., Distinguished Professor Emeritus from the State University of New York Regents and founder of the Center for Sex Research at Cal State Northridge, November 2003

Clara and Alfred Kinsey photographed in their living room for Life *magazine in 1947.*

of the hours Kinsey had spent filming and observing the female orgasm. His films had enabled him to assert authoritatively that the vagina was an insensitive organ and orgasm the result of clitoral stimulation only. Taking on the Freudians, who held firm sway over the minds of both men and women in the early 1950s, he wrote, "Freud recognized that the clitoris is highly sensitive and the vagina insensitive in the younger female, but he contended that psychosexual maturation involved a subordination of clitoral reactions and a development of sensitivity within the vagina itself; but there are no anatomic data to indicate that such a physical transformation has ever been observed or is possible."

The book sold in even greater quantities than its predecessor, but it also provoked a firestorm of disgust and controversy. Although Kinsey came to a fairly obvious conclusion about female sexuality—namely that overall, women had far less sexual experience than men—he also reported in detail and in the same cool scientific tone he had used in the male volume statistics about the incidence among women of masturbation, premarital and extramarital intercourse, oral-genital sex, homosexual encounters. Religious leaders were revolted. Reverend Billy Graham declared, "It is impossible to estimate the damage this book will do to the already deteriorating morals of America." A well-known Baptist minister called Kinsey a "deranged Nebuchadnezzar" who was leading American women "out into the fields to mingle with the cattle and become one with the beasts of the jungle." The indignation of church leaders soon spread to the public at large. "It was not that there was anything intrinsically sensational in the material," wrote Wardell Pomeroy in his 1972 biography, *Dr. Kinsey and the Institute for Sex Research*, "but only the American double standard operating again. We might make disclosures about men that were shocking to prevailing middle-class

Baptist evangelist Billy Graham preaching in November 1949.

morality, but after all, they merely confirmed the conventional wisdom that men were no better than they should be. To talk of girls and women as sexual beings, however—that was too much."

Once again, the Religious Right's reaction was predictable, and came as little surprise to Kinsey. But this time around he had stirred up more than the guardians of morality. Many fellow scientists and scholars fell upon his work with a vengeance, and in a short time, even the press, which had once lionized him, began to denounce him. He was accused of having too small a sample, only 5,940 women, to make the generalizations he made about female sexuality, among them that premarital sexual relations were likely to improve a woman's psychological, social and marital adjustment. Actress Anne Baxter quipped, "So some 6,000 women lined up and confessed. I place my faith in the 80-odd million who weren't contacted." Moreover, the sample he did use was viewed with suspicion. Although Kinsey had clearly explained that he had taken histories from women in all walks of life—teachers, students, dentists, hotel managers, editors, lab technicians, housewives, business executives, policewomen and prostitutes—a widespread belief arose that most of the sample was composed of prostitutes.

It was, of course, a different time altogether from the time when he had published *Sexual Behavior in the Human Male.* That book had appeared three years after the end of World War II, an optimistic forward-looking period. The overseas battles and domestic struggles that had marked the wartime era were over, the returning veterans were starting new lives, business was expanding, peace, prosperity and innovation were in the air. By 1953 the Cold War was on and America had taken a decided turn toward conservatism. Communists were being drummed out of their professions. Schoolchildren were being taught to hide under their desks in the event the Russians drop an atomic bomb. Paranoia was everywhere, and so was conformity.

Kinsey had come forward with his radical new information and ideas just at a time when anything radical or out of the ordinary had begun to be suspect. He could not have chosen a worse time.

1953 at a Glance

Marilyn Monroe, Lauren Bacall and Betty Grable in How to Marry a Millionaire.

- Eisenhower is inaugurated

- Joseph Stalin dies

- Korean armistice is signed

- The Soviets announce they have the H bomb

- Julius and Ethel Rosenberg are executed

- Unemployment is 3 percent

- First-class postage is 3¢

- The Yankees defeat the Brooklyn Dodgers in the World Series

- Little Ricky is born to Lucy and Ricky Ricardo

- CinemaScope is developed to fight the growing popularity of television

- *Playboy* magazine hits the newsstand

- From *Here to Eternity, Kiss Me Kate* and *How to Marry a Millionaire* are at the movies

- American Airlines inaugurates regular commercial flights between New York and L.A.

- Jonas Salk announces the polio vaccine

- The Cuban Revolution begins

- *Casino Royale* is published introducing us to James Bond

- Elvis pays $4 to record a demo as a gift to his mother

- *The Tonight Show* is broadcast as a local variety show

- Tony Blair, Tim Allen and Desi Arnaz Jr. are born

- Dylan Thomas, Eugene O'Neill and Queen Mary die

- Alfred C. Kinsey's *Sexual Behavior in the Human Female is published*

In the next few years, while he would become ever more famous, the national furor he had aroused with *Sexual Behavior in the Human Female* would wreck financial havoc with his beloved project. The havoc began in 1954, a year after the publication of the female volume, when the Rockefeller Foundation, his biggest supporter, withdrew its grants. The new president of the nonprofit organization had heard it rumored that a Congressional committee was going to investigate the Foundation, particularly in regard to its support of Kinsey. At least that was his ostensible reason for parting company with the man his foundation had supported for thirteen years. In reality the Rockefeller Foundation had never been altogether comfortable about Kinsey's work and now they feared that all the negative publicity he was getting

A cartoon published in the New Ulm (Minnesota) Journal, *August 31, 1953.*

Wardell Pomeroy, Paul Gebhard and Alfred Kinsey (left to right) exhausted from working on their manuscript.

would somehow sully their reputation. They were also being pressured by important conservative political figures.

Kinsey was distraught. He became ever more impatient and irritable with his staff and even with some of his film subjects. One of them wrote that until this period Kinsey "had always used 'we' and 'us' when referring to the work...now it suddenly became 'I' and 'me'.... Formerly Kinsey would listen to you, nodding, agreeing, or raising objections. Now his statements became authoritative, almost ex cathedra pronouncements; he no longer listened quietly. Instead he interrupted, issued dicta dogmatically, often turning impatient and snappish, sometimes arrogant."

He continued to gather sex histories—he had declared that he intended to gather 100,000 of them and he still hoped to accomplish that goal. He still worked 'round the clock. But he was failing physically. "He isn't old," wrote a friend who saw him during this period, "nevertheless [he] is nearing his end, with a terrible cardiac deterioration." He and Mac traveled to Europe in an effort to relieve his tension by providing him with relaxing vacation time. But on his return money was on his mind constantly, and he slept badly, even sleeping pills failing to relieve his anxiety. Regularly, he tried to find and woo possible new benefactors for his research. But most of the time, he returned home defeated and empty-handed.

He was, it turned out, terrible at asking for money. One night, when he was soliciting a contribution from the wealthy A&P heir, Huntington Hartford, at a dinner party, he went into such earnest detail about what he was doing and the amounts of money it would take that Hartford grew bored, turned away and talked to someone else.

That night, staying over in New York at a friend's home, Kinsey had a terrible heart attack. "We were pushing the nitroglycerin pills down his throat," his friend recalled, "and eventually he was coming to life again."

He did come to life, at least sufficiently so as to return home to Bloomington and Mac. But she was to say afterward that he never recovered from the Huntington Hartford dinner.

In the next few months he took a few more sex histories in his office, but his heart was dangerously enlarged, his pulse wildly erratic and the diuretics he was taking unable to control his body's fluid retention. He was told by his doctors to rest, that he would die if he didn't take it easy.

But Kinsey had never been a man to take it easy. He took to his bed. But he didn't rest in bed, he kept on working, composing scientific papers and writing letters. In one of these last papers he railed despairingly against "the multiplicity of forces which have operated to dissuade the scientist, to intimidate the scientist, and to force him to cease research in [sexual] areas." He also, as if still recalling the anguish of his own youth, kept dwelling on the agony of frustration that teenagers experienced because of guilt over masturbation. In a letter that suggests he was thinking once again about his old love Ralph Voris, now long dead, he wrote to Voris's

wife to tell her that he had arranged to have Ralph's collection of staphylinid taken by the Illinois State Natural History Society.

Another letter seems to suggest that he'd been recalling how when he was a boy, it had been activity not bed rest that had finally made him into a healthy person; "I shall prove," he wrote to a friend, "as I have in the past 30 years, that you can do more with a physical handicap than [people] sometimes think."

One day he insisted on getting out of bed and going to the campus to talk to the university about appropriating more money for the Institute. He could hardly drag himself up the administration building's steps. Mac, who was with him, begged the university's president, Wells, who had always been a great friend to

Neither Sheep nor Goat

Kinsey's profound legacy is that he gave us both the idea that people are sexual beings and the idea that the world cannot be divided into sheep and goats. He also helped depathologize people's fantasy lives and sexual lives, and in a general broader stroke, to help normalize the concept of being sexual.

There are many misconceptions and misunderstandings about Kinsey and his work—which remains controversial—because of the biases, prejudices and ignorance that still exist. If there's a positive finding reported about healthy sexuality, some in the American public express it as a negative because they believe sexual activity is only proper between a man and woman in a state of marriage for the purpose of procreation.

But, while we do get waves of times that are reactionary followed by times that are more open and positive, things have changed since Kinsey in that more people are feeling comfortable about talking about sexual activities, sexual fantasies and sexual behaviors.

Kinsey's scale, ranging from zero to a six—zero being a person who's sexual behaviors were completely heterosexual and six being a person's behavior who is completely homosexual—revolutionized thinking because most think in terms of black and white. You are either heterosexual or homosexual. What he found was a broad range of sexual behaviors. It helped people understand the fluidity of sexual behaviors, and it had a profound influence on the gay movement.

In that regard, some views are changing because of the popular gay-themed TV shows. Many women who watch the programs enjoy the attitudes, styles and ways of interaction the gay characters portray and wish their boyfriends would follow suit.

—Andrew Mattison, Clinical Professor of Psychiatry
at the University of California School of Medicine
and incoming president of the Society for the
Scientific Society of Sexuality, November 2003

Kinsey, to help her get her husband to rest. "You've got to help me stop him," she said.

"I can't stop him," Wells replied. "But he's got to stop himself, otherwise he'll kill himself."

Mac replied, "That's what he's doing."

Late the following month, on August 25, 1956, Kinsey died. He was sixty-two years old.

Changes in the Wind

Controversy dogged Kinsey even after his death. His methodology continued to be attacked. He was criticized for having done too many interviews in prisons and in homosexual circles. He was excoriated for including too many sex offenders in his sample. He was scorned for taking a mechanistic view of sex—for failing to consider the ineffable and unmeasurable role of love in sexual behavior. And when, gradually, the information about his private sexual proclivities, the sexual practices he urged on his staff and their wives, and the films he produced at his institute leaked out, his very motivations for studying sex began to be viewed as suspect. But in the end, Kinsey triumphed over his critics, for his legacy has been extraordinary.

America has undergone volcanic changes in sexual attitudes and behavior, many of them the result of the openness about sex he so fiercely championed.

Among the changes has been a widespread acceptance of homosexuality. Whether or not Kinsey's figures on the prevalence of homosexuality were inflated, he showed that same-sex experiences in childhood as well as lifelong preferences for same-sex experiences were far more common than had previously been thought; the revelation inspired gays to be take pride in their sexuality and led society to practice understanding and humaneness, where before there had been precious little.

The first issue of
Playboy, *featuring*
Marilyn Monroe, hit the
newsstands December
1953.

Similarly, women have been able to take control of their sexuality. Helped by Kinsey's exploration of the nature of the female orgasm, they battled the notion that clitoral orgasms are immature and women who demand clitoral stimulation hopelessly neurotic.

Other matters changed too. The mid- to late-fifties saw a loosening of strictures against images of nudity. Hugh Hefner, who started *Playboy* magazine in 1953 and credited Kinsey with helping him evolve the magazine's pleasure-preaching philosophy, showed for the first time in a mainstream publication photographs of the naked female form; other publishers and even film makers followed suit, displaying the naked bodies not just of women but of men, too, thereby defying the taboos that implied that the human form was vile. The sixties saw a burst of sexual freedom—not just among hippies who went in for large-scale so-called love-ins featuring mind-altering drugs, ecstatic music, and public copulation, but among more average men and women who in the privacy of their homes began experimenting with bolder lovemaking techniques and a greater variety of sexual positions. The seventies brought frank talk about sexual fantasies and swinging. The eighties and nineties, candor about pregnancy, menstruation, menopause. And in those turbulent decades America got The Pill and *Roe v. Wade*, making contraception and abortion available to millions of women who had been forced to bear unwanted children.

A stirring of sexual liberation was already in the air when he began his research, and indeed was reflected in the very practices his statistics revealed. World War II had exposed average American men to more worldly ways of behaving. Post-war prosperity had made them affluent, and affluence had made them covet and experiment with the kind of personal freedoms that historically had been the province of the upper classes alone.

However, we can definitively see Kinsey's footprints in the strides that have been taken by subsequent sex researchers and by the medical profession. William Masters and Virginia Johnson

Vol. 1 #1
1953

Sex researchers Virginia Johnson and William Masters in 1966.

were Kinsey's most distinguished successors. Building on his work, they used cameras, tape recorders and high-tech electronic instruments to observe the actual physiology of sexual arousal in both men and women. After studying the responses of hundreds of heterosexual couples, in 1966 they published their highly scientific analysis of sexual physiology, *Human Sexual Response*, establishing with modern equipment that had been unavailable in Kinsey's time that the walls of the vaginal canal were without a doubt insensate.

Four years later Masters and Johnson published a second highly important book, *Human Sexual Inadequacy*, this one explaining techniques they had been employing to help people suffering from sexual problems, women who couldn't climax even through clitoral stimulation and men who were impotent or who experienced premature or retarded ejaculation. Among the techniques were "homework" exercises that included nonsexual massage, bouts of genital play that didn't culminate in intercourse, and, for the premature ejaculators, a method Masters had learned from studying the tricks of prostitutes—squeezing the penis just before ejaculation.

Alfred and Clara Kinsey arrive in Paris holding Le Comportement Sexuel de la Femme *alongside its English edition,* Sexual Response in the Human Female.

Worldwide Influence

When you think of psychotherapists, when you think of sexologists, it's Freud, it's Kinsey, it's Masters and Johnson. Those are the triumphant, the giants. And so Kinsey's influence has literally been a worldwide influence. Almost every psychotherapist, clinical sexologist and sex researcher has read Kinsey as part of their educational process and developed theories based on his initial work. Kinsey was simply the very, very top of the field for many years.

The surveys that Kinsey did gave the public the impression that what they were doing at home in their bedroom was normal. It set norms. It gave people a measuring stick to look at. Others have done surveys since then, but Kinsey was the one who started asking us questions, which gave folks permission to talk about sex.

Kinsey was the person who really opened up the doors for succeeding researchers as well. And while there are still very conservative areas of this country and this world, we are much healthier in terms of our own sexuality.

—David Fleming, Executive Director of the
Society for the Scientific Study of Sexuality, November 2003

In the wake of this second book a whole new professional field developed—sex therapy. Sex therapists, generally a male and female team, offered counseling and Masters and Johnson exercises to people all across the country. Some of the new breed of sex therapists were doctors or psychologists. One noted practitioner, Helen Kaplan, published a well-regarded 1979 book called *The Disorders of Sexual Desire*, in which she argued that some couples didn't even desire sex—or didn't desire it with one another—and advised the use of fantasies and pornographic films to treat the absence of desire. Others of the new breed came up with highly questionable "cures," roots and herbs, foot massages, group gropes. But without doubt, sex therapy helped a good many people.

The nineties brought us more sturdy pharmacological assists. The pill Viagra was developed and marketed, making it possible for millions of men to stimulate their sexual desire or stay erect during intercourse. Enzyte followed soon afterward. Today, other medications for men are in the making. And in the near future, we are promised, there will be a pill or a patch or some kind of medical aid that will increase female desire.

Kinsey, who all his life wanted to help people who had sex problems, would surely have applauded the sexual research and sexual therapies that have brought and are bringing relief to countless Americans.

By exposing the hypocrisy about sex that was prevalent in his day, by pleading for greater tolerance and understanding of individual sexual habits, by decrying laws that attempted to regulate what people did in the privacy of their bedrooms, he succeeded in making sex, that central aspect of human life, something we could talk about, something we no longer needed to sweep under a carpet of silence and shame.

He wasn't a perfect man. But he was a pioneer, a teacher, a warrior in a battle that needed to be fought.

Alfred C. Kinsey—scientist, taxonomist, teacher and pioneer—on a gall wasp trip to Mexico in 1935.

The
Reaction

David Halberstam

From his book, *The Fifties*, published in 1993

ALFRED KINSEY was both fascinated and troubled by the vast difference between American sexual behavior the society wanted to believe existed and American sexual practices as they actually did exist. For example, at least 80 percent of successful businessmen, his interviews showed, had had extramarital affairs. "God," he noted, "what a gap between social front and reality!" And he spent the latter part of his career tearing away the façade that Americans used to hide their sexual selves.

Kinsey was no bohemian. He lived in the Midwest, he married the first woman he ever dated, and he stayed married to her for his entire life. Because he was an entomologist and loved to collect bugs, he and his bride went camping on their honeymoon. In his classes at the University of Indiana he always sported a bow tie and a crew cut. He drove the same old Buick for most of his lifetime and was immensely proud of the fact that he had more than a hundred thousand miles on it. On Sundays he and his wife invited faculty and graduate-student friends to their home to listen to records of classical music. They took these evenings very seriously; Kinsey was immensely proud of his record collection. When the wife of one faculty member suggested that they play some boogie-woogie, the couple was never invited back.

Kinsey did not smoke, and he rarely drank. Relatively late in his career he decided to smoke since it would make him more like the men he was interviewing and help put them at ease. Try as he might, he never quite got it right, and his assistants finally suggested that the prop was hurting rather than helping. With drinking it was the same. After his death Pomeroy wrote, "To see him bringing in a tray of sweet liqueurs before dinner was a wry and

Alfred Kinsey photographed in 1948 by Clarence Tripp.

happy reminder that Alfred Charles Kinsey, the genius, the world figure, was a simple and unsophisticated man in the true sense of the word."

He seemed to be the least likely candidate to become one of the most controversial figures of his generation.

When he began his studies of human sexuality, one of his oldest friends, Edward Anderson, by then the director of the Missouri Botanical Garden in St. Louis, wrote to him: "It was heartwarming to see you settling down into what I suppose will be your real life work. One would never have believed that all sides of you could have found a project big enough to need them all. I was amused to see how the Scotch Presbyterian reformer in you had finally got together with the scientific fanatic with his zeal for masses of neat data in orderly boxes and drawers. The monographer Kinsey, the naturalist Kinsey, and the camp counsellor Kinsey all rolling into one at last and going full steam ahead. Well, I am glad to have a seat for the performance. It's great to have it done, and great to know that you are doing it."

Esquire, December 1983

"Alfred Kinsey: The Patron Saint of Sex"

by Stanley Elkin

QUEEN VICTORIA DEAD FORTY-SEVEN YEARS when Alfred Charles Kinsey published *Sexual Behavior in the Human Male* in 1948, fifty-two years and still spinning when *Sexual Behavior in the Human Female* came out in 1953, and though the real effects wouldn't be felt for years, he'd pulled the shades and opened the closets, he'd cleared the cobwebs and aired the attics. He dusted, did windows, and it was the greatest, noisiest spring cleaning sexuality ever had. But it's a Columbus notion finally, for-want-of-a-nail reasoning, the idea that a single man alters history. Rome wasn't built in a day and Kinsey never got anybody laid. History happens piecemeal, in add-ons, in incremental software integers and suffixions and adjunctives. By frill and circumstance and fringe benefit. It's this all-the-trimmings life we live, our starter-set condition, the world continually trading up. (Because only bad men change the world single-handed.) Yet if there'd never been a Kinsey, I'd never have seen Jacqueline Bisset's breasts, Jane Fonda's, Julie Andrews's, for God's sake. If there'd never been a Kinsey, there'd have been no personals in the classified columns of *The New York Review of Books*. MWM would have never found SWM, and most of us would have gone to our graves believing only models or show girls were these lovely flowers of meat under their clothes. (Because what he did, what he did *really*, once we took it all in—and it's still hard to take in—was to democratize flesh, return us to innocence by showing us guilt— Freud did the same but didn't have the numbers—transporting us back to the Garden itself perhaps, hitting us where we lived and breathed, our mutualized lust like a kind of cloud cover and parting our scandalous needs like a red Sea.)

And if Kinsey himself seems to have been uninterested in sex except as a subject that could be measured (*his* subject, as communism was Joe McCarthy's, just that jealous; he even repudiated Freud, was out of sorts with Krafft-Ebbing), it was only because he was a taxonomist, a measurer, a sexual census taker, trained as a biologist at Bowdoin and at Harvard's Bussey Institute, where he began to collect the American Cynipidae—the gall wasp—a collection to which he devoted almost twenty-five years of his life and that ran to over four million specimens before it was finally donated to the American Museum of Natural History after his death. But more sociologist than scientist and finally, more evangel than either. (Because maybe it's different for people with data, maybe the data permits, even obliges, them to fight back, maybe you question their data you question their honor. Maybe it wasn't thin skin or self-righteousness that made him impatient with his critics, that deflected his science and lent him the aspect of someone besieged or gave him this ancient-mariner mentality. It was almost like outrage, like someone trying to clear his name. He was certainly good enough at it, a real sweet talker. A friend of mine, Dr. Lee Robins, professor of sociology in psychiatry at Washington University, heard him at a round-table dinner at the annual meeting of the American Psychiatric Association in 1954. The subject was "Psychiatric Implications of Surveys on Sexual Behavior." The Kinsey report had infuriated them; they questioned the reliability of a sample; they wanted to know, as Lionel Trilling, and Margaret Mead and Reinhold Niebuhr did: where love had gone—and Kinsey told them. Lee remembers his speech—Kinsey never prepared a talk, he didn't even refer to notes—as a sermon, a barn burner, Kinsey, the avenging evangel, the John Brown of sexuality.) The studies that would become Kinsey's famous reports actually began as a noncredited interdisciplinary marriage course offered by Indiana University in the late 1930s. (This was the age of Emily Post, of etiquette columns in the daily papers, of marriage manuals and all the soft instructions.) Asked by the university to coordinate the course and by the students to counsel them, he found that no formal statistical studies of human sexual activity existed, and he began to take data—histories—from the students themselves, to conduct extensive interviews about what people actually did, to themselves and each other. His goal, never achieved, was to collect the sexual histories of one hundred thousand people. When he died, in 1956, there were eighteen thousand such histories in his files, eight thousand of which he had personally taken.

Which makes him a kind of intellectual Casanova, a scientific Don Juan, whatever the boozy, set-'em-up-Joe, torch song and singsong equivalencies are for the ear's voyeurism, all the scandals of the heart and head; all the gossip of the imagination. Because this wasn't even psychiatry, you see. It wasn't, that is, passive, Kinsey came on like a prosecuting attorney. Not did you, but *when* did you; not have you, but how *often* have you—all the D.A.'s bad cop bad cop ploys and insinuations. That he got these people to talk at all—this was 1938, this was 1939, this was 1940 and all the 1940s, this was when men wore hats and women looked like telephone operators, their flower styles and print arrangements like those dumb sexual displays in nature, the bandings and colorful clutter on birds, say, who do not even know that what they are wearing is instinct and evolution, *that* innocent, *that* naïve. Using science, always *Science*, capitalized and italicized too, like a cop pounced from a speed trap, pulling them over to the side, badgering, hectoring, demanding—he was famous now, famous enough to be invited to talk to all sorts of groups, to chambers of commerce and Rotaries and Lions, to Sunday school classes, to cons in the pen, faggot Rush Street's boon companion, the guest of honor on Times Square (who cruises on the weekends: "I am Dr. Kinsey from Indiana University and I'm making a study of sex behavior. Can I buy you a drink?") Kinsey didn't accept fees for those talks he didn't prepare anyway, was paid off in low-down intimacies, other peoples' sex lives, assuring them of perfect confidentiality, on his scientific honor like a high horse, offering his objectivity, pledging all his scientific, nonjudgmental markers and swearing he would never betray them. Which he never did.

But what did he do for love?

Well, that's harder because love had been doing okay. It just hadn't known it is all, until Kinsey's flawed sample and scientific nonjudgmentals dropped by to reassure it.

The Journal of Sex Research, May 1998

From "Alfred Kinsey and the Kinsey Report: Historical Overview and Lasting Contributions"

by Vern L. Bullough

THE MODERN STUDY OF SEXUALITY was dominated by the medical perspective before 1940. Kinsey, a biologist, brought to the study of sexual expression a taxonomic approach—that is, an interest in classification and description. He developed his interview methodology and conducted over 8,000 interviews himself. His results challenged many widely held beliefs about sexuality, including the belief that women were not sexual. His work contributed to both the feminist and the gay/lesbian liberation movements. He was determined to make the study of sex a science, and in large part he succeeded.

The Archives of Sexual Behavior, June 2004

"Sex Will Never Be the Same: The Contributions of
Alfred C. Kinsey"

by Vern L. Bullough

KINSEY BUILT UPON what other European and American researchers had done, but in his male volume he was much more
critical of his predecessors than he was in the female volume. Although he mentioned many of the European sex researchers, several were conspicuous by their absence and, at times, he seemed
very moralistic (e.g., that Hirschfeld was not an objective researcher because of his campaign for gay rights or the failure of
H. Ellis to have face-to-face contact with his participants). He
had little positive to say about psychiatrists in general, although
he imparted a more positive message in the female volume. If bib-
liographical citations are any example, Kinsey explored much
more widely in the social sciences in the female volume than he
did in the male volume, indicating that he himself acquired
greater expertise over the years. Certainly, the female volume was
a more well rounded treatment. Overall, the effect of his books
was to change the way people looked at sex; indeed, sex could
never be the same again.

Redbook, September 1953

From "We Must Face the Facts"

by Ruth and Edward Brecher

THERE IS IMPORTANT SELF-KNOWLEDGE to be drawn from the Kinsey report by both young men and young women. The Indiana University scientists found that:

1. Men differ from one another with respect to sexual attitudes and behavior, but even greater differences exist among women—differences so extreme that some women can hardly believe the facts about others!

2. Although they reach physical maturity earlier, most young women take longer to mature sexually than most young men. Many boys in their teens are already at their peak of sexual activity, while girls may not reach their full sexual maturity until their 20s or even 30s.

3. Women are generally less interested than men in variety of sexual experience.

4. Women talk with one another about their sexual experiences less frankly and less often than men do.

From left: Chris Dilley (Trampolina), Irwin Keller (Winnie), Jeff Manabat (Trixie), and (front and center) Harvard-trained lawyer Ben Schatz (Rachel) make up The Kinsey Sicks—America's Favorite Dragapella Beautyshop Quartet.

Herman B. Wells, Chancellor of Indiana University

From the Foreword of *Kinsey: A Biography*

by Cornelia V. Christenson, published in 1971

As Dr. Kinsey's research into human sexual behavior was conducted while I was President of Indiana University, I have often been asked how it was that the University lent its support to the Kinsey research project. The answer is simple: a member of the faculty with proven competence and judgment in research wished to undertake it. In the process of implementing his research, Dr. Kinsey gained the backing of two respected scientific bodies: the Medical Division of the Rockefeller Foundation voted him funding and the National Research Council's medical Division, through its Committee for Research on Problems of Sex, cooperated by agreeing to administer the funds.

A second question has usually been posed to me, for research into a subject so guarded from mention and revelation as sexual practice did, indeed, embroil the University in a contest to preserve the principle of free scholarly inquiry against numerous and diverse attacks. The question, however phrased, usually called for an assessment of the long-term effect on Indiana University of protecting Kinsey's research. I have said and I believe that it has been beneficial in every way. Throughout history, attempts to keep people in ignorance of human nature and of the world with which they must cope have invariably proved misguided. Moreover, nothing presents so clearly to the public the creative role of the scholar as his penetration through assumptions and traditional beliefs to fact. In the long run, the University's willingness to battle for freedom of inquiry in this

Indiana University President Herman Wells in 1951.

controversial area and to sustain criticism when the results were published has been a source of great pride, even among those who disagreed with Dr. Kinsey on one aspect or another of his research. Events proved that a university can win out on the issue of academic freedom if the university community stands together. The backing of the University's Trustees was critical in maintaining a unified front and they deserve considerable credit for their stalwart stand in the face of public criticism.

For his part, Dr. Kinsey was always ready to cooperate with me by accepting the various administrative decisions which were made for the protection of his research. I found Dr. Kinsey a stimulating and valuable colleague.

At the dinner celebrating the 50th Anniversary of the Rockefeller Foundation, Dr. Robert S. Morison, then head of its Medical Division, told me that the Kinsey research had profoundly affected at least one branch of medicine, gynecology, and that time had proved the wisdom of the Division's initial support.

The Institute for Sex Research is now firmly established. It carries on its work with no more notice than other institutes on the campus receive, and its projects attract the grants which Dr. Kinsey sought in vain during the final years of his life. These developments are a tribute in part to the vision, courage, energy, and persistence of the Institute's founder and to the soundness of the research program he initiated.

Dr. Alfred C. Kinsey has a secure place in the annals of pioneering American scientists.

Look, May 1951

"What Dr. Kinsey Is Up to Now!"

by Albert Deutsch

TWO YEARS AGO, PROF. ALFRED C. KINSEY figured that his monumental sex-behavior study would be completed in about 20 years. Since then, the Kinsey group has struck so many new leads, so many rich mines of unexplored human material, that it is now evident the project will be a lifework even for the Indiana scientist's much younger colleagues, Wardell B. Pomeroy, Clyde E. Martin and Paul H. Gebhard—all in their early thirties.

"I guess I have ten or fifteen years of active work ahead of me," Kinsey told me not long ago. "The others (his present colleagues and new ones that may be added) will have to carry on from there."

When one gets close to it, the Kinsey enterprise looks like a many-ringed scientific circus in which the Kinsey troupe juggles research projects like so many Indian clubs. Right now, Kinsey is intensely interested in investigating the erotic element in art, which will make up a separate report when completed.

Kinsey has already taken the sex histories of several hundred artists—not only painters and sculptors, but also professional dancers, music composers and creative writers.

Some of the most prominent men and women in the world of fine arts have given Kinsey and his colleagues their sex histories. Of each artist, the scientist has asked searching questions as to the motivations and sources of his or her own creative output.

This little-known art project of Kinsey's may yet provide vital clues to the solution of two questions that have puzzled the experts for centuries:

Is there something special in the make-up of the "artist type" that causes him to follow different patterns of sexual behavior from the rest of the population?

How do the sexual behavior and attitudes of artists express themselves in their paintings, sculptures and other works?

The Kinsey study may also clear up decisively the question of "sublimation" in art—whether artists tend to divert their sex drives into the channels of creative art—a thesis elaborately propounded by Dr. Sigmund Freud, founder of psychoanalysis. Kinsey has already disputed this theory of sex sublimation, on the basis of the many case histories he has already studied. His present large-scale study may provide the final check on who is right—Kinsey or Freud.

While the Kinsey team is developing the study of art, it is at present winding up its second report—on sexual behavior in the human female. Meanwhile, the group is already mapping out the report which is scheduled to follow (in about two years). The third volume of the Kinsey reports will be a study of sex laws and sex offenders.

The figures published in the first Kinsey report have already been utilized as standard ammunition for pro and con arguments in court cases involving questions of sexual behavior, or misbehavior.

A German-born professor recently had his application for American citizenship denied by a U.S. District Court in New York because he admitted having had affairs with unmarried women prior to his own marriage.

The applicant's lawyer cited the Kinsey report as indicating that 85 per cent of American men have premarital sex relations. But the Government attorney argued successfully that "society cannot condone practices reserved to parties in the married state," the Kinsey figures notwithstanding. The professor appealed to a U.S. Court of Appeals, which reversed the negative decision and granted him citizenship.

The Kinsey report on males was also cited by another pro-

Marlon Brando, Kim Hunter and Jessica Tandy in Tennessee Williams' A Streetcar Named Desire. *Kinsey took the sexual histories of the original Broadway cast in 1947.*

fessor vainly seeking citizenship in an Illinois court after admitting that he and his wife had lived together for a short period without benefit of clergy before they had legalized their relationship through marriage.

In San Francisco, a 23-year-old parolee—charged with "contributing to the delinquency of a minor" because he admittedly had intimate relations with his 18-year-old fiancée—was saved from a prison term after his lawyer quoted from the Kinsey report and similar sex surveys, indicating the wide prevalence of premarital experience. The judge dismissed the case and blessed the couple's impending marriage; the wedding date had been set before the man's arrest.

In a country court in Philadelphia, Judge Curtis Bok dismissed a case against local booksellers who were charged with distributing obscene books. In his opinion in the case, Judge Bok declared: "Dr. Kinsey's report on the sexual behavior of men is now current. Truth and error, as Milton urged in his *Areopagitica*, are being allowed to grapple, and we are the better for it."

...Another forthcoming volume in the Kinsey project—one which family counselors are awaiting with keen interest—will deal with sexual factors in marital adjustments. This probably will be the most widely read volume in the series.

The Kinsey group already has compiled more than 9000 histories of marriages. Kinsey notes that his research data to date indicates that "sexual factors are usually not the most important in determining the stability of a marriage," but that they do "have some significance in a high proportion of the marriages."

A separate volume will be given to physiological studies of sexual arousal and orgasm; another to what Kinsey calls "the heterosexual-homosexual balance" in human beings. One book will deal with sexual adjustments in institutions, such as prisons, mental hospitals, military establishments and boarding schools.

There will be a volume on prostitution, too. The group has collected the sex histories of about 1200 male and female prostitutes. Kinsey and his colleagues have already obtained knowledge of the personalities of prostitutes, their life stories, the physical setup and management of organized prostitution and other facts about the trade to an extent unequaled by other researchers.

Police Picked Up Kinsey

Both he and his colleagues have narrowly averted disastrous scrapes. Kinsey himself has been picked up as a suspicious character by police in several towns where he was observed loitering about disreputable honky-tonks, criminal hangouts and red-light districts—in search of subjects for interviews. One sheriff nearly put him in the hoosegow as a "snooper," and he was once caught in a house of prostitution when the police raided it. He had to show his credentials to convince the cops he was engaged in a scientific study.

Kinsey, at one time, became a familiar figure among Broadway street-corner touts. He gradually inveigled himself into the good graces of these Damon Runyon characters, who proved helpful in steering him to the riffraff elements he needed to interview.

The interviewing team's newest, and first, woman member—Mrs. Alice Withrow Field—brings to the project a specialized knowledge of sex delinquents. Author of an important study of prostitution in London, Mrs. Field was a member of the probation staff of the New York City Magistrates Courts.

As the Kinsey group's case histories developed, plans were changed. Kinsey had originally planned a separate volume on the sexual behavior of the American Negro, but it became evident to him that there was no essential difference between the patterns of the white sand Negroes, save those based on social-economic factors rather than racial. The data on Negroes, therefore, will be incorporated later in revised editions of the first two volumes.

Gall Wasps Shelved

While his contemporaries await the appearance of his second report, the remarkable adventurer in science looks ahead to the preparation of many more Kinsey reports. He regards with good humor the many barbs about the man who switched his lifework to human sex after spending 25 years scrutinizing the life and loves of the gall wasps.

Not long ago, an American scholar in England was asked by an Oxford University don:

"Tell me about this man Kinsey—hasn't he been neglecting his wasps lately?"

Few people familiar with the aims, methods and accomplishments of the Indiana scientist will express any regret about Kinsey's decision to switch from insects to sex as a socially useful and scientifically valuable contribution to human understanding.

Redbook, May 1956

"What Kinsey Is Doing Now"

by Albert Deutsch

A KINSEY REPORT ON ABORTIONS, now nearing completion, will disclose a remarkably high rate of deliberately aborted births in the United States. The preliminary figures in this survey indicate that perhaps *one out of every six pregnancies* ends in a deliberately induced abortion. This would mean, at a conservative estimate, that each year more than 800,000 abortions are performed in the United States; only a small fraction of these result from legally permitted medical decisions to safeguard the life or health of the mother.

The implications of this Kinsey finding become apparent when it is realized that most illegal or "criminal" abortions are performed on married women who don't want more children, that abortions occur in every social and economic class and that they are often done under sordid, frightfully unhygienic conditions.

Another Kinsey volume slated for early publication is a study of state laws relating to sex. This report will give evidence that many of our sex laws are confusing, contradictory, unenforced, unenforceable, and completely unrealistic.

Most states, for instance, have laws against adultery, but these are rarely enforced. If they were, the Kinsey figures show, about half the married males in America would be jailed at some time during married life. Several states have no laws against adultery, and others make it a crime punishable by up to ten years' imprisonment. A certain sex offense may be only a misdemeanor in one state, punishable by a light fine or short jail term; in another state it may be a felony that carries a life term or even a death penalty. By citing such examples of injustice, the forthcoming Kinsey report is certain to stimulate movements to harmonize and modernize our sex laws.

In so doing, it will be continuing a process started by Kinsey's earlier reports, for it is in the fields of lawmaking and law enforcement that the Kinsey project has had the greatest impact to date. A number of recent court decisions on sex offenses has been based mainly or in part on Kinsey findings. The general effect has been to liberalize interpretations of existing sex laws. Dr. Kinsey has been invited to testify before several state legislative committees, and he has often been consulted by official commissions studying sex laws.

The Kinsey influence is clearly seen in the action last year of the powerful American Law Institute in recommending sweeping changes in our sex laws. A committee of the Institute, composed of leading criminologists and jurists, has been working for years on a model penal code to be submitted to the states to replace existing codes. The committee's draft, approved by the American Law Institute Council, included a lengthy section on sex offenses, based largely on the findings of the Kinsey project.

The model code would clear the state statute books of legal prohibitions against frowned-upon sex acts that properly fall within the realm of morals and religion rather than law. The new code would drop, for instance, the laws against adultery, fornication and sodomy. It is questionable to many experts whether these acts are of proper legal concern, and the laws to regulate them are generally unenforceable and contrary to the efforts the investigators will make to collect this information.

The report will show that, although most courts deal fairly with violators of sex laws, penalties too often depend on the prejudices and whims of individual judges. Some judges may be extremely lenient with one type of sex offender but may throw the book at another. Kinsey and his colleagues have discovered an astonishing prevalence of brutality, frame-ups, and blackmail connected with the handling of alleged sex offenders. Their report will include case

Clyde Martin, Wardell Pomeroy and Alfred Kinsey (from left to right) hit the road.

histories involving policemen, especially those assigned to vice squads, in the systematic victimization of sex-offense suspects.

Dr. Kinsey and his wife last fall made a two-month tour of Europe. Kinsey went to England and six continental countries with three main goals in mind: to lecture before medical, psychiatric and university assemblies; to consult with penologists, police officials and jurists on the operation of sex laws and the treatment of sex offenders in order to compare them with American practices, and to make notes on the masterpieces in the Louvre, the Prado and other great museums in connection with his extensive study of erotic factors in art (which will be the subject of yet another report).

Commenting on his European impressions, Kinsey says, "The Scandinavians in general have the most advanced laws relating to sex and the most professionalized methods of handling sex offenders. In European countries, where attitudes towards sex are far more liberal than ours, the subject hasn't the degree of morbid fascination it has among us. In only one country—England—did I find sex laws and attitudes more stringent than ours."

Austin MacCormick, professor of criminology at the University of California, is one of the very few persons ever allowed to witness a Kinsey interview. With the inmate's consent, he sat in a corner while the interview proceeded.

"I couldn't believe it was possible," he says. "The inmate was uncomfortable at first. Dr. Kinsey started a casual conversation. Within a few minutes, the man was completely comfortable, and when the formal interview began he answered approximately 400 questions on his sex life with ease and I am convinced, with complete honesty. It isn't hypnotism, but there's something in that man Kinsey that inspires trust."

What do the facts about imprisoned sex offenders have to do with the general public? Much more than is generally realized, Dr. Kinsey believes. The Kinsey files contain evidence that "only a minute fraction of one per cent of the persons involved in sexual behavior which is contrary to the law are ever apprehended, prosecuted, or convicted." The ones in prison, in other words, aren't necessarily the worst offenders—they are simply the minority who have been caught.

Here are some topics on which the Kinsey staff is planning publications:
• The influence of drugs on sexual behavior. This report will be based mainly on interviews with 1,000 marijuana users, 150 ad-

dicts of heroin, and other opium derivatives and several thousand individuals whose use of alcohol has affected their sex activities.

• A revision of the first volume, *Sexual Behavior in the Human Male*. This will include several thousand additional case histories and will constitute virtually a second Kinsey report on men.

• Transvestism. This project will be based on intensive studies of 150 men and women who feel they belong to the opposite sex and are impelled to dress accordingly.

• Sexual factors in marital adjustment. This will be a manual for married people and for professionals handling family problems and will be based on information unavailable in current marriage manuals.

• Institutional sexual adjustment. This will draw from sex histories of men, women and children in prisons, mental institutions, hospitals for long-term care, boarding schools, reform schools and the Armed Forces. The book will include controversial facts about what happens to men without women and women without men for prolonged periods, and to adolescents confined for years in one-sex environments.

When I asked Dr. Kinsey what he considered the most significant development since he started his study, he promptly replied:

"The amazing co-operation we now get from all kinds of individuals, groups, and institutions. In the early years we encountered a great deal of resistance in our efforts to obtain interviews and information. People were apt either to fear us or laugh us off. Now we are overwhelmed by invitations to lecture, interview and consult and by eager requests for our data. We know that the great majority of people are with us in our work, and this means a good deal."

It certainly does mean a good deal to have legislators, judges, marriage counselors and ordinary citizens showing serious interest in the Kinsey project. And if the interest leads to positive action, it may mean a good deal to us all.

Life, August 1953

"Nourishing"

by Fannie Hurst

DR. KINSEY'S FIRST BOOK on what now promises to be a continuing study of sex behavior rattled the teeth and inhibitions of the nation. Taboos stirred in their long sleep. Legitimate and needed nouns, nastied only by the nasty in mind, crept out of the mire of their exile to become respectable, via Kinsey. Statistics became more than a sign language.

And now the doctor has done it again, in *Sexual Behavior in the Human Female*—this time with the girls, who for reasons immemorial seem more challenging to popular interest than the less dramatic and dramatized male.

Thanks to the providential snatching of his tomes from the exclusive jaws of science into the realm of popular consumption, sex no longer rears a traditionally ugly head. On the contrary, it now lifts one socially acceptable, clean shaved and fit to enter the drawing room, the schoolroom or even the good graces of Emily Post.

America still rocks with the novelty of it.

What novelist or dramatist, on top or under the ground, whose social investigations are published under such titles as *Nana, Hedda Gabler, Man and Superman, Camille, Forever Amber, Romeo and Juliet, Back Street, This Side of Paradise, Anna Karenina*, can match this: Weeks before the publication of the impending *Sexual Behavior in the Human Female*, representatives from the major newspapers and magazines of the nation journey from its four corners to Bloomington, Ind. to descend, like journalistic locusts, for advance glimpses of the proof sheets of *Sexual Behavior of the Human Female*.

Can it be that Dr. Kinsey is giving us the most comprehensive study on the mechanics of sex on record? Yes, can be and is. Except for scientific studies of groups in colleges or communities, sexual behavior and the resultant social patterns have never been set down on anything like the Kinsey scale. And this publication of his reports on why we are sexually the way we are would seem to mark the first time that these facts, presented scientifically, have hit the mass ear and the mass mind.

But the report is almost certain to be hotly controverted by a world not too far removed from the "birds and bees" approach to sex discussion—like the lady who replied to the psychology professor when he complained that women were too subjective: "I don't believe they are too subjective at all. I'm not." It is the women themselves, drawing their general conclusions from the perpendicular pronoun *I*, who will probably do much of the refuting.

The Kinsey bombshell, stressing the congenital incompatibilities between the sexes and letting us have it in a barrage of hot statistics, will shake the psychiatric couches of the atomic age. Marriage counselors will scurry for revised concepts, and so will the men and women of the courts of domestic relations. Fiction writers will slow down that next novel until the Kinsey dust has settled.

And you, Your Honor, be prepared for this one: "Please don't send me to reform school, Judge. I'm no more a juvenile delinquent than Juliet was with Romeo. The Kinsey report says so."

Dr. Kinsey tells the story of human sexual behavior dispassionately, although it is obvious that he himself scorns our controversial morality. But in general he lets his statistics speak louder than words. And the deductions boil down to almost a cliché: most women are in love with love, rather than with their man.

No novelist who wants to live by something more than bread alone will readily surrender to this antiromanticist philosophy of the statistics. Even the novelist must concede, though, that today masses of women without men are out, not primarily after romance with lace in its sleeves, but after security-in-trousers.

But nature, so seldom caught napping, again has her compensatory little scheme for just exigencies. If women are frigidly geared in their responses to the sexual demands of the male, you need only glance about to realize that their pursuit of him has not abated.

It is not for just the dear dream of surrender that the "career woman" spends her 50 weeks' savings for that two weeks' cruise where she will probably meet no one more eligible that the ship's purser (whose fiancée is coming aboard at Bermuda)? Indeed, the eligible unattached male of this era of the growing economic independence of women boards a cruise ship, enters a summer hotel or embarks upon a business involving secretaries and career women at his peril.

Nature's Traps

It is, of course, conceivable that with women's economic independence only in its infancy, security may some day come to mean something different from mere security-in-trousers. But here again, nature sets her traps with prescience. Whether or not the physical desire of the female for her male matches up to his, her desire for a home does. Be it igloo, ranch house, trailer, manor house, houseboat or a subdivision packingcase with a picture window, and towels on the bathroom rack embroidered "His" and "Hers," these yearnings are obviously plaguing her sufficiently to insure the continuing overpopulation of the world.

Considering the penetrations Dr. Kinsey must attempt into the inhibitions, inaccuracies, faulty memories, distrust, vanities, modesty and shame of the women under his scrutiny, his margin for error seems wide. However, Dr. Kinsey and his aides are masters of the delicate art of probing, with decency and dignity, for the private truths they seek. Without a psychiatrist in sight, the ladies remain vertical in reply to questions that intrude into areas of their consciousness where even angels and psychiatrists might fear to tread.

And his sociological conclusions are not as gloomy as they seem. World War I and the day of the speakeasy did indeed knock the Victorian era higher than a cocked hat. But, though Dr. Kinsey properly does not concern himself with it, there is an encouraging aftermath we must bear in mind. The slim flapper of the '20s, in her short skirts, low waist and neckline, and with her speakeasy-breath, ultimately married her man, frequently the one with whom she had the premarital relations. He, in turn, quickly slipped into the category of tired businessman.

Pushing her perambulator and cooperating with her husband's success story, the erstwhile flapper reared her families in American homes good enough to produce a Grade A crop of youngsters who were to face with glory the wars ahead. So did the subsequent career girl of the '30s. Going to her desk job until the eighth-and-a-half month of her pregnancy, she helped create and era of American, bought-and-paid-for little homes—young families with antennas on their roofs, rumpus rooms in their basements, convertible cars in their garages and strength in their backbones.

Dr. Kinsey's evaluations, vast as they seem to our myopic eyes, are actually only microscopic. His land area under consideration, the United States of America, is only 2,974,726 square miles, compared to the world spread of 58,209,000 square miles. His 5,940 women represent less than 1/100 of 1% of the female population of the U.S.

Yet, I repeat, this is the best measure we have ever had. The Kinsey statistics, like cereal shot from a gun, are not frightening, but nourishing.

Social changes as drastic as the documented ones in Kinsey's two volumes of the sexes have been jittering up the world ever since it went into troubled formation. And good continues to triumph. The scheme of survival, as large as God, seems to have established a permanent protectorate over the squirming, hurting, loving, dreaming, giving, doing and begetting mass of us.

Like the many that have gone before, the social revolution

through which we are now muddling will find its middle of the road. And the Kinsey reports likewise will find their quiet and deserved place in the march of knowledge. Presently their news value, now running a temperature, will sink into yesteryear, along with "Everyday in every way I am getting better and better" and "Peace, it's wonderful."

Perhaps the major concrete conclusion for the layman to reach from the reports is for male and female to better understand the complicated biology of human beings. Similarities can take care of themselves. Dr. Kinsey is chiefly concerned with understanding our differences.

Should such books as the Kinsey reports be written for popular consumption?

Yes.

U. S. News & World Report, November 6, 1953

From "The Story Back of Kinsey: Sex Studies Yield Fame But Not Riches"

WHEN HIS EARLY SEX RESEARCH was translated into the book "Sexual Behavior in the Human Male," Dr. Kinsey was not prepared for the sensation he was to create. The book had been given little advance publicity, no real build-up. It was looked upon by some as a rather dry, scientific work that would interest only physicians, scientists and a few thousand laymen. Now, five years later, 300,000 copies have been sold. There are six foreign editions.

Reaction to the book was violent. Dr. Kinsey was praised, denounced, ridiculed. As the controversy over the book raged on, the public began to realize that a second volume must be in the making, a sex book about women. Thus, the suspense that was generated five years ago helped contribute to the demand for the second book, "Sexual Behavior in the Human Female," when it finally appeared this year.

The colossal publicity that greeted publication of the book led to widespread belief that a slick press agent, hired by Dr. Kinsey, was behind the build-up. One business firm wrote Dr. Kinsey for the name of his press agent, with a view to hiring him. Associates report that Kinsey himself was astonished at the ballyhoo given to the book.

The page 1 publicity in the newspapers and the reams of space devoted to the book in the magazines overshadowed Russia's experiments with the hydrogen bomb, which became public about the same time.

Dr. Kinsey immediately became the center of a raging controversy. Protests came from some large and influential groups that circulation of the report should have been confined to physicians, scientists and scientific libraries. Meanwhile, the book was outselling every other book but the Bible.

According to the Kinsey Report
Every average man you know
Much prefers his lovely doggie to court
When the temperature is low,
But when the thermometer goes way up
And the weather is sizzling hot,
Mr. Gob
For his squab
A marine
For his queen
A GI
For his cutey pie
Is not,
'Cause it's too, too
Too darn hot,
It's too darn hot,
It's too darn hot.

—Ella Fitzgerald's version of
"Too Darn Hot" written by
Cole Porter for the musical
Kiss Me Kate

Ella Fitzgerald, c. 1950.

Dr. Ruth Westheimer, 2004

IN THE JEWISH TRADITION we say that in order to see further, we must stand on the shoulders of giants. At 4'7" that advice is especially apt for me, and in my chosen profession of sex therapist, there is no taller giant whose shoulders I have stood on than those of Alfred Kinsey.

Though far too many people ignore his contributions, without him there might never have been a sexual revolution, and its accompanying increase in pleasure from sex that men and women have enjoyed because of it. Before Kinsey, we, at least in the western world, had been living in the dark ages of human sexuality. On the one hand, so little was known about how we humans function in this area—in fact much of what we did "know" was erroneous—that most people had to struggle with this most basic of human functions. And further cloaking our understanding of sex was the curtain of prudery that descended on us from our Puritan and Victorian backgrounds.

Before Kinsey, there had been some scientific studies done on homosexuality, for example the work of the German physician Magnus Hirschfeld, but Kinsey was the first person to apply scientific principles to the examination of human sexuality in its entirety. Before Kinsey expanded our knowledge of this subject, people had to cope with the damage done to their sexual functioning by the wide variety of myths, rumors, misinformation and religious propaganda that influenced how men and women perceived sex. There were people with a particular agenda, often religious though not always, who were actually trying to make sex as unenjoyable as possible. And as we learn in the movie, one of those people was Kinsey's own father.

Given this lack of understanding, it's not surprising that so many people, especially women, received absolutely no pleasure

Alfred Kinsey, June 1953.

from sex. These women, on their wedding night and forever after, followed the advice of that legendary Victorian mother who told her soon-to-be-wed daughter to just "lie back and think of England." A variation of this philosophy can be seen in the film when one young women states that she believes she is "frigid." This is a word that has since been banished from the lexicon of sexology, in good part because of Kinsey's work, though at that time it was a word that actually was a bit progressive as it implied that women could be something other than frigid. Sadly, for many women in those days before Kinsey did his studies, being frigid could be a life-long sentence.

Now Kinsey's work wasn't perfect. As I point out in my college textbook, *Human Sexuality: A Psychosocial Perspective* (co-authored with Prof. Sanford Lopater), Kinsey wasn't able to sample everyone. Racial minorities were excluded and a disproportionately large percentage of those people questioned had high levels of education. Aging and elderly people and those in rural areas were similarly underrepresented. But the controversy that surrounded his work caused his funding to be severely cut, and I'm sure that had he been given the resources he would have corrected those deficiencies, just as he made significant changes in his methodology between his first book on males and his second one on females, something that is acknowledged in the movie I was glad to see.

But if Alfred Kinsey hadn't had the curiosity, work ethic and courage to pursue his studies, we might all be left thinking that good sexual performance was something perverse rather than a goal to be sought after. I still get hundreds and hundreds of questions from people, both young and old, that show that the myths of the past continue to affect our population and that sexual literacy, though much more widespread, is not universal. The sexual urges are so strong that sexuality is something that no one can ignore. The idea that to abstain from sex is a viable choice is ludicrous, as Kinsey proved, because not only are so few of us capable of ignoring our sexual urges, but why should we? Yes, people can go too far, as did some of those in the movie, but the rest of us shouldn't be punished for the abuses of the minority. Everyone deserves the opportunity to learn as much about their sexual abilities as possible so that they can maximize the benefits of good sexual functioning, an opportunity that might never have come about without the work of Alfred Kinsey.

Showing the ignorance about sex that existed among even educated men and women before Kinsey began his work is an important contribution of this film. Sexual matters still make us uncomfortable, and communications between partners still leaves a lot to be desired. If more people understood how far we've come since Kinsey, and how much less pleasurable their sex lives would be without the body of knowledge accumulated by Kinsey and those who've followed them, they might take more care to hone their sexual skills to an even higher level. As this is an especially important lesson for young people to learn, I strongly suggest that this film be shown to every human sexuality class in colleges across the country.

Kinsey is a wonderfully made movie and I applaud everyone involved, from the screenwriter-director to the actors, most notably Liam Neeson.

Sexual Behavior in the Human Female

From the Introduction to the 1998 edition

by John Bancroft

FROM HIS FIRST MARRIAGE COURSE, Kinsey's work attracted controversy, and this exploded at the national and international level with the publication of *Sexual Behavior in the Human Male* in 1948. In the 50 years since then, the controversy has waxed and waned, in the past ten years resurfacing mainly as a political campaign by those who deplore the change in family and sexual values that have occurred in the United States and elsewhere. They see Kinsey as the architect of this decline, attributing to him enormous influence over a major process of social change which, it should be noted, has affected not only the United States but most industrial countries. They appear to believe that by discrediting Kinsey they will in some sense be able to set the clock back to what they assume were more appealing times.

Kinsey has been described by some as a man with a mission: to change the pattern of sexual behavior in the United States, to bring about a "revolution" in sexual values, even to undermine the social structure of the United States in such a way as to foster communism. (Kinsey was decidedly not a Communist.) What is the evidence that Kinsey had a mission beyond that of a socially aware scientist who wanted his work to be of value to the society in which he lived? Although Kinsey gave many lectures, corresponded extensively, and published a few papers relating to sexuality, there is no doubt that any such impact he may have had was largely the result of the two books from his great project, the *Male* volume and the *Female* volume.

In the *Male* volume, the central theme relating to the need for social change concerns the striking differences in patterns of male sexual behavior between what Kinsey summarizes as the "upper and lower social levels." This was shown in a greater tendency for "upper level" males to engage in masturbation, premarital petting and oral sex, and for "lower level" males to engage in premarital intercourse (mainly in the conventional "missionary" position). Kinsey further described this social class difference as reflecting an awareness, at the upper level, of what is "right or wrong" (i.e., what is moral or immoral), and at the lower level of what is "natural or unnatural." For the upper-level group "all socio-sexual behavior becomes a moral issue. Lower social levels, on the contrary, rationalize their patterns of sexual behavior on the basis of what is natural or unnatural."

In Kinsey's view there are two important consequences of this social class difference; first, a major lack of understanding by one class of the other, and resulting conflicts; secondly, many members of the upper social level "consider it a religious obligation to impose their code upon all other segments of the population." Thus Kinsey describes how marriage counselors, most of whom come from the upper social level, impose their concepts of sexual normality on lower-level couples, where they don't fit. More important, those who determine the laws come from the upper social level; thus, in Kinsey's analysis, most of the sex laws, at the time he was writing, not only had a long background in religious doctrine, but were more consistent with the "sexual morality" of the upper social levels, and inconsistent with accepted standards of "natural" sexual behavior in the lower social levels.

A theme which kept recurring in the *Male* volume was the extent to which the law was out of touch with the real world. At the time Kinsey was researching, virtually all forms of non-marital sexuality were illegal, and some forms of sexual behavior within marriage (e.g., oral sex) were also illegal, at least in some states. "On a specific calculation of our data, it may be stated that at least 85 percent of the younger male population could be convicted as

Clyde Martin and Paul Gebhard examine statistics.

sex offenders if law enforcement were as efficient as most people expect them to be." Yet "only a minute fraction of 1 percent of the persons who are involved in sexual behavior which is contrary to the law are ever apprehended, persecuted or convicted" and "the current sex laws are unenforced and unenforceable because they are too completely out of accord with the realities of human behavior." Kinsey goes on to recount how such laws may nevertheless be capriciously enforced by members of the police, for a variety of often dubious reasons. And when they are enforced, individuals, guilty of some act which is commonplace, often suffer consequences which are grossly out of proportion to the damage caused by the "crime." Kinsey's compassion for the sexual "underdog" comes through time and time again as he describes the consequences of this legal state of affairs, not solely because of the impact of actual conviction, but much more frequently, the chronic effects of guilt about engaging in illegal activities which are, in Kinsey's view, part of the normal range of human sexual experience. He also draws attention to the extent that it has been the male in society who imposes a sexual morality which has longstanding roots in the "property status" of women, leading to such inconsistencies as the impossibility of a husband being accused of raping his wife, while a married couple would be committing a crime by engaging in consensual oral sex.

To some extent, Kinsey's style changed and evolved as he moved from the *Male* to the *Female* volume. Although Kinsey was often critical of those who made assertions about sexual behavior without revealing the evidence on which their assertions were based, Kinsey indulged in a fair amount of this "editorializing" in the *Male* volume. This was less evident in the *Female* volume, where we find much more detailed references to the literature in the form of extensive footnotes, and one senses here a response to criticism.

The last five chapters of the *Female* volume provide a masterly review of the available evidence on the anatomy, physiology, psychology, neurophysiology, and endocrinology of sexual response. Interestingly, in Chapter 14, on the anatomy of sexual response, there are detailed descriptions of common patterns of muscle response and other responses during sexual activity and orgasm. The sources of this data are to a large extent not referenced; one of the sources listed is described as being from "scientifically trained persons who have observed human sexual activities in which they themselves were not involved, and who kept records of their observations." Much of this observational data in fact came from films of sexual activity involving volunteers—films that Kinsey had made in the privacy of his own home. When Kinsey was writing, it would clearly have been unwise to reveal that such filming had been done, though it was subsequently described in Pomeroy's biography of Kinsey. Here, then, for those who have questioned Kinsey's motives for this filming, is the simple explanation: as a scientist, Kinsey was reluctant to rely solely on self-report; he wanted to be able to observe what happened during sexual activity. In the process he paved the way for Masters and Johnson's important work.

There is now general agreement in the scientific community that Kinsey's method of obtaining a sample of Americans did not meet today's standards of survey sampling. Probability sampling was in its infancy when Kinsey started his long-running study.

As Gebhard and Johnson point out in the Kinsey Data, the sampling problem was most marked in the *Male* volume, mainly because of the inclusion of large numbers of prisoners within the non-college sample. When Gebhard, Pomeroy, and Martin confronted Kinsey with the differences in the sexual behavior data between the women with and without prison records, he accepted the need to omit such special groups for the analysis, and in a departure from the *Male* volume, they were excluded from consideration in the *Female* volume.

Some years after Kinsey's death, the Institute staff re-analyzed the data, including the additional interviews which had been collected between the preparation of the *Female* volume until 1963, separating out, for both men and women, a number of special groups which were likely to bias the total sample. This analysis was presented in the Kinsey Data, resulting in "The Basic Sample" of men and women who had never been convicted of any offense other than traffic violations and who did not come from any source which was known to be biased in terms of sexual behavior (e.g., homosexual networks). This involved 4694 white and 177 black men with college education, and 766 white men with no college education. For the women, there were 4358 white and 223 black with college education, and 1028 with no college education. The under-sampling of the non-college educated, for both men and women, was clear. In general, these samples were of most value in studying the college-educated part of the population.

Clyde Martin with punch cards and the IBM machine.

As a result of this "cleaning" of the data, Gebhard and Johnson concluded that "the major findings of the earlier works regarding age, gender, marital status and socioeconomic class remain intact. Adding to and cleaning our samples has markedly increased their value, but has not as yet caused us to recant any important assertion."

One issue which did look different as a result of this process was the incidence of male homosexual behavior. Whereas incidence figures for the college-educated males did not change much, those for the non-college educated, once those with crimi-

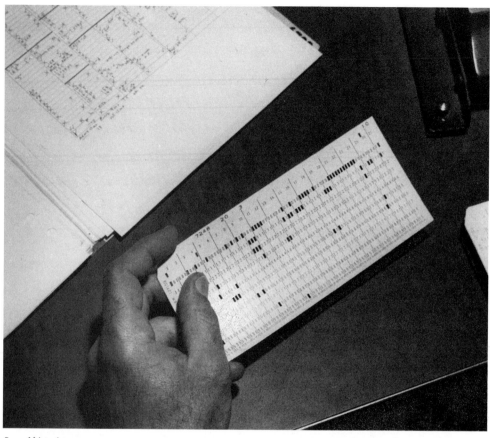

Sexual histories were transferred from written notes onto punch cards, which were then fed into the IBM computer.

nal records were excluded, looked markedly lower. Given the relatively sound nature of the college-educated sample, Gagnon and Simon re-analyzed the data from those groups looking at the occurrence of same-sex behavior. In the *Male* volume we were told that 37 percent of the total male population had at least some overt homosexual experience to the point of orgasm between adolescence and old age. Gagnon and Simon, focusing on 2900 young men who were in college between the years 1938 and 1950, found that 30 percent had at least one homosexual experience in which either the subject or his male partner had attained orgasm. However, slightly more than half of these had no experiences after the age of fifteen, and an additional third had experienced all their homosexual acts during adolescence. This left about 3 percent with extensive and 3 percent with exclusive homosexual histories. Thus Kinsey's original presentation had amplified the occurrence of same-sex behavior, but for the college educated—the largest and most representational part of Kinsey's total sample—the amplification was not as great as is often claimed.

Of course, a number of Kinsey's conclusions have subsequently been proved wrong. For example, reacting to what he regarded as over-enthusiasm at that time for the role of hormones in controlling and influencing sexual behavior, and in particular the current interest in castration as a means of controlling sex offenders, he commented that "the fact that hormones are produced in the gonads is, without further evidence, no reason for believing that they are the primary agent controlling those capacities of the nervous system on which sexual response depends," and he concluded that androgens influenced sexual behavior only in a non-specific way, by increasing general metabolism. There is now further evidence that androgens, at least in the male, have a fundamental part to play in sexual arousability. But the remarkable thing about these two volumes, when re-examined fifty years later, is how much Kinsey got right. One of the more striking examples is his explosion of the myth of the "vaginal orgasm" even though it was Masters and Johnson who received the credit for this. In general, the level of scholarship and the comprehensiveness of the review of the relevant literature, across the *Male* and *Female* volumes, have no equal in the sexological literature before or since.

In the field of sexual science, where intellectual heavyweights have been in short supply, Kinsey remains the pre-eminent sexual scientist. The fact that he was trained as a biologist, yet carried out a massive study of human sexual behavior which was closer to social science than to biology, accounts for some of the mistakes and errors of judgment that he made. He was clearly a stubborn man with strongly held opinions. He needed to be in control, making it less likely that he would accept the advice of others, and this resulted in his taking some wrong directions. However, Kinsey showed himself responsive to criticism when it was backed up with good evidence, and without his stubborn and somewhat arrogant streak he would not have succeeded in what was an exceptionally courageous and monumental piece of pioneering research. While sometimes being hypercritical of his academic peers, he showed strong compassion for those who he believed suffered as a result of their sexual lives. He doubted that the causes for such problems lay within the individual but rather the repressive social environment in which he or she had developed. He wanted sex to play a positive part in people's lives. In this respect, he was a somewhat naïve idealist, whose ideals surfaced at a time when the whole issue of sexual morality was in or near the "melting pot." The extent to which Kinsey is responsible for changes in sexual attitudes and behavior that have occurred since he published his two volumes is debatable. There have been many relevant and powerful socio-cultural factors involved during that half century. But what is beyond dispute is that he opened up the debate about sexual behavior and in several respects "demystified" it. Some will continue to regret this, preferring that sex remains surrounded by mystery, whatever the human cost. As far as I am concerned, he was a man of scientific integrity and great compassion who made a superhuman effort to do what he thought needed to be done, and for this he deserves our greatest respect.

St. Paul Pioneer Press, September 27, 1953

"Graham Sermon Blasts Dr. Kinsey"

"DR. KINSEY'S ONE-SIDED REPORT is an indictment against American womanhood."

"The book will teach young people how to indulge in premarital relations and get away with it."

"It will teach our young people terrifying perversions they had never heard of before."

"It is impossible to estimate the damage this book will do to the already deteriorating morals of America."

Above are a few of the indictments of the Kinsey report made by Evangelist Billy Graham in a sermon, "The Bible and Dr. Kinsey," in which the nation's leading revivalist adds:

"Thank God for women who still know how to blush."

Dr. Graham's sermon, first preached to a nationwide radio audience, has proved so popular the public already has requested 50,000 reprints and additional thousands of requests are pouring in daily to the Billy Graham Evangelistic association headquarters, 1620 Harmon Pl., Minneapolis.

Dr. Graham, who besides his evangelistic services in metropolitan areas and his radio and television programs, writes a daily newspaper column, "My Answer," which appears in the *St. Paul Dispatch* and in Sunday's *Pioneer Press,* has now issued 3 million copies of sermon reprints during the past three years, his representatives in the Twin Cities said.

In his sermon, "The Bible and Dr. Kinsey," Dr. Graham says the private lives of 5,940 women have been exposed by Dr. Kinsey with "no details spared."

Youth Encouraged

The moral laws governing marriage have been scorned and immorality advocated. Young people are encouraged to have pre-marital experiences.

"Happily married husbands and wives are going to start suspecting each other when they read one of every four wives is unfaithful to her husband."

The evangelist also charges the report "shows itself to be completely lopsided and unscientific when it says seven of 10 women who had pre-marital affairs had no regrets.

"He certainly could not have interviewed any of the millions of born-again Christian women in this country who put the highest price on virtue, decency and modesty.

"I do not know any Christian women who would submit themselves to such a probing and analysis," Dr. Graham observes.

The evangelist continues, "Thank God we have millions of women who still know how to blush—women who believe virtue is the greatest attribute of womanhood. Women who would talk to these secret agents about such intimate details of their lives are not typical of the Christian women of America.

"Dr. Kinsey's one-sided report . . . will cause children to doubt the fidelity of their parents and will lead to various types of moral abuses.

"We all agree with Dr. Kinsey that moral conditions in America are bad. But his report for the wholesale public consumption, appealing to the lower instincts of human nature, is aggravating the situation."

Get Away With It

"This book is going to teach young people . . . that what so many people are doing must not be wrong. . . .

"Apparently, Dr. Kinsey has completely disregarded the

teachings of the church and the moral code of the Bible," Dr. Graham concludes.

In the sermon reply to Dr. Kinsey, the evangelist surveys the results of 20th century "behavioristic philosophies," and says their impact has caused many persons to become "convinced the Bible is not God's revelation, salvation is to come through man and not through Christ and morality is relative and not absolute."

Dr. Graham then declared, "Nowhere does the Bible teach that sex in itself is a sin, but from Genesis to Revelation the Bible condemns the wrong use of sex."

He also says the Bible is "one of the world's most outspoken books on the subject of sex. It adopts no 'hush-hush' attitude. It does not try to gloss over sex in either its right or wrong aspects."

Billy Graham's sermon "The Bible and Dr. Kinsey"—a response to the female volume—was first broadcast on the radio, then published.

Immorality Rampant

He asserts the "present generation has put far too much emphasis on the mechanics of sex and far too little insistence on the rightness and wrongness of it.

"Every newsstand and many movie advertisements are an indication of the depths to which we have fallen morally at the present hour.

"Immorality is rampant throughout the nation, but that does not make it right, nor does it justify any college professor's advocating the breaking of moral laws," the evangelist concludes.

Oh! Dr. Kinsey!

PRICE $1.00

A PHOTOGRAPHIC REACTION TO THE KINSEY REPORT

by LAWRENCE LARIAR

From the book *Oh! Dr. Kinsey!* published by Cartwrite Publishing in 1953.

Does your husband think that you've always been true to him?

When your husband leaves town on a business trip—do you stay at home and knit?

Do you agree with Freud that a genuine sexual psychosis militates against the facilitation of a flamboyant neurotic manifestation of the psyche?

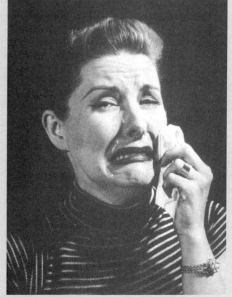

What did you think of your husband on the very first night of your marriage?

The Michigan Catholic, August 1953

PERHAPS THERE IS A LEGITIMATE PLACE for a book like Dr. Kinsey's new study of the sexual behavior of women in the literature of science.

Wiser students of human nature could tell Dr. Kinsey that modesty is the safeguard of virtue. They could remind him of the still valid principle that evil communications corrupt good morals.

Here is an apposite statement from Holy Scripture:

"As for debauchery and impurity of every kind, and covetousness there must be no whisper of it among you; it would ill become saints; no indecent behavior, no ribaldry or smartness of talk; that is not your business; your business is to give thanks to God" (Eph. V, 3, new translation by Msgr. Ronald Knox).

Rock Island (Illinois) Argus, August 20, 1953

DR. ALFRED KINSEY BEGAN HIS SEX STUDIES with good intentions, but his reports have received public attention far out of proportion to their value to society. There is only one explanation—morbid curiosity. As *The Argus* does not cater to morbid curiosity, we are not publishing the results of Kinsey's latest study.

Such hitherto unknown facts as he reveals are the proper subject for scientific discussion and not the public prints. But most of the facts are known generally and the report merely gives them improper advertising.

There are too many important things we should know about human behavior—particularly, why man has not accomplished as much with his heart as he has with his hand and brain; why he contrives wonderful inventions and atomic bombs but has not averted war. Why waste time on unpleasant trivia?

Sacramento Union, August 21, 1953

READERS OF *THE SACRAMENTO UNION* will not find an extended account of Dr. Kinsey's new 842-page book, *Sexual Behavior in the Human Female,* in this newspaper.

This is a scientific report, intended as a guide to scientists, and it is not intended to become a "best seller" or to be read lightly by persons of all ages. Nor do we think it would be helpful in advancing the cause of science to print extracts from the book in the newspaper which is read by all members of the family.

We do not presume to know what Dr. Kinsey hopes to accomplish with his vast array of information in this field, and we do not think his purpose was ever intended to include the newspaper publication at length of the facts he gathered in interviewing less than 6,000 white American women.

We hope our readers will not regard this as an effort to suppress the news, since copies of the book will be available in the libraries and in book stores, but rather as an effort on our part to shield immature minds from what at first blush appears to be something sordid and sketchy.

If there is scientific value to the Kinsey data, let it be digested and analyzed by the scientists.

Time Magazine, August 24, 1953

FOUR MEN COLLECTED THE INFORMATION, traveling across the U.S. for 15 years with the patient persistence of secret agents. They tried to be inconspicuous; they knew that they might be misunderstood. They sought recruits in homes and prisons, saloons and parish houses, burlesque theaters and offices, then interrogated them in private. They took notes in a code which was nowhere written down, and preserved only in the memories of the four. They never traveled together, lest an accident wipe out their secret with them. Coded and catalogued, the facts were locked away, and the book written from them printed in utmost secrecy. Last week presses clattered, turning out pages that were scrupulously counted to make sure that none got away before publication date (Sept. 14)....

"Kinsey... has done for sex what Columbus did for geography," declared a pair of enthusiasts (Lawyer Morris Ernst and Biographer David Loth), forgetting that Columbus did not know where he was when he got there. Perhaps inspired by the accolade, Kinsey opens his second volume with the words: "There is no ocean of greater magnitude than the sexual function." Kinsey, a dedicated explorer, has sailed a long way over that vast and deep ocean, but he has only riffled the surface currents. His interviews are echo-soundings. Kinsey's work contains much that is valuable, but it must not be mistaken for the last word.

TWENTY CENTS

AUGUST 24, 1953

TIME

THE WEEKLY NEWSMAGAZINE

ARTZYBASHEFF

ALFRED KINSEY
Reflections in the mirror of Venus.

$6.00 A YEAR

VOL. LXII NO. 8

St. Petersburg (Florida) Independent, August 24, 1953

"Dr. Kinsey Is Pretty Flimsy"

AT THE RISK OF BEING LABELED a conclusion-jumper and mid-Victorian in attitude, I would like to go on record as saying that Dr. Alfred C. Kinsey is full of condensed canal water. I have not read his volume on the sexual behavior of females, for the very good reason that it is not yet on the market.

All I have read is what millions of other Americans have read, the reviews, along with liberal quotations from the forthcoming book. And while it is always dangerous to base conclusions on quotations pulled from the context, it seems to me that some of the implications he draws head up a pretty dangerous road.

I am not quarreling with his statistics. I'm not a statistics man. But it seems to me that if Dr. Kinsey were permitted to rewrite our sex laws and our code of morals to conform with his statistics, we would be in one sorry mess—sociologically, morally, economically and spiritually.

Dr. Kinsey seems to believe that all our conventions and codes regarding sex are mere superstitions and have no reason for existence. He implies that anyone who goes out and plays it fast and loose in violation of all the conventions is not only justified but will be a better person for it.

He points out, for instance, that women who have sexual experience before marriage make a better adjustment in marriage, but that those who don't indulge are more likely to have marriages that fail.

So what's the conclusion from that? It can be nothing but advice to the effect that if a girl wants a successful marriage, the way to attain it is to engage in premarital sexual experiences.

Then he goes on to point out that only a quarter of those women interviewed who followed that course had regrets for doing so.

He rues the fact that 18 per cent of those who were thus involved became pregnant, pointing out that "there is practically no excuse for such a rate today" with modern, effective contraceptives. Further he implies that the fears of venereal disease should be no barrier to premarital experiences, since they can be easily cured by modern medicine.

Finally, the good doctor insists that the chief damage a girl suffers from experience is not the act itself, or its possible physical and biological results, but the feeling of guilt imposed by legal, moral and religious restrictions.

What Kinsey is advising, it seems to me, is to obey that biological urge and to heck with all the conventions, inhibitions and barriers society has established.

Well, perhaps that's all right if our goal is pure hedonism. But our religious, legal and moral laws weren't established for the simple purpose of denying carnal pleasures or to inhibit our dear little psyches. They were established to protect mankind against his own excesses. Without them our society would be at the moral, economic, and physical level of a group of wayside cows. In fact it would be worse, since all lower animals are far less promiscuous than human beings would be if man weren't held in the road by conventions and restrictions.

Conventions ruling sexual behavior are not an invention of our modern, highly advanced, and ultra "broadminded" age. The most barbaric and unenlightened tribes of the most remote corners of the world have similar restrictions, and have had them nearly from the beginning of time. Why? Because they know, and have learned from experience, that man is an ornery critter, and will eventually destroy himself if he is free to follow his own sexual impulses and desires.

Perhaps some of our conventions are silly. Undoubtedly some of the old rules were actually vicious. There was a time not too long ago when the sins of adulterers were visited upon their illegitimate children. Such a child is not the subject of such vicious scorn and ill-treatment today. Yet if the sin of illegitimacy were removed from the parents, the institution of marriage and family responsibility would quickly become a farce.

What I'm getting down to is this: From what I've read thus far, Dr. Kinsey seems to think that "anything goes."

Well, it just doesn't, that's all. It doesn't, and it can't. And, under the guise of "scientific" findings, to recommend the complete disregard of the conventions of sexual behavior is to further the course of moral decay—indeed, to contribute to the destruction of society itself.

Salina (Kansas) Journal, September 6, 1953

MARRIAGE IS LIKE HEAD CHEESE—if you examine too closely all that goes to make it up, it isn't nearly so appetizing.

As one of our young married friends said, "Gosh, we were dumb enough to think we'd been happy and probably always would be until Drs. Crane and Kinsey came along and directed us to all the could be's, the might have been's and the will be's along the way."

Detroit News,
September 30, 1953

To the Editor:

I AM GLAD TO READ that a minister approves of the Kinsey report, saying that good will come of it. I believe that also. We do not need to stand helplessly by and see women copy men's vulgarity. We can follow this minister's example and teach our sons to keep their finesse, as he believes girls should do, and to have a respect for marriage and parenthood.

My 16-year-old daughter's experiences with boys would indicate that neither the home nor the church have tried to teach this.

I believe that men will set the pattern for the future and that women will be copy cats of their behavior until a moral balance between the sexes is achieved. Kinsey was right in saying that the double standard of morals is fast becoming a single standard, which is only right and the way it should be. We women love virtue in men, also. Society has made a great mistake to expect only one sex to practice purity.

Detroit News,
October 10, 1953

To the Editor:

OBVIOUSLY IT IS THE MISINFORMED who subject Dr. Kinsey to such verbal persecution, unparalleled since Charles Darwin. Dr. Kinsey is sincerely attempting to bring the sexual problem out from the dark ages. Sex is a basic urge of mankind and it cannot and should not be hidden by a mystical cloud of fear and ignorance; the cost is too high. Consider broken homes, crippling diseases, sexual deviates, etc., all due to sexual ignorance.

St. Paul Dispatch, October 28, 1953

A THINLY VEILED SLAP at the Kinsey report was taken by Bishop Francis J. Schenk of Crookston today when he addressed the Minnesota Council of Catholic Women.

Although he failed to mention the report by name, he commended the group for "concerning itself about the virtue of purity instead of permitting itself to become upset and even sidetracked by recent behavioristic studies of men and women."

St. Paul Dispatch, October 31, 1953

To the Editor:

DR. KINSEY REALLY STIRRED a hornet's nest with his remarkable report on women, based on their own testimony.

From my study of Dr. William J. Robinson, Sanger, Ellis, the Bible and Freud, I would estimate Dr. Kinsey's *Sexual Behavior in the Human Female* as a confirmation of what many of us know, or believe, and the rest fairly guess. So I feel convinced that open study is far more conducive to right living and self control than this hush-hush attitude toward one of the most important aspects of life.

Isn't it about time for a people, with the means of education so easily available, to take a more adult view of life and the general welfare of what we boast of as a democratic society? It is gratifying to witness this lively interest in sex education, and our war stained world will be all the better and cleaner for it.

Raleigh News & Observer, March 31, 1954

"Kinsey Statistics Attacked"

DR. ALFRED KINSEY'S WIDELY PUBLICIZED book on *Sexual Behavior in the Human Female* is "both unscientific and dangerous in its implications and assumptions."

This conviction was expressed here yesterday by Roy E. Dickerson of Cincinnati, Ohio, executive secretary of the Cincinnati Social Hygiene Society and a faculty member at the University of Cincinnati, in an address at North Carolina State College.

In a talk entitled "Fact and Fiction in the Kinsey Report," Dickerson charged that Kinsey's book offers "neither trustworthy statistics nor sound reasoning" to back up its assumptions of widespread infidelity among married women and extensive premarital sexual relations.

Furthermore, Dickerson declared that Kinsey's work may lead young people "to disastrous consequences for themselves and others." He spoke in the State College YMCA auditorium under sponsorship of five religious groups at N.C. State and one religious organization at Meredith College.

"Always there are some young people—and others as well—who knowingly or unknowingly are standing so close to the edge of the steep cliff of dangerous sex-behavior that it would take little to cause them to step over the precipice and plunge them down to disastrous consequences for themselves and others.

"Much of the contents of Kinsey's *Sexual Behavior in the Human Female,* as well as the publicity given it, is likely to cause this misstep by stamping two completely false impressions upon the mind of youthful and other credulous readers.

"One false impression is that infidelity is widespread among married women and commonly causes little or no regret or domestic discord. The other is that pre-marital sexual relations and extremes of petting are even more widespread, and actually constitute good preparation for marriage.

"Nothing could be further from the truth. . . ."

225

"Dr. Kinsey, I presume?"

Cartoonist Wesley Thompson's view.

OSCAR G. BEEDLE M.D.

"So I told him I didn't read that Kinsey book 'cause I'm waiting till they make it into a movie."

John Adams' cartoon in *Medical Economics,*

THE GIRLS

"Any more Dr. Kinseys?"

Franklin Folger's cartoon in *The Indianapolis*

"Well, I'm sure Dr. Kinsey never spoke to anyone in Upper Montclair."

Peter Arno's cartoon in *The New Yorker,* September

The Kinsey
Interview

Wardell Pomeroy demonstrates his technique for taking a sexual history.

Female

From *Taking a Sex History: Interviewing and Recording*

by Wardell B. Pomeroy, Carol C. Flax & Connie Christine Wheeler

Have you ever seen anyone having intercourse?
Yes.

Have you seen your parents having intercourse?
Yes. At 12 I barged into my parents' room while they were having intercourse. We were all embarrassed. I left at once.

Were you sexually aroused when you watched them?
No.

Has anyone ever seen you having intercourse?
Yes, my roommate on a double date.

Have you ever had group sex?
Yes.

How often?
Well, I think three times now.

How many people were involved?
Myself, my girlfriend, her boyfriend, and his boyfriend.

Four of you?
Yes.

Did you like it?
Definitely.

Would you do it again?
Yes, in fact we have a date next week.

Cornelia Otis Skinner

From "Trial by Kinsey," *The New Yorker,* May 27, 1950

WORD IS OUT THAT THE KINSEY REPORT on the ladies is almost ready for the press. Doubtless a good percentage of the American male population, whose behavior was so graphically brought to light two years ago, is anticipating, with mixed emotions of dread and glee, the lowdown on the behavior—or misbehavior—of the American female. And doubtless, too, the cartoonists and professional humorists are revamping and changing the gender of their old jokes to be held in readiness for the date of publication. It now appears that the Doctor's researches are not to be confined to the over-all behavior of the American male, the American female, and the mud wasp (whose nationality a divided world has yet to determine); in the new report there will be, I gather, a section devoted to a special study of that happy and unhappy breed, the people whose professions lie in the arts. Just how their patterns differ from those of the male, the female, and the mud wasp we have yet to learn. I heard of this special study one day when I was lunching with a lawyer who is a friend of mine and also of Dr. Kinsey's. What prompted this gentleman suddenly to come out with "How'd you like to be interviewed by Kinsey?" I don't know. Nor do I know for what reason, unless it was the two dry Martinis I had had at the start of the meal, the prospect struck me as fascinating. My reply was a simple "I can't wait."

When the first enthusiasm and the second Martini had worn off, I realized that I *could* wait, after all. In fact, quite indefinitely. But this was a few hours later, and by then the die was cast, as the lawyer's parting words had been to the effect that he would immediately inform the Doctor of my willingness to be interviewed. Oh, well, I figured, maybe nothing would ever come of it, and besides, I could always get out of an awkward situation by saying I'd received a sudden summons from Hollywood—a fortuitous emergency that I have yet to be involved in. I finished my shopping and thought no more about the matter until I reached home and was greeted by my son with the information that someone had been playing a joke on me.

"What sort of joke?" I asked.

"Oh, some dopey friend of yours called up," he answered. "He said to tell you Dr. Kinsey had called."

"And what did *you* say?" I asked.

"I just said 'Oh yeah?' and hung up."

"I'm afraid, my lad," I said, "that it really *was* Dr. Kinsey."

"What would he be calling *you* about?" he asked.

"Oh, I guess he wants to interview me," I replied in an off-hand manner.

My son's eyes bugged out with incredulity. "Why would he want to interview *you*, for heaven's sake!" he exclaimed and, without waiting for an answer, catapulted into the library to tell his father, whose comment was identical except that he didn't say *"heaven's."* It was clear that in the opinion of both the men of my family I could bring as little enlightening material to a Kinsey Report as a child of ten could bring to the Annual Report of General Motors. Indeed, neither one of them appeared to believe that a prospect so fantastic as that of my being interviewed by the Doctor could ever eventuate, and under their influence I began to disbelieve it myself.

Bright and early the following day, as I was drinking my morning coffee in bed, the phone rang, and I pounced to answer it before anyone could pick up a downstairs extension. A pleasant masculine voice asked if this was Cornelia Skinner and I said yes, this was she—an elegance of speech that always sounds as though one were identifying oneself with Rider Haggard's heroine. The man on the phone then quite calmly announced that he was Dr. Kinsey, and at that, I am distressed to say, I heard myself emit a curious whoop followed by a gigglingly shrill, "Oh, Dr. *Kinsey*!"

The Doctor, who by now must be astonished by nothing, seemed to take my vocal flutterings as a matter of course, and in a completely businesslike manner went on to say that our mutual friend the lawyer had told him I was willing to give him an interview and that he was delighted to hear it. I burbled a little lamely that I was delighted to hear it, too. He explained that his time in New York was limited and asked if we could make it Friday. Friday was just two days off. My immediate impulse was to duck out of it all by saying that I couldn't be sorrier but that Friday I had to go out of town. Then something in me murmured that this was no time for American womanhood to show weakness, and in a feeble voice I said that Friday would be just fine. He then said that as the interview usually took two hours, what would I say to starting it at nine in the morning. What I said to myself was a fervent "God, no!" and to Dr. Kinsey, shamefacedly, that nine was a little early for me. Then how about ten, he inquired. I was loath to tell him that 10 a.m. is, for me, about as bad as nine, for fear he'd consider this an indication of my general decadence, so I said with forced heartiness that ten would be just fine, after which he suggested that it might be better if the interview was held at his place rather than at mine.

Not knowing anything about his place, I gave a quick thought to mine. I live in a 1908 apartment building where visitors are still announced in the entrance lobby over a battery phone system so antiquated that the doorman has to resort to the tones of a hog-caller to get across any communication, and the prospect of the entire block's being informed that Dr. Kinsey was calling on me was unsettling. Moreover, our family retainer is an elderly virginal soul who thinks nothing of interrupting any social gathering, whether a large one or a tête-à-tête, with bulletins on our current domestic exigencies. I was further harried by the thought that if she barged into the room with the news that the exterminator had come about the pantry cockroaches at a moment when Dr. Kinsey was putting forth some particularly cozy question, she was quite likely to give notice or faint dead away. I therefore eagerly agreed that the meeting had better be held at his place. This I pictured as a scholarly, yet modernistic office, impressive with chromium trim, steel filing cabinets, mysterious oddments of laboratory equipment, and bookshelves filled with heavy tomes. I imagined it would be in either a medical building or the science department of one of the city colleges. I had something of a shock, therefore, when he said he'd expect me at ten sharp in his room at the Statler Hotel.

Again I was strongly assailed by the impulse to duck out. But again some inner discipline admonished me that, having made my bed, I must lie in it. I could only hope that by 10 a.m. Friday somebody would have made Dr. Kinsey's bed and wondered, a little apprehensively, if, in the manner of the patients on the analyst's couch, I'd have to lie on it. Taking a deep breath, I said that the Statler, too, could be just fine, as casually as though it were an everyday occurrence for me to pay morning visits to gentlemen in their hotel rooms. I have quite conscientiously been giving this hostelry its new name; actually, to me it will always be the Pennsylvania, famous as a headquarters for conventions. The idea of a bedroom in a milling convention center as a setting for a Kinsey interview for some reason struck me as so wildly incongruous that I hung up fast and then gave vent to another loud whoop of nervous laughter.

During the next forty-eight hours, I was in a divided state of mind, wondering whether my engagement with Dr. Kinsey was something to be kept a dead secret or entrusted to a few close friends, like a delicate operation or an illicit love affair. As may be surmised, I started out confiding in one or two boon companions and ended up telling almost everyone I encountered. What chiefly encouraged this wholesale dissemination of the news was a study of the different ways in which people received it. Had I calmly announced that on Friday I was going to go to jail, or receive the Nobel Prize, or elope with the Aga Khan, their reactions could not have been more varied or more intense. Some said,

"*What?*," others were speechless, and several hammed a double take before coming out with a stunned, "I beg your pardon?" It was instructive, then, to wait for the next comments. Women, according to whether their type was the ultra-refined or the lustily earthy, either snorted a horrified "*You wouldn't!*" or eagerly asked if he'd interview them, too. Men reacted in similar ways. The pillars of the Community, with the shocked compassion they'd have for a magdalen, asked why a nice woman would want to do a thing like that, while the heartier fellows burst out laughing, slapped my knee, and said oh boy, they'd sure like to be a fly on Kinsey's pencil. A few of those professional happy-happy-marriage ladies went into frightened postures of modesty, as though they'd just been walked in on in their slips, and stated with misty-eyed piety that in their opinion "those things" were too sacred to mention, especially to anyone who'd put them in a report. I wish now I had kept track of how many times the term "those things" was employed. My secretary, a glorious girl with a heart as big as Ireland when it comes to the welfare of our family, looked panic-stricken and gasped "Jesus, Mary, and Joseph! You're not going to tell him all those things, are you?" and when I asked her all what things, she stammered "Well, I mean *every*thing." I silenced her a bit brutally by asking how she knew I had *any*thing to tell him. She left early that afternoon. I think it was in order to beg Father Murphy to say a special prayer for me.

If the varied adult reactions were surprising, the youthful ones were downright discouraging. It was all too clear that in the estimation of members of the younger generation Dr. Kinsey must be extending his studies into the realm of senile behavior. My son kept reiterating his annoying "Why would he want to interview *you!*" While my best friend's twenty-year-old daughter, with a shrill of amusement, squealed, "What? Miss Prim?" I felt fairly offended by their attitude until I recalled a juvenile one of my own in regard to my elders. To me it was quite unthinkable that the contemporaries of my mother, who was then in her late thirties, could have had any remote interest in matters of the flesh except to cite

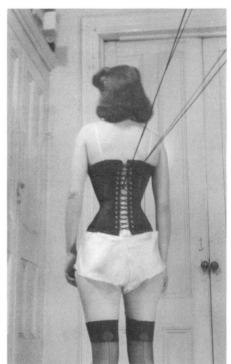

them as horrible warnings to the young. I recall my shock when a neighbor of ours, a forty-three-year-old widow, married a doctor who was verging on fifty, and that I said to my mother, "You don't mean to tell me that they could possibly *still!*" and Mother replied quite crossly "I don't know what you think you're talking about, Cornelia, but I assure you that they can."

Friday morning, my alarm clock went off with its customary shattering effect, and I lay for a time in a state of sleepy malaise, trying to remember what train I must be supposed to catch and to where. Then it dawned on me that this was the day I was taking the Kinsey plunge, and I was seized with the same sort of panic I felt the morning of my wedding. I quieted myself with the realization that, after all, the situations were hardly parallel and that I was not about to pledge myself to journey down life's highway hand in hand with Dr. Kinsey. Nervously pooh-poohing such girlish fantasies, I rose with splendid energy. What to wear was a bit of a problem. The day was bleak and raw, with a gusty wind and a drizzle of rain—weather that called for practical clothes. A tailored suit would have been the obvious choice. I have one but I seldom wear it, because I think it makes me look rather like a dean of a state teachers' college. Fearing that Dr. Kinsey might think so, too, and get off on the wrong track, I selected instead a simple street dress and pinned it at the neck with my great-grandmother's brooch by way of a talisman. Fastening the catch, I wondered if within the next two hours there'd occur a slight upheaval over the quiet Massachusetts grave where the respectable old soul lies.

I was thankful to be able to slip out of the house without any disheartening comments from my family, who seemed to have forgotten about my early-morning appointment. I hailed a taxi and with debonair nonchalance announced my destination. The driver proved to be the chatty type. He told me he was about to have a session with a doctor, and, just to be folksy, I told him I was about to have a session with a doctor, too. He said his was throat and I said well, mine wasn't throat, exactly, and we let it go at that.

The anticipated convention was swarming in the lobby of the Statler. My qualms returned as I made my way through the crowd and up to the information desk, which was so beset that I had to stand waiting my turn. When it came. I had to summon all my courage to ask for the number of Dr. Kinsey's room. Because of the surrounding hubbub, the clerk failed to catch the name and I was forced to repeat it twice, in an increasingly amplified voice. The clerk, with an enlightened "Oh, yes," told me the number while the rest of the petitioners stared at me with evident interest. Blushing prettily, I took a couple of steps over to the house phone.

The Doctor's wire was busy. For a few uncomfortable seconds, I waited, and then tried again. The wire continued busy and the petitioners continued to stare. I am fairly adept at outstaring on occasions, but this didn't seem to be one of them. I was, however, damned if, under their searchlight scrutiny, I'd wait with lowered eyelids until the phone was free.

Giving up any idea of announcing my arrival to the Doctor, I walked with womanly decorum over to the elevators and got into a car. The only other occupant, besides the operator, was a gentleman wearing a convention plaque that announced that he was J. W. Truby. His manner indicated that the convivial aspects of the local convention must have been of twenty-four-hour continuity. The doors closed with a portentous clang and my heart sank in ratio to the elevator's rapid rise. I felt panicky and as if I'd have to turn to someone—Mr. Truby, perhaps. For an insane moment I struggled with the impulse to tell him what I was about to do. What quickly restrained me was the sobering thought that Mr. Truby might decide to come along with me, and his presence would be difficult to explain to Dr. Kinsey. The elevator came to a stop and I hurried off.

The Statler is one of those hotels that employ gray-haired, highly proper looking matrons to sit behind a desk on every floor, hand you your key and your mail and a motherly smile, and, from their vantage positions, take discreet note of where you are going. These ladies, the Association of Innkeepers would lead us to believe, convey that "homey" touch, but to me, even under such innocent circumstances as when I am merely bound for my own room, they convey an indefinable sense of guilt. On this occasion, the sense was more definable. I felt like a call girl. Taking comfort in the thought that I didn't *look* like a call girl—which as comfort was not too morale-building—I set my hat at a dignified angle, smiled cozily at the matron, and started briskly for Dr. Kinsey's room, which, I soon realized, was in a direction completely opposite the one I was taking. This involved about-facing and repassing the desk, and this time I avoided looking at the matron.

I found the room and I found Dr. Kinsey, who turned out to be a scholarly gentleman of humor and charm. He put me completely at ease, and the interview I had dreaded proved to be as simple as it was fascinating. I came away with a high opinion of Dr. Kinsey and, I don't mind saying, a pretty good one of myself.

It may be of interest to note in conclusion that, within the ensuing twenty-four hours, of those persons who had evinced such outraged scruples at the prospect of my interview not one failed to call me up and say, "What did he ask you?" My answer to each and every one was the same: "If you think I'm going to tell you what he asked, you're as crazy as you would be if you thought I was going to tell you what I answered!"

Doctor to Doctor

HE WAS A FULL PROFESSOR, married with adolescent children. While carrying on his teaching duties in the zoology department he worked every available hour, day and night, traveling anywhere that people would give him interviews. He was training a couple of young men in his method of interviewing. Dr. Yerkes and I submitted separately to his technique. I was astonished at his skill in eliciting the most intimate details of the subject's sexual history. Introducing his queries gradually, he managed to convey an assurance of complete confidentiality by recording the answers on special sheets printed with a grid on which he set down the information gained, by unintelligible signs, explaining that the code had never been written down and only his two colleagues could read it. His questions included subtle tricks to detect deliberate misinformation.

—George W. Corner
A physician member and later the chair of the Committee for Research in the Problems in Sex (CRPS), the Rockefeller-funded grant-giving body operating under the umbrella of the National Research Council

Coding and Recording

From *Taking a Sex History: Interviewing and Recording*

by Wardell B. Pomeroy, Carol C. Flax & Connie Christine Wheeler

THE CODE FOR RECORDING information developed by Dr. Alfred Kinsey is what is known as a position code. The meaning is derived from the position of the symbols on the page as well as from the symbols themselves. For example, a check mark at one place on the page will mean "Yes, I like to cook," while in another position on the page the same symbol will stand for "I learned about masturbation by being told about it." A "14" in one position will mean "I had my first menstrual period at age 14," and at another place it will mean "I've had two years of college."

The code was designed with two features in mind: first that it would be virtually impossible to break, thus ensuring the confidentiality of the material, and second that it would be compact and therefore easy to use and economical to file. The *Kinsey Reports* are proof that an enormous mass of data can be recorded securely in a relatively brief time, requiring little storage space and few materials. The code is secure, economical, and, once learned, easy and quick to use. Minor modifications of the coding by each interviewer will ensure confidentiality.

Dr. Kinsey's code evolved from his early laboratory work with gall wasps, when he was using twenty-eight different measurements to record color and length of wings, size, and other characteristics. He was dismayed by the tedium of the task since there were millions of gall wasps to record, so he devised a brief shorthand system. When he became interested in taking sexual histories, he quite naturally adapted this code.

Soon after Kinsey became interested in studying human sex-

One single code sheet—like the mock-up at right—was sufficient to record most histories.

uality, he devised a brief questionnaire which he handed out to graduate students in biology. One question he asked of the male students was, "Are your testes descended?" To his surprise, a majority of the responses stated that only one was descended. He knew this couldn't be true, because undescended testes are uncommon; consequently he discussed this question with his students and soon realized that they had misinterpreted it to mean, "Does one testis hang lower than the other?"

At that point, Kinsey abandoned the questionnaire and began to ask questions of his subjects directly. Believing that note taking during the questioning would interfere with his rapport with the subjects, he tried to commit the entire interview to memory and would rush to another room after it was over and write down everything he could recall. But this method was obviously inefficient and time-consuming; besides, data were lost because total recall was impossible. Thus he was forced into recording. As he began to code the material, he found that he was able to maintain his rapport with people and that the interview and coding moved along at a fluid pace.

Eighty percent of the questions on the history were developed within two weeks and the remaining 20 percent during the next six months.

The interview is recorded on a prepared form on a standard 8 1/2" by 11" sheet, easily filed or slipped into a notebook. The paper should be of high rag quality so that it will not yellow or become brittle with age. It is best to write with a fine-point pen because the coding is written in a very small area, with the marks close together; the pen will not smudge as a pencil would. It is advisable to print rather than to use cursive writing, and some practice may be needed to improve one's legibility.

The recording sheet is composed of 24 well-defined blocks which contain a varied number of spaces. As noted, the meaning of a symbol depends upon its position within a particular block. The 24 specific aspects of the sexual history recorded in the blocks are as follows:

Background Information	Premarital Intercourse
Health	Incidental Prostitution
Recreation	Premarital Coital Attitudes
Family Background	Marital Coitus
Marriage	Extramarital Coitus
Sex Education	Contraception
Puberty	Erotic Arousal
Preadolescent Sex Play	Anatomy
Self-Masturbation	Group Sex
Dreams	Incidental Homosexuality
Premarital Petting	Animal Contacts
First Coitus	Other Sexual Behaviors

There is sufficient space on the bottom of the recording sheet for expanding, adding, or exploring replies. An asterisk is used to indicate when a response is continued at the bottom of the sheet. Remarks recorded in the space below the blocks are written in an abbreviated style—that is vowels are omitted and only the consonants are used to represent the word, along with common symbols. In this way, ideas can be recorded in a very limited space.

Example of code in abbreviated style: Marr. Bd bcs ♂ alcol + Cx. Translation: The marriage is bad because the husband abuses alcohol and has extramarital intercourse.

The code is flexible enough to record a vast spectrum of human behavior, the usual and the unusual, the anticipated and the extraordinary.

The code is comprised of mathematical signs, numbers, letters, and other simple symbols. Because it is the position of a symbol in the block that indicates its meaning, relatively few symbols can be used. For example, in the Family Background block, "M" stands for mother; where marital status is noted, "M" represents marriage; "M" also symbolizes masturbation; in the religion block "M" may be used to indicate that the respondent is a Methodist; and in addition, "M" is the symbol for masochist.

When the interview is over, the interviewer quickly scans his coded sheet to check whether there are any blanks indicting that a question was not asked. Before the respondent leaves, the interviewer can easily ask these questions to ensure that a complete history has been taken.

Christine Jorgensen

From the book *Christine Jorgensen, A Personal Story,*
Published in 1967

I HAD RECEIVED A LETTER from Dr. Alfred Kinsey, inviting me to be interviewed at the Institute for Sex Research at Indiana University in Bloomington. Previously, with my permission, the Danish doctors had forwarded reports of my case for Dr. Kinsey's files at the university. His initial letter to me read in part:

Certainly you would be contributing very materially to our research and the ultimate benefit to all the people who are utilizing the material on our research. We can guarantee, of course, that we will keep all of the material confidential. Dr. Benjamin must have assured you of this.

In order to prevent the disturbance which we are sure would occur if your name and our name were connected, we wonder if it would not be simplest to put you up in our own home . . . I would also suggest that I send someone to meet you at either the airport or train in Indianapolis in order to help keep your visit confidential.

You have a good deal to contribute and we shall very much appreciate the time you give us.

At the time, Dr. Kinsey was preparing material for his exhaustive report, *Sexual Behavior in the Human Female.*

I believed that since my name had become synonymous with problems of a sexual nature, it was important that a recognized scientific agency should have as much data as possible, and with my desire to contribute to the Kinsey project, I accepted his invitation.

I traveled under a fictitious name, having already found it a convenience that saved a lot of trouble. I was beginning to be

fairly artful at dodging reporters. My arrival at the Indianapolis airport went unnoticed and I was met by a private car and whisked off to the home of Dr. and Mrs. Kinsey in Bloomington. I spent several days in that pleasant atmosphere, and submitted myself to the complex cross-questioning at the Institute.

Christine Jorgensen photographed by the Institute's staff photographer, William Dellenback, in 1953.

Probably no one would have known of my visit had it not been for my desire to spend an evening at the movies, after an afternoon of conferences. I went alone and was instantly recognized. It didn't take long to connect my presence in Bloomington with Dr. Kinsey and the work then in progress at the Institute of Sex Research. Within a few hours, newsmen from all over the country were calling the Institute for information.

Already much overworked and upset by the intrusions of the press, Dr. Kinsey suffered a heart attack and was rushed to a nearby hospital. Fortunately, the research on my case was nearly finished and I left within a day or two.

I was afraid Dr. Kinsey would be angry at this invasion and hold me responsible, but he took it with good grace and I enjoyed a friendly correspondence with him until his death in August of 1956.

I remember him personally as a shy, quiet man and a gracious host, but in his work he was a supreme egoist, and left me with the impression that he believed his books on sexual behavior were the definitive ones, and there was not much left to be said on the subject. Perhaps his professional conceit was warranted, for above all, he was a dedicated research scientist, and I was happy to have made even a small contribution to his studies.

Male, Eighth-Grade Education, Age 43

From *Taking a Sex History: Interviewing and Recording*

by Wardell B. Pomeroy, Carol C. Flax & Connie Christine Wheeler

How tall are you?
I'm 6 feet tall.

How much do you weigh?
I weigh 160 lbs.

What's the most you ever weighed in your life?
Uh, 200 lbs.

How old were you then?
I was in the Army.

Well that made you about 20.
Yeah, that's right.

When your penis is soft, how long would you guess it is?
Oh, it ain't more than 4 inches.

How long is your penis when it's hard?
I don't know, I never measured it.

Well, make a guess. Would you say it's this long, this long, or this long? (Interviewer demonstrates possible length, with his or her hands, in no progression.)

About 6 inches.

Have you ever been circumcised? Have you ever had skin cut away from the head of your penis?
No, I guess I never did.

When your penis is hard, do you have any trouble pulling the skin back over the head?
No, no trouble.

Is the opening on your penis about here on the tip end or underneath?
No, it's right there on the tip end.

Do you have two balls?
Uh, yeah.

Does one hang lower than the other?
Uh, I guess the left one does.

Would you want to change your body in any way at all? Is there any way you would change it?
Oh, I guess I like my body pretty well.

Anything about your height or your weight or your hair or your skin?
Oh, I'd like smoother skin. I had acne when I was a kid.

Anything else about your body that you'd like to change?
No, I like it all right.

Is there anything about your sex partner you'd like to change? Anything about her body?
Well, she weighs about 30 pounds more than I'd like her to weigh, but outside of that, she's a pretty good-looking broad.

How do you think your sex partner feels about your body?
She don't care.

What kinds of things do you like in a sex partner?
I like 'em tall, redhead, good teeth, fun loving, and pretty smelling.

Fine. Anything else?
Yeah, big tits.

O.K.

Talk of the Town

From *The New Yorker*, March 27, 1948

WE KNOCKED AT THE DOOR of a fifth-floor room in the Hotel Astor the other afternoon, by appointment, and Dr. Alfred C. Kinsey poked his head out and said, "I'm running behind schedule. Would you mind coming into the next room?" He closed the door, and we walked down the corridor to the next door. Kinsey opened it, handed us copies of *Time* and the *Saturday Review of Literature*, and disappeared, with an apologetic murmur, into the room whence he had come. All was silence. Half an hour later, Kinsey beckoned us into the other room, and we got our first real look at him—a big, husky fellow, appearing to be younger than his fifty-three years, wearing a double-breasted blue suit, a dark-red bow tie with white dots, unruly brown hair, a friendly smile, and an air of repose. He told us that he was making his first visit to New York since the Report came out, that he had had a couple of long conferences with a local authority on erotic literature of the past, that he was flying back to his home in Bloomington, Indiana, the next morning, and that he planned to return soon, with his three colleagues, for six weeks of intensive case-history interviewing in Manhattan. They expect to average seven histories a day apiece, at the rate of one every hour and a half, except for old people, who may take up to two hours. Kinsey told us that an eleven- or twelve-hour working day is routine with him and that he'd been lining up subjects here—both sexes—through factory and other labor groups, educational institutions, nursery schools, the underworld, and the *Social Register*. "You mean the Social Register Association has been helping?" we asked. Not exactly, Kinsey said, but a good many people in *Register* circles have. "I've been astonished to discover that you can get *anybody* to give you a record of his most intimate activity," he told us. "I think they do it out of altruism. I've been so busy I've had no time for the theatre, which I love, but I *have* been able to go to a lot of foreign restaurants. I bet I know more eating places here than the average person." His taste is wide. He likes Turkish, Syrian, Greek, Armenian, Hindu, Italian, and Chinese cooking, and revels in sea food.

He took sixteen hundred case histories himself in three years, and paid all the expenses, before the subsidies came along. "My wife—she was doing graduate work in chemistry at Indiana University when I married her—has been a mainstay in my research," Kinsey said. "The Salvation Army has been one of my strongest supporters. A few years ago, when I got thrown out of a hotel here for having too many underworld characters who didn't wear ties coming in to see me, the Salvation Army invited me to use its men's-employment-bureau quarters, on West Forty-eighth Street. I still use that place to interview subjects without ties. The police have put the heat on underworld groups recently and they're lying low, but the situation will loosen up soon and I'll be able to get at them again." Kinsey told us he had turned down several requests to appear on radio programs.

There was a knock at the door. Kinsey opened it and poked his head out, and we heard a cultured, female voice. "I'm running behind schedule," he said. "Would you mind coming into the next room?" He went through the inside door, let the lady in, and returned to us. "I like the Astor because it's accessible," he told us, "and because, as I look out on Times Square, I get the feel of the tremendous variety of people that must be sampled. The mass and variety of people who go through this square! I used to stand on Broadway and watch them for hours, thinking of the sampling problem."

Reliability and Validity in Interviewing

From *Taking a Sex History: Interviewing and Recording*

by Wardell B. Pomeroy, Carol C. Flax & Connie Christine Wheeler

RELIABILITY REFERS TO THE CONSISTENCY and dependability of a given answer. For example, if a respondent in the first interview is asked, "How old were you when pubic hair first began to grow," and the answer is "10"; and in a second interview, the answer is "I think it was age 10 or 11" to the same question, that answer is reliable. On the other hand, if the answer is "age 10" in the first interview and "age 15" in a subsequent interview, the reliability of the response is low.

Validity refers to the truth of the answer. In the above example, even if the answer to the pubic hair question is highly reliable (on both occasions the respondent answered "age 10"), this is not proof that in *actuality* pubic hair began to grow at age 10. So in interviewing we are faced with two problems: (1) can the respondent accurately recall specific details of his or her sexual life, and (2) to what extent does the recollection reflect the reality of the respondent's life?

Reliability has been established for this sex history inventory with a minimum of two years and an average of four years between taking and retaking sex histories of the same people.

Validity is almost always more difficult to measure than reliability. In the example above, to measure validity the respondent would have to have observed and recorded when pubic hair growth began and then, years later, compare his or her recollection with the original observation. When such comparisons have been made, the responses have been virtually identical.

Several other ways of testing validity have been used. For example, the sex histories of a husband and wife should be the same in certain areas. For example, did they have intercourse with each other before marriage, what are their frequencies of marital intercourse, how long does it last, what positions are used, what are their petting techniques, how many abortions did the wife have in marriage? A high degree of validity has been found with all of these items.

There are also many clues that an interviewer receives while taking a sexual history which give indications of taboo overt behavior. For example, there are ten or twelve clues about homosexual behavior that are given before one asks the question, "How old were you the first time you had a homosexual experience?" If many of these clues are in a positive direction and the respondent nevertheless denies overt homosexual experience, he is confronted with the inconsistency and asked to explain it. In most cases, the respondent will then admit homosexual behavior or will be able to explain the inconsistency.

A sexual history can be falsified in three ways: exaggeration, misremembering, and cover-up. We have found that exaggeration is almost impossible to maintain because of the pace of the interview and because of the complexity and detail of the information sought. Persons who have deliberately tried to exaggerate have reported that it is almost impossible to accomplish. In addition, because of the nonjudgmental nature of the interview, there is little motivation to exaggerate. As indicated above, misremembering is minimal and is as often in one direction as the other.

It is most difficult for the interviewer to deal with cover-up. Establishing rapport, giving permission, and being alert to the many clues to overt behavior are the best ways to overcome this difficulty.

So far we have spoken about the reliability and validity of the subject's responses. But the interviewer must sometimes make subjective judgments, particularly when estimating the intensity of a respondent's feeling. In taking histories at the Kinsey Institute, occasionally the interviewer is cross-checked to determine how accurate their judgments were by sitting in on one another's history taking and recording independently. The judgments were found to be about 98 percent reliable, suggesting that familiarity with the technique gives the interviewer increasing confidence in his ability to interpret responses correctly.

cept to me, that it would be meaningful to Dr. Kinsey only as a fraction of a tremendous mass of information. All this did little to relieve my anxiety.

Anyway, I mustered my altruism and appeared for the interview as scheduled. I arrived at Dr. Kinsey's hotel suite doing my best to hide tenseness with a casual objective demeanor. He greeted me cordially by name, showed me to a comfortable seat and invited questions. I wasn't ready to ask questions. Instead, I leaned upon and commented on my interest in his work. As a professional interviewer, Dr. Kinsey must have known I had many questions. My not asking any must have signaled that I didn't feel sufficiently secure to raise them. An inexperienced interviewer might have missed this point or have been baffled by my simultaneous presentation of both secure and insecure behavior. Or, being in a hurry to get the answers to a few hundred questions, he might have noticed only my indications of comfort and interpreted them as signs of my readiness to proceed with the interview proper. Or he might have become anxious himself over my apprehension and introduced petty talk in an attempt to put me at ease. This, in turn, might have made me lose confidence in the interviewer's ability to keep the interview focused objectively upon history taking—led me to feel his tendency to become subjectively involved in my personal problems. The variety of ways in which I could have been mishandled are too numerous to mention. Now, as an interviewer myself, I know so well!

Dr. Kinsey did not mishandle. In a winning way, he picked up on my expression of interest in the research. In telling him of this interest, I was soon talking about myself, and, before I knew it, about my sex history. When, at any point, I indicated feelings that my experience was unusual, he had a way of sympathetically asking me how I felt this to be so. His manner seemed to say, "I am interested that you see this as unusual. What does this mean? How has this influenced your behavior?" His manner distinctly did not say, "That does (or does not) seem unusual to me." Clearly, I was being regarded as a human being with individual

characteristics—not as Jo Caro, inadequate, deviant, or immoral.

Already, in those first ten minutes, Dr. Kinsey had learned my origin, what kind of a family I came from, why we had moved from one cultural group to another, how I was alike and unlike my associates, something of my failures, achievements, and goals. This information must have helped him comprehend my frame of reference—an important step in accurate interpretation of interviewee behavior. At the same time, his getting this material increased my confidence that I would not be misunderstood.

With little awareness of doing so, I intently watched Dr. Kinsey's face and listened to the inflections of his voice. For what? For some sign of personal judgment, I suppose, which would signal me not to trust him. No such signs appeared. I tested him by telling of small mischievous "sins." By the time my words reached his ears, they were void of sinfulness and magically had become sheer interesting fact.

I ventured greater and greater deviations (or so I assumed them to be), and before I knew it, not only was Dr. Kinsey getting the facts he wanted, but I was looking at some of my own behavior in a shining new light. How many times, for example, had I laughingly told others of sex exploration with my childhood friends? Although I smiled again in telling the same details to Dr. Kinsey, he didn't seem at all amused—just interested. Suddenly I no longer needed to smile or laugh.

During the interview, Dr. Kinsey handled my questions as I raised them. I recall wondering whether certain kinds of behavior might be physically harmful. He asked how I felt they might be so. In explanatory response I, most often, would discover from myself whether or not my fears were reasonable. On occasion, Dr. Kinsey would straighten me out on some scientifically groundless fear. At no time did he in any way discourage or encourage me to alter my sex behavior. Yet he opened new avenues of expression simply by enabling me to ponder over some of my attitudes and ideas.

By the end of the interview I had answered some three hundred questions. Even though I know some people are more easily embarrassed than I, it is difficult to imagine the most timid person being uncomfortable in the Kinsey interview. I also believe that those who ordinarily need to exaggerate would be quite at ease in letting Dr. Kinsey ferret out the true facts.

As I departed, I had no thought or feeling that my behavior would abruptly or drastically change. I felt intact—still myself. More at ease and more aware—but still undeniably myself. Freer to experiment and live without hiding guilt with laughter or fear with denial. Any regrets were my own—unfed by disapproving attitudes from educator Kinsey. I walked away a bit wearily—the kind of weariness that comes with feeling relieved after having been tensed for a fantasied ordeal. Most of all, I felt the awe of having just lived through a rather profound experience.

Incidentally, I know Dr. Kinsey must have been making a record as we went along because I recall his showing and explaining to me the form on which he would be noting symbols. Yet I truly can recall no awareness of his record taking.

Female, Age 54, Divorced at Age 39

From *Taking a Sex History: Interviewing and Recording*

by Wardell B. Pomeroy, Carol C. Flax & Connie Christine Wheeler

Have you ever paid a male for intercourse?
Yes, I have.

How young were you the first time you
ever paid a male for intercourse?
I was 43.

And when was the last time you paid a
man?
Just last year.

O.K.

Between the ages of 43 to 53, how
often did you pay for intercourse?
Oh, I used such services quite regularly.

How regularly would you say?
I can't really remember precisely.

Was it every week, or twice a year, or
once a month?
*I started with one gentleman on a
regular basis for the first six years.*

How regularly did you see him during
that period?

I saw him about twice a month.

Did you pay anyone else for intercourse during those first six years, say
from age 43 to 49?
No, he was the extent of my interest.

And from age 49 to 53, how often did
you pay for coitus?
*Oh, that's easy. I only saw two other
men I paid, each one one time only.*

Then you paid for intercourse approximately 146 times, that is twice a
month for six years is 144 plus the two
single experiences?
*I didn't realize it was that much, but
the calculations are correct.*

What is the total number of different
males you've paid for intercourse?
*Well, there was my regular partner of
six years and then two others.*

That's right. What were their ages?
Now?

No, at the time you were having intercourse with them.
*Let's see. One was 28, one was about 23
and the other I'm guessing was probably
somewhere in between, maybe around 26.*

O.K.

How much did you pay the men for
intercourse?
You mean including gifts?

I mean cash on the barrelhead each time
you had intercourse.
*My regular man was always $100. And
the other two were less.*

How much were they?
One was $50 and the other about $35.

Great.

What techniques did you use?
Oh, we just had sex.

You mean intercourse?
Yes.

Was there any mouth genital contact?
No. I never allowed that.

Was there any anal intercourse?
Once, but we always had straight sex.

Fine.

Have you ever been paid for intercourse?
*Well, it's funny that you should ask. One
time I was in a singles bar, and a man
insisted on paying me $40 for intercourse,
which I would've been happy to have had
without payment, but he went ahead and
paid me.*

What other times?
That was the only time.

Photographs

3

13

14

15

Jo Caro

From *Sex Life of the American Woman*

edited by Albert Ellis

FROM THE TIME I VOLUNTEERED to be interviewed, until the appointed hour, I underwent a transformation. I had regarded myself as a reasonably intelligent, sexually sophisticated, and objective person—interested in contributing my sex history for the benefit of mankind. Others might be timid, but not I.

How mistaken I was.

As the hour approached I began to face the fact that it was my personal experience which was sought—not my intellectual ideas and evaluations. There I was, a grown woman, suddenly fearing embarrassment. What about my own sex life? What about my attitudes? How could I really talk about myself? My "perversities" would seem grotesque. Or would they? Was my behavior really perverse or did it just suddenly seem so because it was somewhat contrary to what my parents had instilled in me as being proper? Perverse? Why, no! Doubtlessly, just the reverse! I thought of friends whose behavior covered experiences different from mine—behavior which I had been able to think was all right for them but not for me. I recalled earlier discovery of biased attitudes and realized I had replaced some of them with other biases. Perhaps I was—under the guise of sophistication—quite repressed, inhibited, and grossly moralistic.

In short, I became anxious. I felt I was about to make a fool of myself. I tried to remember my initial impression of Dr. Kinsey's warm, accepting personality. I reminded myself that he had interviewed thousands of people, that my history was insignificant ex-

21   22   2

24

33

34

42

43

All photographs by Ken Regan/Camera 5.

1. Liam Neeson *(Alfred Kinsey)*

2. John Lithgow *(Alfred Seguine Kinsey)* and Benjamin Walker *(Kinsey at 19)*

3. Liam Neeson and Laura Linney *(Clara McMillen)*

4. Laura Linney and Liam Neeson

5. Liam Neeson

6. Laura Linney

7. Liam Neeson and Laura Linney

8. Laura Linney and Liam Neeson

9. Laura Linney and Liam Neeson with Bill Buell *(Dr. Thomas Lattimore)*

10. John Lithgow, Laura Linney and Liam Neeson

11. Laura Linney, Liam Neeson, Jenna Gavigan *(Joan Kinsey)*, Luke MacFarlane *(Bruce Kinsey)* and Leigh Spofford *(Anne Kinsey)*

12. Liam Neeson

13. Liam Neeson

14. Oliver Platt *(Herman Wells)*

15. Tim Curry *(Thurman Rice)*

16. Liam Neeson

17. Liam Neeson and Peter Sarsgaard *(Clyde Martin)*

18. Liam Neeson and Peter Sarsgaard

19. Peter Sarsgaard, Liam Neeson and Laura Linney

20. Peter Sarsgaard

21. Chris O'Donnell *(Wardell Pomeroy)*

22. Peter Sarsgaard

23. Timothy Hutton *(Paul Gebhard)*

24. Dagmara Dominczyk *(Agnes Gebhard)*, Timothy Hutton, Julianne Nicholson *(Alice Martin)*, Peter Sarsgaard, Heather Goldenhersh *(Martha Pomeroy)* and Chris O'Donnell

25. Chris O'Donnell, Timothy Hutton, Liam Neeson and Peter Sarsgaard

26. Peter Sarsgaard

27. Liam Neeson and Peter Sarsgaard

28. John Epperson, Jefferson Mays and Liam Neeson

29. Peter Sarsgaard, Liam Neeson, Chris O'Donnell and Timothy Hutton

30. Chris O'Donnell and Timothy Hutton

31. Liam Neeson

32. Laura Linney

33. Laura Linney and Liam Neeson

34. Liam Neeson and Laura Linney

35. Liam Neeson

36. Dylan Baker *(Alan Gregg)*

37. Romulus Linney *(Rep. B. Carroll Reece)*

38. Liam Neeson and Laura Linney with reporters

39. John Lithgow and Liam Neeson

40. Lynn Redgrave

41. Liam Neeson

42. Liam Neeson, Bill Condon and Laura Linney

43. Bill Condon

Part Two

Kinsey:
The Movie

A Conversation with Bill Condon

by Rob Feld

THE IDEA OF PSYCHOLOGICAL REPRESSION, of those forces which bubble hungrily beneath the surface of an individual psyche or the collective consciousness of a culture, is common in art and narrative. Scholars such as Joseph Campbell find it in ancient myth, and with the advent of psychoanalysis, an endless stream of Western artists set about exploring the concept and using its symbolism in their work. Though his model isn't predominantly in use anymore, Freud argued that some of our drives and memories—many of them sexual—are so horrific to our conscious mind that we must repress them, if only as a pragmatic means of getting through our days and lives. Nevertheless, these repressed desires, emotions, and tendencies play a heavy hand in our actions because we can be successful in denying their presence for only so long.

With his latest film about Dr. Alfred Kinsey—a man who

spent his life trying to free sexuality from the shame which society imposes on it—writer/director Bill Condon examines explicitly what in his past work has been more thematic and contextual. While it would be far too simplistic to cubbyhole a talent as diverse as Condon as a *gay filmmaker*, it would be hard to view his work outside the context of his experience growing up gay in 1960s America. In his earlier screenplays, including the horror film *Sister, Sister*, the intimate depiction of the last days of James Whale in *Gods and Monsters*, and the adaptation of the Broadway musical *Chicago* (*Chicago* being the only one he didn't direct), Condon's characters have all suffered for their socially unacceptable sexuality.

Condon grew up in New York City, where he remained for college, studying philosophy at Columbia University. Though he had only audited a few film classes as an undergraduate, Condon hoped to enter UCLA's graduate film program, and moved to California to establish residency in the state. Condon had also been doing some freelance journalism, and submitted a twenty-page critical think-piece to *Millimeter* magazine. Although the article didn't fit with the magazine's technical orientation, at the last minute *Millimeter* found itself with a large amount of extra advertising space, and decided to print the article in its entirety.

The result was the first in what Condon describes as a number of lucky breaks he has experienced in his career. Producer Michael Laughlin (*Two-Lane Blacktop*) had just moved into Alan Pakula's house, where he happened to see a stray copy of *Millimeter*. Condon never made it to UCLA because Laughlin tracked him down and offered him a job. At the age of 22, Condon got an early taste of how frustrating the studio development process could be. He was a fan of Hitchcock, however, and because of John Carpenter's recent success with the low-budget *Halloween*, the horror and suspense genres seemed viable ways of getting smaller movies made outside the studio system. Condon sat down to write a script called "Dead Kids," which was a riff on 1950s mad scientist movies, with some more contemporary horror tropes thrown in. With Laughlin as director, they succeeded in financing the project and shot the film for $1 million in New Zealand, which stood in for small-town Illinois. The film, which was released under the title *Strange Behavior*, was in no way a financial success, but it was reviewed well enough to afford Laughlin and Condon a bigger budget for an unofficial sequel, *Strange Invaders*. Having given UCLA a miss, being involved in the making of these films became Condon's version of film school.

Working with producer Walter Coblenz, Condon next wrote a script for himself to direct. Although Bob Rehme at New World Pictures was interested, he felt the project was too ambitious for a first-time director. Instead, he offered Condon a script he owned called "The Louisiana Swamp Murders." By this point, it was several years into the cycle that *Halloween* had started, with films like *Friday the 13th* and *Nightmare on Elm Street* taking up the mantle. "Swamp Murders" was a particularly basic tale of an incestuous brother and sister who run a crocodile farm/bed and breakfast, and serve their guests to the crocs. "It wasn't as fun as it sounds," Condon notes.

However, hungry to direct, Condon sat down with the script and his friend, Joel Cohen (*Toy Story*), and a month later they emerged with the screenplay for *Sister, Sister*, keeping only the core elements of the original (namely, Louisiana and crocodiles). The resulting mesh of slasher film and Southern Gothic ("In retrospect I'm not sure those things necessarily belong together," Condon admits) contained many of the thematic elements that were to become constants in Condon's work to follow. In the film, Lucy (Jennifer Jason Leigh) and her older sister, Charlotte (Judith Ivey), live together in a dilapidated plantation house, sharing the unmentionable secret of the murder of Charlotte's boyfriend many years earlier, when he had tried to rape them. Lucy has since spent time in an institution, though she is, arguably, in fine health. Charlotte, as mother figure, prevents Lucy from acting on her sexual urges, ostensibly because of her fragile state, and the guilt for their crime consumes them both.

Lucy's sexual confusion sends her in many directions, and it is not until she has freed herself—by making love to what turns out to be the wrong man—that can she achieve redemption. This was something of a break from genre convention, in which the psychotic killer typically wreaks vengeance at the moment when his victim transgresses sexually. (Think Janet Leigh in *Psycho*, or any of the teenagers in *Halloween*.) A self-described lapsed Catholic, Condon observes, "When I look back on my attempts to fit into that form I realize one thing: that the people who get punished in the scripts I wrote are the people *doing* the repressing. Only the act of freeing yourself from repression is rewarded."

Sister, Sister was neither a financial nor critical success and Condon spent some time in "movie jail," directing cable movies, writing the script for *F/X 2*, and directing *Candyman: Farewell to the Flesh*. It was almost a decade before Condon was able to find financing for a project that he would both write and direct, *Gods and Monsters*. It might be more appropriate to view this long prison sentence as boot camp, however, because that film showed the masterful touch of a sensitive and mature filmmaker, while continuing to expand on the themes that interested him. "I envy directors who are able to shift genres from picture to picture," Condon says. "I've found that for me each movie seems to emerge from the one I've just done. You're exploring a certain set of ideas, and then you look around for new opportunities to develop them further. Even *Gods and Monsters* grew out of my experience of making horror movies."

Condon's Oscar-winning screenplay, which he adapted from the Christopher Bram novel *Father of Frankenstein*, draws a fictional portrait of the final days of director James Whale (Ian McKellen). While he made many films outside the horror genre, Whale is largely remembered for his classics *Frankenstein, Bride of Frankenstein,* and *The Invisible Man.* When the story joins him, it is 1957 and Whale has for the most part cloistered himself, having fallen from Hollywood grace years before. He has also suffered a series of small strokes, which have weakened his concentration and left his mind prone to wandering. Memories, unwanted and merciless, now force themselves into his consciousness at whim—the young man who died in the trenches of the Great War, not properly mourned as a lover as he hung from the barbed wire; his *Frankenstein* monster, that misunderstood patchwork of a man, somehow fallen from grace and searching for love; and the mob with their torches, oppressive and angry, who demand conformity on pain of ostracism, or worse. It is not until these repressed demons of identity are fully exorcized, through an unlikely friendship with his gardener, Clay Boone (Brendan Fraser), that Condon's Whale can make enough peace to leave this mortal coil behind.

Chicago was many years in development before Condon came on board to write the screenplay, but it was his and director Rob Marshall's approach to the story that made the Broadway musical's transition to screen work, by placing the musical numbers into the fantasy world of Roxie Hart (Renée Zellweger). The fantasies, which play out Roxie's repressed and forbidden desires, drip with sex and eroticism, as compared with her drab, unfulfilled reality. In an effort to rise to stardom through the ultimate societal transgressions, murder and adultery, she weaves a public identity for herself as an American angel led astray, co-opting social norms to her own advantage. Hypocrisy in all its forms runs rampant through the story, as the manipulated public embraces this selfish, murderous woman, and leaves her husband—the one person in *Chicago* who acts with love—out in the cold. A variation on a theme for Condon, Roxie is driven by the desire not just to conform, but to become an icon to the conforming mob, worshiped and adored by them. The public's love is fickle, however, and at the apex of her success, Roxie is discarded in favor of the next idol on whom the masses can project their hopes and longings. Again in Condon's work, one's identity and sense of worth can never be defined from without.

The idea for making a film about Kinsey came to Condon

from producer Gail Mutrux, who sent him the biography *Kinsey: Sex the Measure of All Things*, by Jonathan Gathorne-Hardy. Condon was immediately taken by the complexity of Kinsey's character. "Dr. Kinsey was a scientist who tried to categorize everyone," Condon says, "and then used that process to prove that everyone was different. That's a wonderful contradiction. In trying to separate sex from everything imposed on it by culture, religion, and society, he also, like an artist, tried to work out some very deep conflicts within himself, and then share what he'd discovered with the world." By using the mob's own tendency to categorize and label, Kinsey subverted that very process by showing its impossibility.

Kinsey was on a very personal quest to bring to the surface all that the shame instilled in him as a child had forced him to repress. The fact that we are capable of denying our essential nature shows us to be malleable creatures, subject to the external pressures of a culture that either affirms or rejects us. In addition to being well-rendered, Condon's characters are so compelling because their inner selves come into such sharply defined conflict with these external forces—the very essence of drama. Crudely put, it is our quest for happiness. This was Kinsey's quest, as it was Roxie's and Whale's and Lucy's. Condon's characters seem to argue that unless we look within—rejecting the unnatural and stifling categorizations of the group—that quest will ultimately fail.

ROB FELD: There were so many stories to tell in Kinsey, *which you could have taken in a lot of different directions. But somehow you managed to break out of the standard biopic model, which you successfully avoided in* Gods and Monsters *as well. What guidelines did you set for yourself?*

BILL CONDON: There are so many pitfalls to the biopic form. One of the problems is that the private lives of noteworthy people are often less interesting than whatever achievement they're famous for. There are a lot of films about writers, for example, where you find out about their love lives and health problems, without ever really getting a sense of them as artists. That's why I think you have to so careful in choosing a subject. With James Whale, for example, the films he's remembered for are completely idiosyncratic projections of his own identity. Those movies intertwine so closely with who he is that it's possible to give equal dramatic weight to the work and the private life. In other words, scenes about Whale's movies can tell you as much about him as scenes from his private life. I felt that same thing when I first started reading about Kinsey. By getting people to talk and think about sex, he had a staggering effect on the culture. There's a direct link between his two studies and the sexual revolution of the 1960s. But the work sprang from a very personal need. And as he discovered things, he applied them to his private life. For example, Kinsey was stunned by the amount of homosexual activity he was encountering in the sex histories, which in turn made him feel more comfortable in exploring this aspect of his own sexuality.

ROB FELD: You've also used flashbacks to great effect in your films, but they come with their own pitfalls.

BILL CONDON: Absolutely. I think people are rightly wary of flashbacks, which can often seem either convenient or unmotivated. With James Whale, a series of small strokes had left him incapable of controlling where his mind took him. It was a terrible ailment in real life, but it's also a godsend to a filmmaker, since it allows you to introduce crucial memories in quick painful stabs. With *Kinsey* it was harder. I knew I wanted to depict scenes from his youth, but it wasn't until I was deep into writing the script that I found a way to introduce them. One of the truly remarkable things about Kinsey was his genius for sitting opposite total strangers, from all social backgrounds, and getting them to open up about the most intimate aspect of their lives. He would ease people in by starting with simple biographical details: age, religious upbringing, education. He'd then move on to more personal questions, like a subject's relationship with his parents, before launching into questions about sexual activity. Kinsey described these sex histories as a kind of prism through which you could understand a person's entire life. So one day it hit me—what if the movie was nothing more than Kinsey's own sex history? The fact is, he did train his team of researchers by having them take his sex history, which he was very candid about. It's always exciting when you stumble onto something like that, and things finally fall into place.

ROB FELD: Talk to me about adaptation, and especially adapting the lives of real people and what that responsibility is. You must have felt a great responsibility to Kinsey and Whale.

BILL CONDON: Yeah, it's hard. I talked to so many people who knew James Whale, and when Ian McKellen came to Los Angeles to prepare for the movie, I introduced him to many of them. Then one day he called up and said, "This has been very helpful, but I think I'm done now." It was time to start creating his own version of Whale—which is all it ever could or should be. Obviously, you need to be truthful to the essence of who someone is, and there's no better compliment than when a relative or friend says, "God, you really captured him." I have to say I was thrilled to get a few of those calls last week from people who are currently working at the

Kinsey Institute. They didn't know him, of course, but they do spend their lives surrounded by him. But I think that you have to recognize that all you're really creating is your version of this person. Just by virtue of the choices you make, you're defining what interests you about him. And of course you're going to have to leave a lot out. I remember going to London for the *Gods and Monsters* premiere, which happened long after the American run of the movie, and meeting James Whale's two grand nieces, who are in their sixties now. They remember him as Uncle Jimmy from Hollywood, who would show up back in England for the occasional holiday. You know, at a certain point, if you have a movie that's been well received, you get used to being introduced to people who say nice things. But as soon as the film was over, they expressed their disapproval, especially about the sexual content in the movie. They weren't even convinced Uncle Jimmy was homosexual. And why should they be? They'd been young girls when he died. That was their experience of him. They had every right to express those things, and I had certainly left James Whale the family man out of that movie.

ROB FELD: Kinsey seemed to turn his own life into something of a Petri dish, encouraging partner swapping among his team, for example. In some ways, it did leave him open to attack—scientists aren't supposed to experiment on themselves.

BILL CONDON: Well, again, it's odd because his whole idea was to study sex as something separated from emotion, but—because he was so full of empathy himself—he did feel it was important to understand what people were talking about. So he would sometimes dabble in things in which he didn't have much interest, in order to experience them at least once. You have to remember, Kinsey started thinking about sex and teaching the marriage course in the late 1930s, and really launched into this project in the early 40s. He then spent fifteen years doing nothing but talking and thinking about sex every day, for sixteen hours a day. He wasn't someone who relaxed or took vacations. Sex became his new religion. So, as he delved deeper into the subject, new possibilities presented themselves. One was this kind of wacky notion that he could create a sort of sexual Utopia among a small group of friends and associates. There would be open sexual activity, but without the romantic and emotional entanglements that threaten hearth and home, marriage and stability. He was trying to separate sex from emotional involvement and make it into a pure outlet for pleasure. And, of course, it didn't work. All it takes is one person to fall in love and suddenly all the rules go out the window.

ROB FELD: *Did you meet any people who had been interviewed by Kinsey?*

BILL CONDON: This wild thing happened while we were prepping the movie in New York. I was subletting a place and my phone number was listed. A woman called one day and said she was one of the first people whom Kinsey had interviewed in the 1940s. She's actually in the movie as one of the interview subjects—the older woman in the cross country montage, who talks about how, if you weren't a virgin, you were a fallen woman, and no one would want you.

ROB FELD: *You approached the visuals of film with the idea of a grid design, didn't you?*

BILL CONDON: A few years ago, the Kinsey Institute, which has in the past been secretive about their vast collection of erotica, published a book called *Peek,* which was, literally, a tiny peek into their amazing archives. There was a series of photographs that really inspired me as I was writing the script. A naked man stands in front of a piece of graph paper, his penis becoming progressively more erect in each picture. It kind of captured what Kinsey was all about—taking human beings and trying to get them onto that grid, into those graph paper squares. I showed the photos to

Richard Sherman, the production designer, who said, "Why don't we use that as a visual motif for the entire film?" So as Kinsey's project comes to life, the grid starts to appear, whether as a room divider, or a lamp, or even the exterior of a building. Then, when things go wrong, the squares disappear. For example, when Kinsey is at his lowest point, after the publication of the *Female* volume, he gives a lecture where people walk out on him. We decided to place the scene in a vast marble rotunda, and [cinematographer] Fred Elmes created a series of ever tighter circles around Kinsey. The grid has collapsed.

ROB FELD: *I know the Kinsey Institute was very helpful in the making of the film. You borrowed examples of erotica from them, didn't you?*

BILL CONDON: We went into the library and duplicated a few things. I also begged to see some of the famous "attic films," but they're very protective of the people who appeared in those films, even though they're mostly close-ups of genitals.

ROB FELD: *There are a few genital close-ups in the movie, and they're actually pretty shocking.*

BILL CONDON: There's another movie to be made about Kinsey that would be quite confrontational, but I decided on a more classical approach, where you're lulled into a kind of pretty Merchant/Ivory universe. When you come to Kinsey's first marriage course, Bruce Finlayson's wonderfully evocative costumes make you feel as if you're in an idealized American university setting of the early 1940s. Then Kinsey projects a black-and-white slide—just as he did over sixty years ago—and it's a ten-foot tall image of an erect penis entering a vagina. I think it takes you by surprise—imagine penises and vaginas in *The Remains of the Day*!—and hopefully gives you an idea of how revolutionary Kinsey was.

ROB FELD: *And there's no need to embellish it.*

BILL CONDON: No, no.

ROB FELD: *Your stories tend to involve characters and worlds which are particularly eccentric and fringe. Are you deliberate about the ways in which you lead an audience into those worlds? It can be difficult to just drop people into them.*

BILL CONDON: I really learned that lesson with the first movie I directed, *Sister, Sister*. The central characters were a damaged, repressed woman (played by Jennifer Jason Leigh) and her equally strange sister (Judith Ivey). The setting was also fairly exotic, a rundown plantation house on the bayou in Louisiana. There wasn't a relatively "normal" character until Eric Stoltz showed up, about twenty minutes in, which made it difficult for an audience to connect with the movie. I realized later that it would have made more sense to start with the Eric Stoltz character, and then take him into this strange world and see it through his eyes. To give the audience an anchor. That's one of the nice things about early failures. You learn lessons that you never forget.

ROB FELD: *And you applied that lesson to* Gods and Monsters?

BILL CONDON: Yes. James Whale was also a pretty exotic character. So I opened the movie with Clayton Boone (Brendan Fraser) waking up, starting his day, finally driving up to Whale's house. He gave us a point of view with which to approach Whale. That's true for *Kinsey* too. Alfred Kinsey is in some ways an unlikely character to build a movie around. He's pedantic, socially maladroit, a bit dense; he misses the point in some crucial ways, and that can become wearying after a while. But as soon as Clara (Laura Linney) appears and is charmed by him, we start to see him through her eyes. I think she provides the way in.

ROB FELD: *Do you find yourself drawn to misfits and outsiders?*

BILL CONDON: Certainly outsiders. Even in *Chicago,* Roxie is someone who has her face pressed against the window, desperate to get in. That story had been told in several previous movies and theatrical versions, but this aspect of Roxie—her yearning to belong— was something I tried to make more explicit.

ROB FELD: *Do you think that identification with the outsider is an outgrowth of growing up gay in America?*

BILL CONDON: Sure, I think being gay contributes to a lot of these issues—sitting on secrets and feeling, in some basic way, that you don't belong.

ROB FELD: *In your films, themes of dreams, aspirations and eroticism play themselves out as primary motivating factors for your characters. What role do you think that sex plays in our psyches, at least in the world of film?*

BILL CONDON: Like so many people, one of my first movie loves was Hitchcock. His treatment of repressed sexual desire and voyeurism really fascinated me. And I think part of what attracted me to Kinsey was that he made films. He was a literal voyeur, although he was rarely aroused by what he was observing. A movie is something you experience in the dark. You enter a dream state for a couple of hours, often seeing idealized versions of what Kinsey liked to call the human animal. So even when a movie isn't explicitly about sex, it's always part of the experience.

ROB FELD: *In Larry Kramer's play,* The Normal Heart, *which describes his experiences founding the Gay Men's Health Crisis in the 1980s, Ned Weeks (the Kramer character) is on a crusade to get the gay community to stop having sex until they can get a handle on AIDS. The opposing argument in the play is: "This is what we are. You can't tell us not to be what we are." Which frustrates Weeks, because he insists that a gay identity shouldn't be wholly defined by one's sex life, which of course is not the way in which the straight population is defined.*

BILL CONDON: One of the people I interviewed was Clarence Tripp, who met Kinsey in 1948 and then became part of the project. I asked him what Kinsey would have made of the gay movement. "Oh, he would have been horrified," Tripp said. Kinsey's basic idea, if you were to put it in a nutshell, is that everyone's sexuality is unique. Having collected over a million gall wasps, he discovered that none of those tiny insects was identical to another. He then took that notion of individual variation and applied it to human sexuality. The problem, as he saw it, was that, though we're all different, we all need to feel part of the group to feel reassured that what we do is *normal.* But there's no such thing as normal—there's only common or rare. That's all that Kinsey was trying to figure out: what was common and what was rare. He was shouting to people: Be yourself! Break away from the group! So for him there's no freedom in defining yourself by your sexual acts. We live under the delusion that we've come so far, but I think Kinsey would say that—while the group imposes different expectations and demands today—the impulse to belong still overwhelms our individual desires. I mean, is it that much easier being a teenage girl now, with the pressure to be sexually active, than it was to be young in the Sandra Dee era, when virginity was so prized? What happens to the person who doesn't feel comfortable with the dominant mores? The pressure to fit in—that never goes away.

ROB FELD: So in a way Kinsey is saying overtly what had been more thematic in your previous work?

BILL CONDON: Maybe. I think of those great scary images of the vengeful townspeople in *Frankenstein*, gathering to kill the monster. It was an idea that was unique to Whale's telling of the Frankenstein story—that the mob was more frightening than the monster. And that's what's so moving about Kinsey. He was always speaking out for the individual.

ROB FELD: But he kind of created a group of his own, right? He was, himself, something of a movement.

BILL CONDON: I think he probably would have understood that there were political reasons for forming a group—obviously, there's safety in numbers. And, like it or not, Kinsey is one of the unofficial fathers of the gay movement. The Mattachine Society had its first meeting soon after the *Male* volume was published. A few influential homosexuals said, "Well, there are a lot more of us than we thought. What are we going to do about this?" Gore Vidal puts it well when he says that people aren't homosexual or heterosexual, just homosexualist and heterosexualist. Everybody has his own sexual makeup. And I guess every movie has a unique sexual identity too. *Kinsey* depicts hetero-, homo- and bisexual activity. But because Kinsey was speaking to everybody, I thought it was important to keep the sexual equation balanced. When you're an openly gay director, it's easy for your movie to be ghettoized as a gay film. But I say that with some trepidation, because I don't want to suggest that I'm not happy to take on that mantle, which I certainly am.

ROB FELD: But you hope what you've created has universal appeal.

BILL CONDON: That's right. It reminds me of something that happened at Sundance the year *Gods and Monsters* played there. They always have one screening in Salt Lake City, and it was fascinating to watch a predominantly Mormon audience—who knew nothing about the movie—gradually become complicit with Ian McKellen as he tries to talk Brendan Fraser out of his pants. This was a character they might shun in real life, but in a movie, the issues of aging, unresolved yearnings, and loneliness connected on a level that crossed sexual identity boundaries. It was my favorite screening of that movie.

ROB FELD: There's a scene at the end of Kinsey *with Lynn Redgrave as an interview subject. Kinsey at that point has been questioning what he's accomplished, but his encounter with this woman helps him to see that he has, in fact, brought liberation and happiness to at least one life. I'm wondering if that's really the best any filmmaker can hope for. To reach at least one person and let him know he's not alone.*

BILL CONDON: That's what movies have done for me. And some of the bleakest movies have made me feel the most reassured; when you see a kind of behavior, or even a thought pattern, to which you can relate, it makes you feel that you're not out there on your own.

The
Final
Shooting
Script

KINSEY

by

Bill Condon

FINAL SHOOTING SCRIPT

FADE IN:

IN DARKNESS

                    KINSEY (V.O.)
          Don't sit so far away. Anything that
          creates a distance should be avoided.

We hear a wooden chair being dragged across the floor.

                    KINSEY (V.O.)
          And try not to frown.

                    MARTIN (V.O.)
          I'm sorry. Was I frowning?

                    KINSEY (V.O.)
          You have to relax. How can I be
          expected to open up if you're not
          relaxed?

                    MARTIN (V.O.)
          Right.

                    KINSEY (V.O.)
          Take a deep breath. Start again.

INT. LAB ROOM - DAY (1942) (B&W)

A blank, anonymous space. CLYDE MARTIN, 24, open-faced and amiable,
stares across at Kinsey, who remains unseen. Martin holds up a
piece of paper.

                    MARTIN
          As you can see, this piece of paper's
          been divided into 287 squares. Your
          sex history will fit on this single
          page, in a cryptic code.

                    KINSEY (O.S.)
          Don't forget to mention that there's no
          written key to the code. The interview
          subject will only be candid if he knows
          he's speaking in the strictest
          confidence.

                    MARTIN
          Right. Okay, so...when were you born?

                          KINSEY (O.S.)
          June 23, 1894.

                          MARTIN
          Are you single or married?

                          KINSEY (O.S.)
          Married.

                          MARTIN
          What is your race?

                          KINSEY (O.S.)
          Don't waste time asking the obvious,
          Martin. Fill it in yourself.

Martin writes a W in a top box, near 6-23-94 and the familiar
circle-with-arrow symbol for the male gender.

                          MARTIN
          What is your religion?

                          KINSEY (O.S.)
          I was raised a Methodist.

                          MARTIN
          How often do you attend church?

                          KINSEY (O.S.)
          Not at all now, but I did regularly
          until I was 19.

Martin writes MXf(-19).

                          MARTIN
          How did you get along with your father
          and mother when you were growing up?

                          KINSEY (O.S.)
          That's a multiple question. It allows
          me to ignore any part I don't want to
          answer.

                          MARTIN
          Sorry. How did you get along with your
          mother?

                    KINSEY (O.S.)
          Fine. We had a loving relationship.

                    MARTIN
          And your father?

Now we see ALFRED KINSEY. A grey-blond buzzcut and penetrating,
black-encircled eyes. He wears a rumpled suit and bowtie.

                    MARTIN (O.S.)
          How did you get along with your father?

INT. METHODIST CHURCH BASEMENT - HOBOKEN - DAY (1904)

AL KINSEY, 10, gangly and pale, sits in the front row, next to his
8-year-old sister MILDRED and his mother SARA, who cradles her
newborn baby, ROBERT. His father, ALFRED SEGUINE KINSEY, 40,
handsome and charismatic, preaches to the sparsely attended church
elders meeting.

                    KINSEY SR.
          Lust has a thousand avenues. The
          dance hall, the ice cream parlor, the
          tenement saloon, the Turkish bath —
          like the hydra it grows new heads
          everywhere. Even the modern
          inventions of science are used to
          cultivate immorality. The gas engine
          has brought us the automobile joy
          ride and an even more pernicious
          menace, the roadside brothel.
          Electricity has made possible the
          degrading picture show. Because of
          the telephone, a young woman can now
          hear the voice of her suitor on the
          pillow next to her.

Al shifts uncomfortably, trying not to be titillated by his father's
imagery.

                    KINSEY SR.
          And let us not forget the most
          scandalous invention of all: the talon
          slide fastener — otherwise known as the
          zipper — which provides every man and
          boy speedy access to moral oblivion.

Al's mother turns and smiles sweetly, which makes the boy blush with
guilt.

INT. LAB ROOM - DAY (1942) (B&W)

WARDELL POMEROY, 30, sits opposite Kinsey now. He's movie star handsome with a confident, engaging personality.

> POMEROY
> Are you currently in good health?

> KINSEY
> I suppose so.

> POMEROY
> What makes you doubtful?

> KINSEY
> Every doctor I've ever seen. Early disease left me with a weakened heart.

> POMEROY
> Did you have any illnesses that kept you out of school?

> KINSEY
> I had typhoid fever and rickets. Also rheumatic fever, measles, chicken pox, pneumonia and several bouts of influenza.

Pomeroy shifts slightly as he makes notations.

> KINSEY
> Pomeroy, what are you doing? You're worse than Martin.

Pomeroy looks up, surprised.

> KINSEY
> Never make judgments about people.

> POMEROY
> I wasn't.

> KINSEY
> Your body posture told me that my list of ailments made you uncomfortable.

> POMEROY
> Maybe it did. Sorry.

                         KINSEY
          Maintaining a non-judgmental attitude
          is harder than you think. The best way
          is to smile and nod your head while
          looking me directly in the eye.

Pomeroy makes the adjustment, a quicker study than Martin.

                         KINSEY
          Where were we?

                         POMEROY
          Your health as a boy.

                         KINSEY
          It improved greatly when I finally
          discovered the outdoors. I never got
          over the excitement of setting off into
          the wild. Escaping bed, illness.
          Family.

                         POMEROY
          Alone?

EXT. WOODS - DAY (1908)

Al stands in a clearing. He is 14 now.

                         KINSEY (V.O.)
          No, never alone. I was surrounded by
          friends.

Al observes creatures through a small retractable telescope.
Woodpeckers and squirrels. Grasshoppers and butterflies. And
birds, countless varieties of birds.

Al lowers the scope, compares the robin he just observed to a
drawing in a book. He makes a few notes, a quick sketch.

                         KINSEY (V.O.)
          Being in the outdoors taught me to rely
          on my own judgment. I started to
          learn about things by grasping them,
          tasting them... looking at them.

                         POMEROY (V.O.)
          Biology.

                         KINSEY (V.O.)
          Yes, biology. The science of life.

The fields and woods became my new
place of worship. My cathedral.

Late in the day, Al checks his watch. He retracts his scope.
Suddenly alone.

                    KINSEY (V.O.)
          The only sadness they brought was when
          I had to leave them.

INT. LAB ROOM - DAY (1942) (B&W)

PAUL GEBHARD is also 30, with a mustache and reddish hair that
recedes into a widow's peak.

                    GEBHARD
          How old were you when you first tried
          to pleasure yourself?

                    KINSEY
          No, no, no euphemisms. If you're
          talking to a college graduate, use
          masturbation, testicles, penis, vagina-
          vulva, defecation, urination. With a
          lower level male, it's jacking off,
          balls, prick, cunt, piss, shit. I
          don't know, Gebhard. Maybe your
          Harvard degree is too ivory tower for
          our purposes.

                    GEBHARD
          I was brought up out West. I've rubbed
          shoulders with ranchers and miners my
          whole life.

                    KINSEY
          And I thought you were going to shave
          that mustache.

                    GEBHARD
          I like it.

                    KINSEY
          It's a disguise, a cover-up. Look at
          any movie. The villain's always the
          one with the mustache.

                    GEBHARD
          My wife likes it.

                         KINSEY
          You have a chance to make an important
          contribution to knowledge and science.
          Are you telling me you'd give that up
          for a little facial hair?

                         GEBHARD
          Yes. I suppose I am.

Kinsey is stumped.

                         KINSEY
          Well keep it trimmed.

Gebhard can't suppress a smile.

                         KINSEY
          Let's get back to masturbation.

EXT. WOODS - LAKE WAWAYANDA - DAY (1914)

Al, 19, climbs onto a promontory. Dressed as an Eagle Scout, he has
become a tall and handsome teenager, almost radiant, with curly hair
that glistens in the sunlight. He is followed closely by a junior
scout, KENNETH HAND, 16.

EXT. WOODS - LAKE WAWAYANDA - DAY (LATER)

Kenneth stares at a chirping blue jay through a pair of binoculars.
Al gazes at the boy.

                         AL
          That's a mating call.

                         KENNETH
          So how'd you wind up at the Stevens
          Institute, Al? I thought you wanted to
          be a biologist.

                         AL
                 (imitating his father)
          "There are enough scientists, son.
          Engineers are what society needs now."

He angrily hurls a rock across the valley.

                         KENNETH
          I had one of the old fits again.

An uncomfortable silence as Kenneth returns Al's gaze.

                              KENNETH
                I tried to stop —

Kenneth steps closer to Al, who pulls a manual from his pack.

                              AL
                         (reading)
                "Any habit which causes the sex fluid
                to be discharged must be resisted.
                Doctors link it to an assortment of
                illnesses, including insanity,
                blindness, epilepsy, vertigo, deafness,
                and even death."

                              KENNETH
                What if it happens while you're asleep?

                              AL
                "It is said that the loss of one ounce
                of seminal fluid equals the loss of
                forty ounces of blood."

                              KENNETH
                I'm killing myself and I'm not even
                awake. What are we supposed to do?

Fortunately, the manual does suggest some helpful treatments:

                              AL
                "Keep your bowels open. Read the
                Sermon on the Mount. Sit with your
                testicles submerged in a bowl of cold
                water. Think of your mother's pure
                love."

The two boys lower their heads, contemplating their options.

                              AL
                Why don't we pray?

Al and Kenneth kneel.

EXT. WOODS - LAKE WAWAYANDA - KINSEY'S TENT - NIGHT

Al lies awake in his sleeping bag. He places his hands under his
pajamas, slowly caressing his thighs and chest. All the while
keeping his eyes closed.

Finally Al starts to masturbate. He ejaculates quickly, then breaks
into frightened sobs.

INT. LAB ROOM - DAY (1942) (B&W)

Questions come in quick succession now.

                  POMEROY
        How young were you the first time you
        had an orgasm while dreaming?

                  GEBHARD
        How frequently did you have wet dreams?

                  MARTIN
        What did you dream about?

                  POMEROY
        How young were you when you first
        experienced hugging or kissing?

                  GEBHARD
        Necking?

                  POMEROY
        Petting?

                  GEBHARD
        Oral sex?

                  MARTIN
        How young were you when you no longer
        thought of your parents' home as your
        own?

INT. KINSEY CHILDHOOD HOUSE - AL'S BEDROOM - DUSK (1914)

A finished attic that serves as Al's bedroom. It's a perfectly
ordered space that reflects his hobbies and obsessions, from the
stamp and butterfly collections to the pancake classical music disks,
one of which plays on a portable phonograph. Al opens a trunk,
revealing a Bunsen burner and a lock box hidden under some clothes.

                  KINSEY SR. (O.S.)
        Al, it's getting late. Let's make the
        rounds.

Al flexes his jaw muscles, tense with anger and resentment. He opens
the metal box and adds a stack of bills to his already considerable
savings.

                  AL
        Be right down.

EXT. GROCERY STORE - DUSK (1914)

Kinsey Sr. and Al bicycle up to a roadside store. Kinsey Sr.
remains by his bike while Al enters the store.

INT. GROCERY STORE - DUSK (1914)

Al steps up to the immigrant Irish GROCER.

                    AL
          Pack of Fatimas.

                    GROCER
          You don't seem like a boy who'd take up
          smoking.

                    AL
          How do you know what kind of boy I am?

                    GROCER
          Okay, son. That'll be fifteen cents.

As soon as the money changes hands, the door swings open.

                    KINSEY SR.
          You are a criminal, sir. I shall
          report you at once to the local
          authorities.

                    GROCER
          Dear Jesus, a goddamn Protestant.

Kinsey Sr. grabs the pack of cigarettes from Al's hand. Al
retreats, embarrassed and angry.

                    KINSEY SR.
          Did you not just sell this vile weed to
          a minor?

Al presses his hands against his ears.

                    KINSEY SR.
          It's the Lord's work to protect the
          young from temptation.

                    GROCER
          Get the hell out of my store.

                    KINSEY SR.
          Men like you, men of weak character...

The grocer grabs a broom and brandishes it.

>   GROCER
>   I've given you a proper warning,
>   mister.

>   KINSEY SR.
>   (yelling over him)
>   ...are offensive to the great mass of
>   right-thinking American citizens!

>   AL
>   Shut up!

Kinsey Sr. wheels around. Al stares at him with strained features.
A tightly wound coil finally unsprung.

>   AL
>   You know what you are, father? A prig!

>   KINSEY SR.
>   Al...

>   AL
>   A skinflint, a petty tyrant, and a
>   hypocrite to boot! You think you
>   matter? You don't matter!

Al bursts into tears. Kinsey Sr. turns to the grocer, shaken.

>   KINSEY SR.
>   Something's wrong with him.

Kinsey Sr. looks around, nervous that someone might see them.

>   KINSEY SR.
>   Maybe your workload's too heavy, son.
>   You could drop mechanical drawing...

>   AL
>   I've withdrawn from Stevens.

>   KINSEY SR.
>   That's impossible, I'm a senior member
>   of the faculty. Someone would have
>   informed me.

>   AL
>   Why? Everyone there hates you.

Kinsey Sr.'s face reddens.

> AL
> I'm going to Bowdoin to study biology.

> KINSEY SR.
> And how do you intend to pay for that?

> AL
> They've given me a partial scholarship.
> And I've socked away most of my
> scouting money.

> KINSEY SR.
> You've become a shady person, Al. A
> person who keeps secrets.

> AL
> I had no choice.

> KINSEY SR.
> What a disappointment you turned out to be.

Kinsey Sr. leaves. Al watches.

> POMEROY (V.O.)
> How many years of schooling did you
> complete?

> KINSEY (V.O.)
> Twenty. After taking my undergraduate
> degree at Bowdoin, I received my
> doctorate from the Bussey Institute at
> Harvard.

INT. LAB ROOM - DAY (1942) (B&W)

Pomeroy writes 20, then Ph.D.

> KINSEY
> I took a position as assistant
> professor of zoology here at Indiana
> University. At first I studied the
> Rhaetulus Didieri, or stag beetle.
> Then I discovered a far more
> fascinating insect.

EXT. INDIANA UNIVERSITY - BIOLOGY HALL - DAY (1920)

The campus is Charles Addams Gothic.

                    KINSEY (V.O.)
          This is the American Cynipidae, or gall
          wasp.

A BLACK-AND-WHITE SLIDE (1920)

pops onto the screen. An insect stands on its hind legs, boring a
tiny hole into the bud of a tree.

                    KINSEY (V.O.)
          Here the wasp deposits an egg into its
          host plant, in this case an oak tree.
          A gall, or abnormal growth, forms at
          the point of entry. Hence the name
          "gall wasp."

The next slide shows a gall, a round growth about three inches in
diameter, attached to the bark of the tree. A quick series of
images illustrate the life cycle of the gall wasp.

                    KINSEY (V.O.)
          The adult wasp chews its way out of the
          gall, copulates, and begins searching
          for a place to lay its eggs. At which
          point it has the good sense to die.

INT. CLASSROOM - DAY (1920)

Kinsey is 26 now, tall and charismatic, with bright blue eyes and
blond hair standing straight up like a shock of Kansas wheat. His
soulful eyes and air of inaccessibility have made him an intriguing
figure, especially to the women who comprise over half the class.

                    KINSEY
          The animal kingdom includes at least
          two million insect species. So what
          makes the gall wasp so fascinating?

In back, a COED shows her friend a sketch of herself in a romantic
clinch with the handsome teacher. Near them, another young woman,
with lively eyes and dark hair cut in a Dutch bob, tries to ignore
their giggling and concentrate on the lecture. This is CLARA
McMILLEN, 22.

                    KINSEY
          I've spent the last three years
          crisscrossing the continent collecting
          gall wasps. And what have I learned
          from my tiny friends, half the size of
          the household ant?

The coed whispers to her friend.

                    COED
          That you need a date?

Clara silences them with a look.

                    KINSEY
          After studying thousands of these pesky
          creatures under the microscope, I've
          yet to find a single gall wasp that's
          the same as another. In fact, some are
          so different that the offspring of one
          generation bear no more resemblance to
          their parents than a sheep bears to a
          goat. There are those of us who might
          take comfort in this fact.

Clara smiles, appreciating the irreverence.

                    KINSEY
          Consider the implications. If every
          single living thing is different from
          every other living thing, then
          diversity becomes life's one
          irreducible fact. Only variations are
          real. And to see them, you simply have
          to open your eyes.

EXT. INDIANA UNIVERSITY - DAY (1920)

The annual zoology department picnic. Kinsey, sitting apart from
the others, takes in the easy laughter and casual intimacy of two
GRADUATE STUDENTS across the lawn.

                    CLARA (O.S.)
          Hello. Mind if I sit here?

Kinsey looks up and squints at Clara, silhouetted in the midday sun.

                    KINSEY
          Why?

                    CLARA
          Because you're the only unattached male
          and I'm the only unattached female.

                    KINSEY
          That's very sensible.

Clara sits on the blanket. Kinsey sizes up her outfit, untailored
pants and loose-fitting blouse.

                    CLARA
          How refreshing. A man who cooks.

He tends a tiny cooking fire, over which he is heating a can of
tomato soup.

                    KINSEY
          I picked it up when I went out West to
          collect galls. I was gone for eleven
          months and I don't think I saw more
          than a dozen people the whole time.

                    CLARA
          Sounds lonely.

                    KINSEY
          I enjoyed it.

                    CLARA
          I've been reading up on gall wasps. I
          think I know why they appeal to you.

Kinsey smiles politely.

                    CLARA
          They have great big wings, but they
          can't fly. They're incapable of
          getting from this hill to that hill
          unless it's close enough to walk.

She repositions Kinsey's salt and pepper shakers to illustrate her
point.

                    CLARA
          Which means it's possible to retrace
          each generation's steps, hill by hill,
          all the way back to the beginning. The
          gall wasp Garden of Eden, so to speak.

                    KINSEY
          Very interesting, Miss Millen. You've
          managed to bridge the gap between
          Darwin and the Book of Genesis in a
          single phrase.

                         CLARA
          McMillen.

                         KINSEY
          Hmmm?

                         CLARA
          Clara McMillen.

                         KINSEY
          Oh...I'm Prok.

                         CLARA
          Sorry?

                         KINSEY
          It's a nickname my graduate students
          have given me. Pro-fessor K-
          insey...Prok.

                         CLARA
          Prok. It suits you.

                         KINSEY
          At first I worried that it suggested an
          inappropriate level of intimacy between
          teacher and student, which could lead
          to a loss of respect down the line.

                         CLARA
          I think it just means they like you.

                         KINSEY
          Yes. Eventually I realized that.

He pours a cup of soup and hands her a plate.

                         KINSEY
          Tomato bisque and sandwiches.

Clara catches his eye and smiles.

INT. BOARDING HOUSE - PARLOR - ANOTHER DAY (1921)

Kinsey plays a Chopin etude on an upright. Clara is moved by his
passionate, sensitive performance.

INT. BOARDING HOUSE - KINSEY'S ROOMS - DAY (1921) (LATER)

Music continues as Kinsey shows Clara his classical music
collection. Hundreds of albums, all sorted and labeled.

                         KINSEY
            ...they used to be categorized by
            period but I've recently rearranged
            them alphabetically by composer. I
            find it's more efficient.

                         CLARA
            Did you ever think of playing
            professionally? You're very good.

                         KINSEY
            Thank you. But very good isn't good
            enough.

He reaches for a box wrapped in brown paper.

                         KINSEY
            I got you a present.

Kinsey shyly glances as Clara unwraps the present. A compass and
hunting knife, and a pair of hiking boots.

                         CLARA
            How marvelous.

She hugs him and he squeezes tight. They share a first tentative
kiss.

INT. LAB ROOM - DAY (1942) (B&W)

Clyde Martin's page is dotted with numbers and checks and symbols,
indecipherable to the untrained eye.

                         MARTIN
            At what age did you first have
            premarital intercourse?

                         KINSEY
            I didn't.

                         MARTIN
            So at the time of marriage, you were a
            virgin?

                    KINSEY
          Yes.

                    MARTIN
          Was your spouse also a virgin?

                    KINSEY
          Yes.

                    MARTIN
          When you got married, did you want to
          get married?

                    KINSEY
          Very much.

EXT. WOODS - CAVE - INDIANA - DUSK (1921)

Kinsey and Clara stand silhouetted in a small cave.

                    KINSEY
          ...I see marriage as a lifetime
          partnership between equals. You're a
          brilliant scholar with a keenly
          perceptive mind and a profound respect
          for nature. You're also a capable hiker
          and camper, and a champion swimmer.

Clara smiles opaquely.

                    KINSEY
          And you're the one girl in a million
          who's as interested in insects as I am.

                    CLARA
          To be honest, Prok...I'm just not sure.
          I've always considered myself something
          of a free-thinker. Frankly, I find you
          a little churchy.

                    KINSEY
          Churchy?

                    CLARA
          And I've had another proposal.

Kinsey looks shocked, and crushed.

                    CLARA
        I'm not saying no. I just need some time.

Kinsey backs away.

                    CLARA
            Prok, please...

                    KINSEY
                (sudden and sharp)
        I think you're mean. Mean, heartless,
        and cold.

Kinsey stops, surprised by his own outburst. Clara moves toward him
but he runs off.

INT. GALL WASP HALLWAY - NIGHT (1921)

It's after midnight. Kinsey sits at his desk, green eyeshade in
place. He peers through a microscope, a study in total
concentration. From his POV, we see a gall wasp.

                    KINSEY
                (softly)
            Astounding!

Kinsey carefully inserts a two-inch steel pin through a clip of
cardboard, applies a dab of clear cement, and mounts the specimen.

On minute labels, Kinsey records the insect's locality and date of
emergence, as well as the host plant name and his own name as
collector, all inscribed in India ink. He sets the impaled clip in
a cork-bottomed wooden case.

The specimens are placed about a quarter inch apart, all facing
right. Dozens of insects fit in one box, and, as we pull back to
reveal that it is now morning, we see that there are hundreds of
such boxes, stacked to the ceiling.

Clara stands in a corner watching Kinsey. CAMERA remains at a
distance as she steps into his office.

                    CLARA
            If you'll have me...

Kinsey's face lights up. He stands and embraces her.

EXT. HIGHWAY - OHIO - DAY (1921)

Kinsey and Clara drive East after their wedding ceremony.

                         CLARA
              How old is it?

                         KINSEY
              Oh, eighty million years or so.

She holds up a fossilized gall wasp, a specimen beautifully
preserved in amber.

                         KINSEY
              Does Mrs. Kinsey like her wedding
              present?

                         CLARA
              It's perfect.

They share a smile, then anxiously study the passing countryside.

INT. HOTEL ROOM - CINCINNATI - NIGHT (1921)

In the dark, Clara slips into bed next to Kinsey. Their bodies are
covered from neck to ankle. They kiss, becoming more fevered, until
Kinsey's groping makes Clara pull away.

                         KINSEY
              I'm sorry.

                         CLARA
              No, it's...

They start again, more slowly this time. Kinsey unbuttons Clara's
nightgown and opens it, revealing her breasts.

                         KINSEY
              How beautiful.

Clara stares at the ceiling, more embarrassed than she expected to
be.

                         KINSEY
              May I?

He starts to fondle her, then fumbles awkwardly with the buttons of
his pajama bottoms. He climbs on top of Clara and tries to enter
her, but he's clearly having trouble holding an erection.

                         KINSEY
              Sorry, I'm a little nervous...

                         CLARA
              That's alright, we don't have to...

Kinsey shuts his eyes and concentrates.

                    KINSEY
          No. I'm ready.

Kinsey enters her. Clara's face registers intense pain, but she
closes her eyes as Kinsey starts to grunt. On the verge of passing
out, she screams and presses her hands against his chest.

                    CLARA
          I'm sorry, it just hurts too much.

Kinsey pulls out, quickly. Clara rebuttons her nightgown.

                    KINSEY
          Forgive me, Mac.

                    CLARA
          No, it's me...

They turn away from each other, mortified.

                    KINSEY
          It's a long drive to my parents. We
          should get some sleep.

INT. KINSEY CHILDHOOD HOUSE - DINING ROOM - DAY (1921)

A family dinner, with MILDRED, 26 and dour, and ROBERT, who at 18
has settled into the role of perfect son.

                    KINSEY SR.
          ...Robert's had a 92 in mechanical
          drawing, a 95 in mathematics, and a
          clean 100 in shop practice!

                    KINSEY
          That's excellent, Robert.
          Congratulations.

                    KINSEY SR.
          I worried that his teachers were
          showing him favor due to my senior
          position. But they tell me he's the
          most gifted student in his class.

                    ROBERT
          Living with the best teacher at Stevens
          doesn't hurt, father.

                    KINSEY SR.
          At this rate, he'll finish his degree
          in three years.

                    SARA
          Al, tell us what you've been working
          on.

                    KINSEY SR.
          Don't bother, Al. You know your mother
          only has a fourth grade education.

                    KINSEY
          I'm studying gall wasps, Mom. I've
          gathered over a hundred thousand
          specimens, which is really only a drop
          in the bucket...

                    KINSEY SR.
          Ten years of higher education and he's
          still collecting bugs.

Clara ignores Kinsey Sr., turns to Sara.

                    CLARA
          Prok's also written a biology textbook.
          It's read in colleges across the
          country.

                    SARA
          Really!

                    KINSEY SR.
          So I assume you plan to start a family
          soon.

Picking up on his son's discomfort:

                    KINSEY SR.
          No need to rush it. Once you have
          children, you're tied down forever.
          Your life is over.

A pall hangs over the table.

INT. KINSEY CHILDHOOD HOUSE - AL'S BEDROOM - NIGHT (1921)

Kinsey and Clara try to get comfortable in the tiny bed.

                    CLARA
        I don't know what I expected exactly,
        but...he's much worse than I ever
        imagined.

                    KINSEY
        He is pretty awful, isn't he?

                    CLARA
        "I once read that the decline of the
        Roman Empire was the result of too
        frequent bathing."

Kinsey lets out a booming laugh that echoes in the still house.

                    CLARA
        Shhh. You'll wake him.

                    KINSEY
        "Some speculate that rampant adultery
        is a possible cause of earthquakes."

This time the laugh gets caught in his throat, turning into a sob.

                    KINSEY
        I'm sorry you had to witness that.

                    CLARA
        I think I really fell in love with you
        tonight. Seeing you here...

Kinsey gazes over at her, suddenly quiet.

                    KINSEY
        Do you think we can make this work,
        Mac?

                    CLARA
        I don't know. I've heard some people
        just don't fit together.

                    KINSEY
        There's no one I'd rather be with.

                    CLARA
        Physically, I mean. Some people aren't
        compatible. If only there were some
        way to know...

                    KINSEY
          That's it, Mac!

He jumps up, pulls on the overhead light.

                    KINSEY
          Every problem has a solution, even this
          one.

He opens the closet, grabs a suitcase.

                    KINSEY
          We just need to talk to someone. An
          expert who's studied the matter.

                    CLARA
          What are you doing?

                    KINSEY
          Why waste any more time?

INT. DOCTOR'S OFFICE - DAY (1921)

DR. THOMAS LATTIMORE sits with Kinsey and Clara, sketching on a
piece of paper.

                    LATTIMORE
          Your hymen shows an inordinate
          thickness. Dr. Kinsey, how large is
          your penis?

                    KINSEY
          Excuse me?

                    LATTIMORE
          When erect, how large is it?

Lattimore picks up a ruler.

                    LATTIMORE
          How long from the scrotum? Here?
          Here? Or here?

Clara points to the largest size, then adds an inch.

                    LATTIMORE
          I'm surprised you didn't pass out.

                    CLARA
          Is there anything we can do?

                          LATTIMORE
          It's a common enough problem. Would
          you like to take care of it today?

Kinsey and Clara laugh and nod.

EXT. BOARDING HOUSE - LATE AFTERNOON (1921)

A few COUPLES and a FAMILY stroll past, dressed in their Sunday
best. We move to an open window on an upper floor.

INT. KINSEY'S APARTMENT - BEDROOM - LATE AFTERNOON (1921)

Kinsey and Clara fall onto the pillow, having finally consummated
their marriage. They turn to each other, amazed and elated.

INT. LAB ROOM - DAY (1942) (B&W)

We shift rapidly from Kinsey to Clara, who answer identical
questions during separate interviews.

                          POMEROY (O.S.)
          What was the maximum number of times
          you had intercourse with your spouse in
          any seven-day period?

                          KINSEY
          I'd say twenty or so.

                          CLARA
          At least three times a day that first
          week, so twenty-one at a minimum.

                          POMEROY (O.S.)
          Is there tongue kissing during
          foreplay?

                          KINSEY
          Yes.

                          POMEROY (O.S.)
          Hand on breast?

                          CLARA
          Yes.

                          MARTIN (O.S.)
          Mouth?

                         GEBHARD (O.S.)
          Hand on female genitalia?

                         POMEROY (O.S.)
          Hand on penis?

                         CLARA
          Yes.

                         GEBHARD (O.S.)
          Mouth on female genitalia?

                         MARTIN (O.S.)
          Mouth on penis?

                         KINSEY
          Yes.

                         CLARA
          Yes.

                         KINSEY
          Yes.

                         CLARA
          Yes. Yes. Yes.

MONTAGE (1922-1936)

A series of photos illustrate the growth of the Kinsey family, first
ANNE, then JOAN and finally BRUCE. Each photo is taken on a field
trip, everywhere from a reservation in Nevada to a village in
Guatemala to the mountains outside Mexico City.

INT. LAB ROOM - DAY

Clara and Kinsey interrupt each other.

                         CLARA
          I became pregnant with Anne in 1923. I
          decided to give up my graduate work...

                         KINSEY
          ...by the time Anne was born, I had
          collected over 200,000 gall wasps...

                         CLARA
          Joan arrived a year later...

                    KINSEY
          ...just after Joan's fifth birthday, I
          reached my goal of half a million
          wasps.

                    CLARA
          ...and Bruce is our youngest.

                    KINSEY
          ...Bruce found the gall that hatched
          the millionth wasp. It was in the
          mountains outside Mexico City.

                    CLARA
          They grow up so fast.

INT. HALLWAY OUTSIDE KINSEY'S OFFICE - DAY (1938)

We move past thousands of interred gall wasps until we come to
Kinsey's office.

INT. KINSEY'S OFFICE - DAY (1938)

Kinsey sits opposite BEN and EMILY, a young married couple, both
graduate students.

                    BEN
          We heard you had good advice for some
          of the biology students...

                    KINSEY
          Sexual difficulty among newly married
          people is more common than you think.
          It's nothing to be ashamed of.

Emily nods without believing him.

                    KINSEY
          How long have you been married?

                    BEN
          Two months now.

                    KINSEY
          And Emily, you've had absolutely no
          response during that time?

                    EMILY
          It's like I'm dead down there.

                         BEN
          We went to the doctor and he said
          there's nothing wrong.

                         KINSEY
          Does Ben ever use his fingers to excite
          you?

                         BEN
          Why bother, now that we can do the real
          thing?

                         KINSEY
          What is your most common sexual
          position?

                         EMILY
          There's more than one?

                         KINSEY
          Mac and I are still discovering some.

Ben and Emily grin, disarmed by his candor.

                         KINSEY
          Emily, were you sexually experienced
          before you got married?

                         EMILY
          No, I still thought babies came out of
          women's navels.

                         KINSEY
          Did you ever masturbate?

She shakes her head, then breaks into agonized sobs.

                         EMILY
          It's all my fault. I'm damaged in some
          way. Frigid.

                         KINSEY
          I don't think that's the problem at
          all. Ben, do you ever perform oral sex
          on Emily?

                         BEN
          I'm not sure what that means, sir.

                         KINSEY
          Genital kissing.

                    BEN
          My brother told me that causes problems
          later on. With having babies.

                    KINSEY
          Oh I don't think that's true.

                    EMILY
          No, I heard that too.

                    KINSEY
          I can assure you, there is no relation
          between oral sex and pregnancy.

                    BEN
          But how do you know?

                    KINSEY
          How do I know the Earth is round? It
          just is.

                    BEN
          But has anyone actually proven there's
          no connection?

                    KINSEY
          If you're asking whether there's been a
          scientific study devoted to the subject
          of oral copulation and fertility, well,
          frankly...

He glances up at a shelf lined with books about biology.

                    KINSEY
          ...I don't know.

                    BEN
          Then how can you be sure?

Emily nods in agreement.

                    KINSEY (V.O.)
          ...I felt like a blundering amateur.

INT. KINSEY HOUSE - BEDROOM - NIGHT (1938)

Clara moves from bedroom to bathroom, dressing for a black-tie
event.

                    KINSEY
          I couldn't imagine where this crazy
          idea came from, so I consulted an
          expert.

Kinsey picks up a weighty tome. "Ideal Marriage — Its Physiology
and Technique."

                    KINSEY
               (reads)
          "Oral contact, while acceptable as a
          means of stimulation, is pathological
          if carried through to orgasm, and
          possibly injurious."

                    CLARA
          Well I must be in grave danger then.

                    KINSEY
          And wait. "The hand should never be
          used for the purpose of sexual
          excitation. There is but one finger of
          love with which to approach the female
          genitals, and that is the male organ."
          It's all just hooey. Morality
          disguised as fact.

                    CLARA
          Just...do your tie.

INT. WELLS HOUSE - NIGHT (LATER) (1938)

A small reception in Kinsey's honor. HERMAN WELLS, at 35 the
youngest president in IU history, holds a copy of Kinsey's latest
book. Wells is short and rotund, with dark wavy hair, a trimmed
mustache, and a smile that could melt ice.

                    WELLS
          Professor Kinsey's method of collecting
          vast numbers of gall wasps over a wide
          geographic range has made him a starred
          scientist, one of only five on our
          faculty. It's also earned him his
          immortal nickname, "Get-A-Million-
          Kinsey."

Kinsey and Clara join in the mild laughter.

                    WELLS
          His new book, "The Origin of the Higher
          Categories in Cynips..." Did I get
          that right, Prok?

                    KINSEY
          Close enough.

                    WELLS
          ...traces the gall wasp back to its
          birthplace in the upper Cretaceous,
          over 85 million years ago. So, back
          among us after 42,000 miles on the road
          — I give you Dr. Kinsey.

Kinsey joins Wells and shakes his hand.

                    KINSEY
          Thank you, President Wells, for that
          incisive description of twenty years of
          work. I thought you might have
          actually read my book, until I saw
          those crib notes in your palm.

Wells lets out a booming laugh.

                    KINSEY
          Of course, my other book hasn't been
          checked out of the library in six
          years. I'd be surprised if a dozen
          people have read it. But I guess I
          always knew that gall wasps weren't
          going to make them beat a path to my
          door...

Kinsey hesitates, surprised by where the speech has taken him.

                    KINSEY
          In any case, thank you, Herman. This
          is splendid. A very fine event indeed.

A warm round of applause from his colleagues. Clara twines her
fingers through Kinsey's.

INT. WELLS HOUSE - NIGHT (LATER) (1938)

Wells talks with DR. THURMAN RICE, the burly head of the medical
school.

                    WELLS
          Some reform-minded undergraduates paid
          me a visit the other day. They're
          campaigning for a sex course.

                    RICE
          I already cover sex in the hygiene
          class.

Kinsey turns, interrupting the conversation.

                    KINSEY
          Which the student paper called the most
          useless course on campus.

                    RICE
          Ah, Kinsey. I'm glad to see middle age
          hasn't softened the edges.

                    KINSEY
          Not only is your class irrelevant, it's
          irresponsible. There's a VD epidemic
          sweeping this country, Thurman.

                    RICE
          And that's my fault? I don't know
          whether to be insulted or flattered.

                    KINSEY
                 (turns to Wells)
          Herman, the trustees appointed you to
          shake things up around here. Why not
          address the need for sex instruction
          that deals frankly with students' real
          questions and concerns?

                    RICE
          Open sex instruction promotes
          daydreaming. It's better to address
          such things in a general medical
          course.

                    KINSEY
          You mean an anti-sex course, with
          irrelevant gabble about dahlias and
          bees.

                         WELLS
              Gentlemen, please. I plan to take the
              students' proposal under advisement.

Kinsey nods vigorously.

                         WELLS
              But since I just got this job and would
              like to hold on to it for another week
              or two...I think I'll stick with the
              hygiene course for now.

Rice savors the victory with a tight smile.

EXT. INDIANA UNIVERSITY - MEDICAL SCHOOL - DAY (1938)

Students and faculty bustle into the building.

                         NARRATOR (V.O.)
              ...medical authorities state that of
              the type of teenage girls applying at
              public health stations for aid, the
              percentage that is infected with
              venereal disease is always very high.

CLIP (EXISTING FOOTAGE)

A black-and-white mental hygiene film from the period. A dour
NARRATOR reads stiffly from cue cards.

INT. CLASSROOM - DAY (1938)

Moving across a row of MALE FACES, bored to stupefaction.

                         NARRATOR
              In all of these cases where youthful
              energy and inquisitiveness are
              unrestrained, the sex urge is always
              present and promiscuity nearly always
              follows...

The students perk up at the suggestive images. Boys and girls
kissing in cars, even a glimpse of panties at a wild dance party.

                         NARRATOR (V.O.)
              ...with its inevitable harvest of
              abortions, illegitimate births
              and...disease.

Onscreen, an avuncular doctor sits opposite a distraught young man.

> DOCTOR
> What's your trouble, Jerry?

> JERRY
> Well I've...I've got a pretty bad sore
> down here.

> DOCTOR
> Hmmm. Just stretch out on that table
> over there, we'll have a look at you.

> NARRATOR
> This story vividly portrays the misery
> caused to innocent victims by the
> ignorance or selfishness of individuals
> infected with syphilis.

The students groan as the screen is filled with disgusting images.
Tongues with open bloody sores, backs covered with hideous warts.

> DOCTOR (V.O.)
> You had to learn the hard way that you
> can't tell by the looks of a woman
> whether she has syphilis or not.

> JERRY
> I guess that finishes me. I'll have to
> leave home, quit school and go
> someplace where people don't know who I
> am.

An animated graphic presents the proverbial fork in the road, one
path leading to health, the other to disease.

> NARRATOR (V.O.)
> The cure for juvenile delinquency is an
> education in the dangers and
> consequences of breaking the time-
> tested rules laid down for the
> regulation of human conduct.

The narrator finishes with a wooden nod.

INT. CLASSROOM - DAY (CONTINUOUS) (1938)

Thurman Rice opens the blinds.

                         RICE
          The idea that men need sex is a lie.
          If it were true, the boy who exercises
          his sex organs regularly would have the
          greatest sexual experiences in later
          life. Whereas in fact, that boy is
          likely to be sexually dead by the time
          he reaches adulthood. Abstinence poses
          little difficulty for the college-age
          male. Men don't reach their sexual
          peak until the age of forty.

Herman Wells observes from a back row.

                         RICE
          It is only the lower-class male, often
          Negro, who finds it difficult to
          control his urges.

The sole BLACK STUDENT sits apart from the others, expressionless.

                         RICE
          However, perfect inhibition, although
          an ideal to be striven for, is not
          always achievable. Stress and the
          worries of the day can lead to a
          weakening of resolve, opening the door
          to temptation.

He looks up from his prepared notes and smiles.

                         RICE
          When tense at bedtime, I find there are
          little tricks to relaxing. If I can't
          get to sleep, I like to close my eyes
          and think of all the Johns I know.

There is a stifled collapse of laughter in the room. Rice is
confused, tries to play along.

                         RICE
          Well, not only Johns. Sometimes
          Peters.

More tittering.

                         BLACK STUDENT
          How 'bout Dicks?

The class erupts.

                    RICE
          I'm sorry?

INT. HALLWAY OUTSIDE KINSEY'S OFFICE - DAY (1938)

A stern STAFF SECRETARY walks down a long line of APPLICANTS.

                    STAFF SECRETARY
          If you're here to enroll in Dr.
          Kinsey's class, it's open only to
          faculty members and their wives,
          graduate students, seniors, and married
          undergraduates.

The single UNDERGRADUATES fall out of line. Clyde Martin, 20, looks
around, catches a FEMALE STUDENT's eye. The secretary points at
him.

                    STAFF SECRETARY
          Are you a senior?

Martin grabs the student's hand.

                    MARTIN
          We're engaged.

The young woman nods nervously. The secretary moves on.

INT. LECTURE HALL - DAY (1938)

The room is packed, almost as many women as men. A tense silence
falls over the crowd as Kinsey strides in and starts to speak,
loudly, and without notes.

                    KINSEY
          Why offer a marriage course? Because
          society has interfered with what should
          be a normal biological development,
          causing a scandalous delay of sexual
          activity which leads to sexual
          difficulty in early marriage. In an
          uninhibited society, a twelve-year-old
          would know most of the biology which I
          will have to give you in formal
          lectures as seniors and graduate
          students.

In the back, Clara listens intently.

                         KINSEY
          So...let's start with the six stages of
          the coital sequence. Stimulation,
          lubrication, erection, increased
          sensitivity, orgasm, and nervous
          release.

Clyde Martin sits with his new friend in the front row.

                         KINSEY
          Both sexes experience all six stages
          equally.

                    (writes on the blackboard)
          Stimulation.

He gazes out at the students.

                         KINSEY
          Who can tell me which part of the human
          body can enlarge 100 times?

Dead silence. Kinsey points to a pert young COED.

                         KINSEY
          Miss?

                         COED
          I'm sure I don't know. And you have no
          right to ask me such a question in a
          mixed class.

Kinsey looks at her coldly.

                         KINSEY
          I was referring to the pupil of your
          eye, young lady. And I think I should
          tell you, you're in for a terrible
          disappointment.

An explosion of laughter cuts the tension. The coed smiles good-
naturedly.

                         KINSEY
          It is often with the eye that
          stimulation begins.

He motions to a STUDENT, who switches on the slide projector.
There are stifled gasps as an image of a penis penetrating a vagina
fills the portable screen.

> KINSEY
> The actual adjustments which are made
> in the male and female genitalia are
> shown on this slide. The vagina must
> be spread open as the erect male organ
> penetrates.

Kinsey nods and another slide appears. He uses a ruler to
illustrate his points, with an air of detachment that's almost
deadpan.

> KINSEY
> You will see that the clitoris is
> swollen, thus providing the erotic
> stimulation necessary for the
> completion of the act on the part of
> the female. You will also see that
> this point on the penis, which is the
> most sensitive point, is similarly
> stimulated.

EXT. INDIANA UNIVERSITY - DAY (1939)

Clyde Martin runs through a torrential downpour. He crashes into a
man wearing an enormous yellow hat.

> MARTIN
> (blurts out)
> Where on earth did you get that cap?

He catches himself when he recognizes Kinsey.

> MARTIN
> Oh, Professor Kinsey. Sorry.

> KINSEY
> It's a whaler's hat. Not pretty, but
> extremely practical in a storm. Do I
> know you?

> MARTIN
> I'm in your marriage course. Clyde
> Martin.

> KINSEY
> How are you finding it, Mr. Martin?

                         MARTIN
                   (a born flirt)
              It's the most enlightening class I've
              ever taken.

Kinsey smiles, flattered.

                         MARTIN
              I better be off. I have a job
              interview at the zoology library.

                         KINSEY
              Forget that. Come with me.

INT. HALLWAY OUTSIDE KINSEY'S OFFICE - DAY (LATER) (1939)

A student fills in the last empty slot in Kinsey's office hours
chart. Martin hands out coffee to other students who wait in the
outer office.

INT. KINSEY'S OFFICE - DAY (1939)

A series of TALKING HEADS, male and female students sharing their
most intimate concerns with Kinsey.

                         MALE STUDENT #1
              Can too much sex cause cancer?

                         FEMALE STUDENT #1
              Will wearing high heels make me
              sterile?

                         FEMALE STUDENT #2
              I think my vagina is abnormally shaped.

                         MALE STUDENT #2
              Can you get syphilis from a whistle?

                         MALE STUDENT #3
              Is homosexuality a form of insanity?

                         FEMALE STUDENT #3
              I think about my cat. A lot.

                         MALE STUDENT #4
                   (stuttering)
              Does suppressing sex lead to
              stuttering?

INT. LECTURE HALL - DAY (1939)

                    KINSEY
          "Does too much masturbation cause
          premature ejaculation?" "Is it unusual
          for my boyfriend to touch my anus?"
          "Is my penis smaller than most?" All
          excellent questions, and they all have
          the same answer: "I...don't...know."

He passes out some questionnaires.

                    KINSEY
          From a sexual standpoint, it's hard to
          say what's common or rare, because we
          know so little about what people
          actually do. This leaves most of us
          feeling anxious, or guilty. Am I
          interested in the right things? Do I
          do things the normal way?

It's clear from the rapt faces that Kinsey has struck a nerve.

                    KINSEY
          One of the ways of finding out what
          people do is to find out what they've
          done. So please, take the time to fill
          out these sex questionnaires.

Students leaf through the five pages of questions.

EXT. KINSEY HOUSE - GARDEN - DAY (1940)

A garden paradise, two-and-a-half acres dotted with rock gardens,
lily ponds, and terraced slopes; there's even a man-made stream
running through the property. Kinsey, shirtless and brown as a
berry, crouches in a tall patch of day lilies, while Clyde Martin
digs in a bed of irises.

                    MARTIN
          These colors are incredible.

                    KINSEY
          It's the most complete collection east
          of the Mississippi. We have over 250
          separate varieties of irises.

Kinsey stands, naked.

> KINSEY
> No, Martin, you're doing that wrong.
> You're making extra work for yourself.

It's only when he steps out of the lily patch that we see that he's
actually wearing flesh-colored shorts. Kinsey adjusts Martin's
shoveling technique, as Clara appears with a pitcher of lemonade.
She observes the physical connection between the two men, which is
broken when Kinsey notices her.

> KINSEY
> Ah. Lemonade.

EXT. KINSEY HOUSE - GARDEN - DAY (IMMEDIATELY FOLLOWING)

Kinsey makes notations on a pad.

> KINSEY
> Mac, these responses will floor you.
> The gap between what we assume people
> do and what they actually do is
> enormous.

> MARTIN
> You know the thing that amazes me?
> There's no relationship between how
> sexy a girl looks and her sex life.
> The ugly ones seem to get all the
> action.

> CLARA
> I always thought 'ugly' was an ugly
> word.

> MARTIN
> Sorry.

> KINSEY
> Not only does every male in the class
> have a history of masturbation, most of
> the women do too.

> CLARA
> That doesn't surprise me. How about
> premarital sex?

> KINSEY
> About a third of the married men claim
> at least one experience. It's only one
> in ten for the women.

                    CLARA
          If they're telling the truth.

                    MARTIN
          And there's extramarital sex too. Not
          just heterosexual but homosexual.

                    KINSEY
          I just wish we could get more
          volunteers. A hundred cases is hardly
          representative.

                    CLARA
          Maybe it's because it's a
          questionnaire. It feels like homework,
          or a test.

                    MARTIN
          I agree. Also, people don't know if
          they can trust you.

Kinsey looks up.

                    MARTIN
          Well, not you personally. It's just
          ...they have to be sure their secrets
          are safe.

                    KINSEY
          That's ridiculous. Everyone knows I
          keep those questionnaires under lock
          and key.

                    CLARA
          Clyde might have a point. You're asking
          people to reveal information that's very
          sensitive and possibly even damaging.

                    MARTIN
          What if you just talked to them? Then
          all their secrets would be in your head.

                    KINSEY
          Martin, you should have spoken up
          months ago.

He heads toward the house. Martin turns to Clara.

                    MARTIN
          I can't tell, was that a compliment?

                         CLARA
              Yes. I think it was.

INT. KINSEY HOUSE - KITCHEN - EVENING (1940)

Kinsey takes okra from the refrigerator while Clara grabs a pot
holder. ANNE, 18, and JOAN, 17, move in and out, setting the table
for dinner.

                         KINSEY
              People resist at first, but I'm trying
              to choreograph the questions so they'll
              be disarmed into answering...

Kinsey unpeels a blackened banana and drops it into a large pot of
soup.

                         JOAN
              Daddy, how many different things have
              you put in there?

                         KINSEY
              It's the Kinsey stew.

                         ANNE
              Clean-out-the-refrigerator night, you
              mean.

                         KINSEY
              Martin's been surprisingly helpful. He's
              an ideal practice subject, since he's had
              relations with both men and women.

Clara's jaw tenses slightly as she takes the casserole from the
oven. BRUCE, 15, enters through the kitchen door.

                         KINSEY
              Where have you been?

                         BRUCE
              Swim practice.

                         CLARA
              How'd it go?

                         BRUCE
              Pretty good. Coach said he might start
              me at the next meet.

                         CLARA
              Bruce, that's wonderful.

                              KINSEY
              I told you, there won't be any more
              swimming unless your science grades
              improve.

                              BRUCE
              I can't help it, Dad. I hate biology.

                              KINSEY
              That's because you've never developed
              your intellect. Physical activity is
              important, son, but your interest in
              sports is excessive.

                              CLARA
              Yes, maybe he should take up
              engineering instead.

A pointed look at Kinsey, who scowls.

EXT. KINSEY HOUSE - BACK PORCH - DUSK (LATER) (1940)

The family eats al fresco as the sun sets.

                              KINSEY
              ...talking to people yields more
              information than I ever imagined. I
              think it will prove to be a ground-
              breaking technique.

                              ANNE
              What if they make things up? That's
              what I'd do.

                              KINSEY
              I'm building in little tripwires to
              catch lies and inconsistencies.

                              JOAN
              Would you like to take my sex history,
              Daddy?

                              KINSEY
              Do you have a sex history, sweetie?

Joan shakes her head, disappointed.

                              JOAN
              No.

                         KINSEY
          How about you, Anne? You've been
          dating Jim for a while now.

                          ANNE
          We've done some petting. I figured we
          wouldn't try intercourse until college.

                         KINSEY
          That's probably better.

                          JOAN
          If Anne can have intercourse, I should
          be able to too.

                         KINSEY
          Your sister's eighteen, and seriously
          involved with someone.

                          JOAN
          Does it hurt?

                         CLARA
          What, dear?

                          JOAN
          Breaking the hymen.

                         CLARA
          Oh just a little. Nothing too bad.

                         KINSEY
          It helps if you spread the vulva to
          facilitate penetration.

                         BRUCE
          Can we please talk about something else
          for once? Other families don't do
          this, you know. It isn't normal.

                         KINSEY
          When did you become such a prig?

Bruce pushes out his chair and stands.

                         BRUCE
          Most of my friends aren't even allowed
          to come over here. Their parents think
          you're a menace.

He picks up his plate and heads into the house.

                    KINSEY
          You've spent too much time in the water,
          Bruce. All that chlorine's done something
          to your brain! Sometimes I don't know
          where he came from.

                    CLARA
          Have you learned nothing?

Clara throws down her napkin and follows Bruce into the house.

EXT. RUSH STREET - CHICAGO - NIGHT (1940)

A winter night. Kinsey and Martin walk down a deserted inner city
street.

                    KINSEY
          ...I heard about this community from a
          former student of mind. This is my third
          trip and already the results have been
          astounding. By my calculation, there are
          over 300,000 cases here in Chicago, and no
          one's even bothered to talk to them. It's
          a gold mine of information, Martin, and
          we've got it all to ourselves.

They stop at a storefront where the windows have been painted black.
A blue bulb offers the only hint of life inside.

INT. GAY BAR - NIGHT (1940)

The place is packed, and it's a wildly diverse group, old men and
young, white and black, Irish and Poles. Men in business suits mix
easily with blue collar types. The BARTENDER ignores Kinsey, smiles
at Martin.

                    BARTENDER
          What'll it be, handsome?

Kinsey leans in, oblivious to the spark between them.

                    KINSEY
          Two Scotch and sodas.

Not Martin's first choice, but he goes along.

                    KINSEY
          I find liquor an essential tool of
          social lubrication. Although it has
          involved more drinking than I thought
          I'd ever do in a lifetime.

The bartender slides a drink to Kinsey and carefully places the other in front of Martin. Kinsey hands the bartender a fifty cent piece.

                    KINSEY
          We might as well get started.

The bartender gives Kinsey a dime, which he pockets. He turns to an effete middle-aged MAN whose acne scars are covered by a thin veil of makeup.

                    KINSEY
          Hello. I'm Professor Kinsey from
          Indiana University and I'm making a
          study of sex behavior. Can I buy you a
          drink?

                    EFFETE MAN
          I assume you're joking.

                    KINSEY
          No. I'm not. I'd be very grateful if
          you'd answer some questions about your
          sexual history.

The man turns to a couple of FRIENDS.

                    EFFETE MAN
          Mary here is a professor. She says she
          wants to study my sex behavior.

                    FRIEND
          Tell her to stick around and watch.

The men walk away, laughing. Undaunted, Kinsey turns to a rough-looking MAN of Slavic descent.

                    KINSEY
          Hello. I'm Professor Kinsey from
          Indiana University and I'm making a
          study of sex behavior. Can I ask you a
          few questions?

A tense moment as the man stares at Kinsey. Then he breaks into a smile.

                    SLAVIC MAN
          Yeah, I heard about you. You're the
          sex doctor, right?

                    KINSEY
          I guess I am. If you'd be kind enough
          to talk to me, it would be of great
          help to science.

                    SLAVIC MAN
          Sure. What do you want to know?

INT. GAY BAR - NIGHT (LATER) (1940)

It's almost four in the morning and only the barflies are left.
Kinsey and Martin sit opposite JAKE, a young man with a Kansas
twang.

                    JAKE
          Same boy. Tommy Potts. We were
          messing around in a haystack, the way
          kids'll do. Pop found us and he locked
          us in the barn. Then he called my
          brothers in.

He takes a swig of beer.

                    JAKE
          They branded us. Took turns doing it.

He lifts his shirt, shows the scars on his chest and belly.

                    JAKE
          Then they beat us raw. Broke a couple
          of ribs, my collarbone. Tommy, he
          didn't make out as well as I did.

                    KINSEY
          How old were you?

                    JAKE
          Thirteen.

Kinsey's eyes water, moved by the young man's story.

                    KINSEY
          And you've been on your own since then?

                    JAKE
          I get by. It's not that I mind being
          queer, cause I don't. I just wish
          other folks weren't so put out by it.

                    KINSEY
          Homosexuality happens to be out of
          fashion in society right now. That
          doesn't mean it won't change some day.

                    JAKE
          Right.

He downs his beer with a skeptical laugh.

                    KINSEY (V.O.)
          Why didn't I see it before?

INT. HOTEL ROOM - CHICAGO - NIGHT (1940)

Martin opens his suitcase on one of the two single beds, while
Kinsey sits on the other, talking long distance to Clara.

                    KINSEY
          Human beings are just bigger, slightly
          more complicated gall wasps. There's
          infinite variation, most of it
          unexplored. All I have to do is
          collect more than anyone else, and
          homosexuals are the perfect place to
          start!

Clara lets out a laugh.

                    KINSEY
          What?

INT. KINSEY HOUSE - BEDROOM - NIGHT (INTERCUT) (1940)

We INTERCUT with Clara, who is awake in bed.

                    CLARA
          Sorry. I just had an image of some of
          our friends hearing you right now. As
          if the marriage course isn't bad
          enough.

Kinsey steals a glance at Martin, who casually strips down and heads
for the shower.

                    CLARA
          Now promise me, Prok. You'll get at
          least four hours sleep before heading
          back.

                        KINSEY
         Of course.

                        CLARA
         And let Clyde share in the driving.

                        KINSEY
         Okay, Mac. I'll sign off now. I love
         you.

Clara hangs up, with an anxious look.

INT. HOTEL ROOM - CHICAGO - NIGHT (LATER)

Martin emerges from the bathroom, towelling himself dry. Kinsey is
already under the covers, making notes on a pad.

                        MARTIN
         You know what impressed me tonight?
         The way you talk to people.

Martin drops the towel and slips on a pair of boxer shorts.

                        MARTIN
         You can get just about anybody to open up.

Never one to take a compliment gracefully:

                        KINSEY
         It's just a matter of putting yourself
         on their level.

                        MARTIN
         No, it's more than that. You really
         seem to care.

Martin sits on his bed.

                        MARTIN
         This idea of yours...this rating scale.

                        KINSEY
                 (sits up, shows him the notes)
         0 to 6. 0 being exclusively
         heterosexual and 6 exclusively
         homosexual. The majority of people
         line up somewhere in the middle.

                        MARTIN
         What makes you think that's true?

                    KINSEY
          Common sense. About a third of our
          predominantly heterosexual histories
          have homosexual acts, and vice versa.

                    MARTIN
          I guess I'm about a 3, huh?

                    KINSEY
          Based on your sex history, I'd say
          that's likely.

                    MARTIN
          How about you?

Kinsey takes a moment to answer.

                    KINSEY
          I suppose I've been a 1 or 2 most of my
          life, even though it's taken a long
          time to recognize it.

                    MARTIN
          And now?

                    KINSEY
          Probably a 3.

                    MARTIN
          Ever done anything about it?

Kinsey's voice trembles; he's a teenage boy again, his father's
frightened son.

                    KINSEY
          No.

                    MARTIN
          Would you like to?

He leans across and presses his lips against Kinsey's. Kinsey's
eyes flutter involuntarily as he holds his mouth shut.

Martin moves to withdraw when Kinsey pulls him back. He opens his
mouth and welcomes Martin's kiss with a deep groan.

INT. KINSEY HOUSE - PARLOR - NIGHT (1940)

Clara sits quietly in a wing chair, while Kinsey paces in front of
her.

                         KINSEY
            I'm sorry, Mac. I've taken on so many
            other people's secrets, I can't keep
            any more of my own.

Clara stares down at the rug.

                         KINSEY
            You still haven't said anything.

                         CLARA
            It's not like I'm surprised exactly.
            I've observed certain things over the
            years.

                         KINSEY
            Such as?

                         CLARA
            Oh, a look or a gesture. The pet
            student who suddenly becomes a part of
            the family, and just as suddenly
            disappears when you tire of him.

                         KINSEY
            I think you must know me better than I
            know myself.

                         CLARA
            But I'm not sure I understand. Haven't
            I always been open to whatever you
            wanted?

                         KINSEY
            It's not you, Mac. You're the best
            partner any man could have.

                         CLARA
            I'm just not enough. Is that it?

Kinsey doesn't answer. Clara closes her eyes, wounded.

                         KINSEY
            Every day I hear the most heartbreaking
            stories and my advice is always the same.
            What you're doing isn't wrong or unnatural.
            Have courage. Be true to yourself. Well
            this is inside of me. To what extent, I
            don't know. But I'd be a hypocrite if I
            pretended it wasn't there.

Clara turns away from him.

                    KINSEY
        Mac, please...if anyone can understand,
        it should be you. When I took your
        history, didn't you admit to having
        sexual feelings for other men?

                    CLARA
        Don't...don't you dare use that against
        me.

                    KINSEY
        I'm sorry, but what keeps you from
        acting on your feelings? Convention.

                    CLARA
        No, it's our marriage. It's our
        children.

                    KINSEY
        Exactly. Social restraints.

                    CLARA
        Did you ever think that those
        restraints keep people from hurting
        each other? I don't sleep with other
        men because it might hurt you.

                    KINSEY
        But what if it didn't hurt me?

                    CLARA
        Then I'd be hurt.

                    KINSEY
        You're just afraid that I don't love
        you anymore, which is ridiculous. The
        human animal is capable of all kinds of
        sexual expression. Not all sex has to
        be sanctioned by love, enriched by
        emotion. To the Greeks and Romans...

                    CLARA
        Stop doing that, Prok, stop lecturing.
        And don't try to use science to justify
        what you've done.

Kinsey kneels in front of her.

                         KINSEY
          You're my girl, Mac. The bond we have,
          the life we share...sex is nothing
          compared to that.

                         CLARA
          I can't talk about this anymore.

She walks past him and leaves the room.

INT. KINSEY HOUSE - PARLOR - DAY (1941)

A Sunday musicale in the parlor, which is dominated by Kinsey's
record collection, now numbering in the thousands. A dozen
PROFESSORS and WIVES sit in a circle, listening to an LP recording
of Sibelius' Violin Concerto in D Minor.

                         KINSEY (V.O.)
          Most people think that what they do
          sexually is what everyone does, or
          should do. But nearly all of the so-
          called sexual perversions fall within
          the range of biologic normality. For
          example, masturbation, mouth-genital
          contacts, and homosexual acts are
          common among most mammals, including
          humans. Society might condemn such
          practices on moral grounds, but it's
          ludicrous to call them unnatural.

Martin sits stiffly between two faculty wives darning socks. He
gazes over at Kinsey. Clara watches from across the room.

INT. LECTURE HALL - DAY (1942)

Kinsey lectures to a rapt audience, as the Sibelius plays under.

                         KINSEY
          Based on the first Book of Genesis and
          according to public opinion, there is
          only one correct sexual equation. Man
          plus woman equals baby. Everything
          else is vice. But the orgasm record of
          the males in this classroom alone
          proves the ineffectiveness of social
          restrictions and the imperativeness of
          the biologic demand.

Clara and Martin listen from different parts of the classroom.

                    KINSEY
          Why are some cows highly sexed, while
          others just stand there? Why do some
          men need thirty orgasms a week, and
          others almost none? Because everyone
          is different. The problem is, most
          people want to be the same.

Kinsey aims these remarks to the back of the classroom, where
Thurman Rice is observing.

INT. KINSEY HOUSE - DINING ROOM - NIGHT (1942)

MUSIC continues under. Clara retypes a student's sex diary, while
Kinsey edits notes and Martin works on a graph.

                    KINSEY (V.O.)
          They find it easier to simply ignore
          this fundamental aspect of the human
          condition.

Kinsey takes a bite of a sandwich, then absentmindedly starts to
place it in a bowl of soup. Clara and Martin both notice and grab
the sandwich. They share a smile.

INT. LECTURE HALL - DAY (1942)

Kinsey lowers his voice for dramatic effect.

                    KINSEY
          They're so eager to be part of the
          group that they'll betray their own
          nature to get there.

INT. KINSEY HOUSE - PARLOR - DAY (1942)

Back to the musicale. Kinsey, Clara and Martin share looks.

                    KINSEY (V.O.)
          If something pleasurable and strongly
          desired is prohibited it becomes an
          obsession.

INT. LECTURE HALL - DAY (1942)

Kinsey takes a pregnant pause.

                    KINSEY
          Think about this.

Thurman Rice looks as if he's about to explode. MUSIC ends.

EXT. KINSEY HOUSE - BACK PORCH - DAY (1942)

Martin helps Clara carry groceries from the car.

> CLARA
> ...surely you have better things to do
> than help a middle-aged lady with her
> groceries.

> MARTIN
> Prok got worried when he couldn't reach
> you. He has to spend the evening
> taking some histories, so he'd like an
> early dinner, preferably five o'clock.

> CLARA
> That hardly gives me time to boil an egg.

> MARTIN
> Can I help?

> CLARA
> Thank you, I'll manage. But I'm sorry
> he made you play messenger.

> MARTIN
> No. I volunteered.

INT. KINSEY HOUSE - KITCHEN - DAY (IMMEDIATELY FOLLOWING)

Clara pushes open the kitchen door, calls out.

> CLARA
> Do you hear that?

> MARTIN
> What?

> CLARA
> The sound of an empty nest.

> MARTIN
> It must be a big adjustment. Have you
> heard from him yet?

> CLARA
> Oh Bruce is loving college. Or maybe
> it's just being away from here.

Martin puts the groceries on the counter.

                    CLARA
          Would you like some pie?

                    MARTIN
          Rhubarb?

Clara smiles, opens the refrigerator. Martin sits.

                    CLARA
          You know, Clyde...I didn't like you
          very much at first.

                    MARTIN
          I don't blame you. Most women would
          have had me murdered.

                    CLARA
          Oh I considered it. But I hate to
          think of myself as conventional.

Clara pours a glass of milk.

                    CLARA
          But if this had to happen...I'm glad it
          was you.

Clara serves the pie and milk, sits.

                    CLARA
          And I'll admit there have been benefits.
          It's certainly sparked things up sexually.
          I suppose we'd both grown bored, without
          even realizing it.

                    MARTIN
          I think you've handled it remarkably well.

                    CLARA
          I learned something a long ago time.
          Once Prok has his mind set, it's no use
          trying to stop him.

                    MARTIN
          Yes. He is relentless.

He stares down, a bit glum. Behind them, we see Kinsey step into
the open doorway.

                         CLARA
                Clyde?

Kinsey stops to listen.

                         MARTIN
                This thing between Prok and me. It was
                fine for a while, but now...

Martin shakes his head. Kinsey looks stricken.

                         MARTIN
                I guess I really miss sleeping with
                women.

                         KINSEY
                That's perfectly understandable.

He enters, kisses Clara on the head.

                         KINSEY
                It's clear from your history that you
                have greater sexual interest in women
                than men.

                         MARTIN
                Good. So you won't mind if I ask Mac
                to have sex with me?

Kinsey, for once, has nothing to say. Martin turns to Clara, who is
also stunned.

                         MARTIN
                Only if it appeals to you, of course.

                         CLARA
                I don't know. Would it be separately,
                or together?

                         MARTIN
                No, definitely just you and I.

                         CLARA
                Well...I think I might like that.
                Prok, what do you think?

Kinsey forces a tight smile.

INT. KINSEY HOUSE - FRONT HALLWAY - DAY (1942)

Kinsey waits at the foot of the stairs while Clara and Martin have sex in a bedroom. He checks his watch impatiently.

                    KINSEY
               (calling out)
          Mac, the Rockefeller Foundation is
          coming today!

There's no response.

INT. KINSEY HOUSE - BEDROOM - DAY (1942)

Clara and Martin snuggle after sex.

                    KINSEY (O.S.)
          We still have to catalog those prints,
          Martin!

                    CLARA
          Clyde, you know I enjoy this
          tremendously but...

                    KINSEY (O.S.)
          Mac, please!

                    CLARA
               (calling out)
          I'm coming, Prok!

She reaches for her blouse.

                    CLARA
          It's just a very full day.

INT. ZOOLOGY DEPARTMENT OFFICES - DAY (1942)

In the library, Kinsey lays out some prints and photographs.

                    KINSEY
          One key to understanding a foreign
          culture is its pornography. Every
          culture produces its own peculiar
          sexual imagery, as distinct as its
          cuisine and in most cases as difficult
          to export.

Kinsey lays out the pornographic material for Herman Wells and DR. ALAN GREGG, 55, the highly cultivated Director of the Medical Division of the Rockefeller Foundation.

                    KINSEY (V.O.)
          As you can see, Brazil's imagery tends
          toward zoophilia, while Italy favors
          nuns and priests. In England, one
          often sees depictions of the stern
          headmistress — spankers and wankers —
          whereas in the Far East, it's soft
          flage and light bondage.

Gregg gingerly picks up a Japanese print.

                    GREGG
          You've amassed an impressive
          collection.

Wells examines a primitive toy made of sticks and nails, a Rube
Goldberg-like contraption of a man entering a woman from behind.

                    KINSEY
          Only what I've been able to afford from
          my own savings. But if the Rockefeller
          Foundation agrees to our grant, I'll be
          able to turn this into a world-class
          library. Do you have any idea when you
          might decide?

                    WELLS
          Please, Prok. Dr. Gregg just got here.

                    KINSEY
          Sometimes I'm amazed anything has
          survived. The Library of Congress has
          a policy of destroying whatever it
          considers too erotic. The loss to
          science has been incalculable.

Gregg fingers a Roman wax seal of copulating figures.

                    KINSEY
          There's plenty of time to take your sex
          histories before dinner. Who'd like to
          go first?

The two men turn to each other, caught off guard.

INT. KINSEY HOUSE - DINING ROOM - NIGHT (LATER)

Kinsey sops up the last bit of gravy on his plate.

                    KINSEY
          Early in my bug hunting days, someone
          asked me what I was looking for. I
          said I wouldn't know until I saw it
          statistically.

He lays down his utensils and shoots a glance at Gregg's plate,
which is almost full.

                    KINSEY
          A scientist can only generalize with
          reliable certainty if he gets enough
          statistical information.

                    CLARA
          Is this your first time in Bloomington,
          Dr. Gregg?

                    GREGG
          Yes, it's lovely. Hillier than I
          expected.

                    KINSEY
          That's why I've broken the American
          population down into 200 major social
          subgroups. We'll get anywhere from 400
          to 1000 histories from each group, for
          a total of 100,000, give or take a few.
          It could take twenty years, but at the
          end we'll finally be able to answer
          most of the basic questions about human
          sexuality.

Clara interrupts again, touches Wells' arm.

                    CLARA
          Herman, is the pot roast dry?

                    WELLS
          No, it's delicious.

                    KINSEY
          The first publication will be a Male
          volume, followed a year later by the
          Female study. Then another nine books,
          dealing with sex offenders,
          homosexuality, pregnancy, birth and
          abortion, and art studied from a sexual
          standpoint.

                    CLARA
          With the children gone, I don't get to
          cook big meals anymore.

                    GREGG
          Where are they?

                    CLARA
          The oldest is a graduate student in St.
          Louis, and the other two are at Oberlin.

                    KINSEY
          Let's get to the point. This project
          is one of the greatest ever undertaken
          in connection with the human animal,
          but without support from the
          Rockefeller Foundation, it will never
          get off the ground.

Gregg gives up, rests his utensils on his plate.

                    GREGG
          There are those who argue that sex is
          largely a matter of feelings and
          psychological attitudes. Things beyond
          your training as a zoologist.

                    KINSEY
          That's like saying a biochemist can't
          analyze cooking because he's not a
          chef. It's inane.

Clara catches his eye across the table. He tries to soften the
remark.

                    KINSEY
          That is, it's really a...very stupid
          way of looking at things.

Clara shakes her head.

                    KINSEY
          One of the aims of science is to
          simplify. The only way to study sex
          with any scientific accuracy is to
          strip away everything but its
          physiological functions.

                    GREGG
          And this team you're proposing?

                    KINSEY
          I'll need two bodies at least, both
          with advanced degrees in science. And
          Clyde Martin of course.

                    GREGG
          Since you're working in such a delicate
          area, they need to be as clean as
          Fuller Brush men.

Kinsey is confused by the reference.

                    CLARA
          Door-to-door salesmen, Prok.

                    WELLS
          I think Dr. Gregg's point is that
          anyone working on the project must have
          motives that are entirely pure and
          scientific, and above reproach morally.

                    KINSEY
          I couldn't agree more.

                    GREGG
          And one more thing. I hope you're not
          going to dwell on sexual oddities and
          perversions.

                    KINSEY
          Science is always interested in the
          rare.

                    GREGG
          Yes, but it's advisable to stick to
          what's normal. You don't want to shake
          people up.

Clara gives Kinsey another warning look.

                    KINSEY
          Of course not. I'm just a taxonomist,
          a measurer. I'm happy to leave the
          social policies to others.

Gregg nods approvingly.

                    GREGG
          Good.

INT. LAB ROOM - DAY (1942)

We've caught up to our recurring scene, the team learning how to take a sex history, in color now. Gebhard interviews Clara, with Kinsey and the others observing.

>   GEBHARD
>   So if you're ready I'd like to begin
>   with a few background questions.

>   KINSEY
>   No, all wrong. Start by putting the
>   subject at ease. Would you care for a
>   drink, Mac?

>   CLARA
>   A glass of water would be nice.

Kinsey pours water from a pitcher.

>   KINSEY
>   Do anything fun this weekend?

>   CLARA
>   My daughters were home so I never
>   stopped. We had a marvelous meal on
>   Saturday night.

>   KINSEY
>   Really? What did you cook?

Before Clara can answer:

>   KINSEY
>   See how much more relaxed she's become?
>   If you ease in with innocuous
>   questions, people forget they're giving
>   sex histories.

Another day. Martin talks to a retired FEMALE SCHOOLTEACHER.

>   MARTIN
>   How did you first find out about
>   masturbation?

>   FEMALE SCHOOLTEACHER
>   I invented it, son.

Kinsey interviews a nervous young MALE CLERICAL WORKER.

                    MALE CLERICAL WORKER
          Sometimes I tie a rope around my balls
          when I jerk off.

                    KINSEY
          And what other masochistic acts do you
          enjoy?

                    MALE CLERICAL WORKER
          Does that mean queer?

Gebhard interviews a FEMALE ASSISTANT PROFESSOR.

                    GEBHARD
          How often do you have intercourse?

                    FEMALE ASSISTANT PROFESSOR
          Two or three times.

                    GEBHARD
          A month?

                    FEMALE ASSISTANT PROFESSOR
          No, a day.

He smiles and nods encouragingly.

                    GEBHARD
          That's good.

Gebhard then talks to a MIDDLE-AGED BUSINESSMAN.

                    GEBHARD
          How often do you reach orgasm?

                    BUSINESSMAN
          Once.

Careful not to assume anything this time:

                    GEBHARD
          A day?

The man shakes his head.

                    BUSINESSMAN
          No. Only once, about twenty years ago.
          I was sitting on a piano stool,
          listening to music.

Again, an encouraging smile.

                    GEBHARD
          That's good.

Pomeroy interviews a JANITOR with a thick Armenian accent.

                    POMEROY
          How old were you when you first
          ejaculated?

                    JANITOR
          Fourteen.

                    POMEROY
          How?

                    JANITOR
          With horse.

Pomeroy maintains eye contact with the man.

                    POMEROY
          How often were you having intercourse
          with animals at age fourteen?

The man looks at Pomeroy, amazed, almost spooked.

                    JANITOR
          Yes, is true I fucked a pony. You are
          a genius. How did you know?

                    POMEROY
          You just said you had sex with a horse.

                    JANITOR
          No. Whores, not horse.

In quick succession, the interviews conclude, with each of the
subjects visibly more relaxed.

                    FEMALE SCHOOLTEACHER
          That was quite enjoyable. I hope I've
          been of help.

                    FEMALE ASSISTANT PROFESSOR
          Do you find my answers typical?

                    BUSINESSMAN
          Am I normal?

                    FEMALE SCHOOLTEACHER
          Is this normal?

                        JANITOR
          Am I normal?

EXT. HIGHWAY - OHIO - DAY (1943)

Martin behind the wheel of the Kinsey family Oldsmobile. Kinsey
rides shotgun, with Gebhard and Pomeroy in back, as the team moves
across the country collecting sex histories. Various road signs
zoom past. WELCOME TO MAINE. LOUISIANA. NORTH DAKOTA. OREGON.

MONTAGE (1943)

A red line inches across a map of the United States, tracking the
team's progress. The face of an older POETESS fades on:

                        POETESS
          ...I found a book in the dining room
          buffet under all the tablecloths. I
          used to put it under my shirt and go
          into the bathroom and sit and read but
          I was very frightened...

As she continues to speak, a second face emerges. A prison INMATE
in his mid-20s:

                        INMATE
          ...she told her mother she didn't like
          it. Or maybe it was just her mother
          who didn't like it. Before you know
          it, the police were banging on the
          front door. Hell, I didn't even know
          it was illegal. Now I'm in here for
          five years...

Next an elderly BLACK MAN, followed by a BERRY PICKER and a WAC:

                        SHARECROPPER
          ...well you know some old gal caught me
          out in the field. She said she was
          goin' to show me a new game called
          puddin'. I guess I kind of liked it...

                        BERRY PICKER
          ...as a young boy watching the animals
          on the farm. It was very exciting...

                        WAC
          ...we didn't talk about that too much.
          It was just something that you did.
          But it felt good....

The information is registered on small Hollerith data cards, which are fed into a primitive IBM computer, large as a chest of drawers. The machine spits out results with a loud ker-chunk, ker-chunk.

INT. HOTEL ROOM - ALABAMA - NIGHT (1944)

Kinsey writes at a desk where the clock reads 3:15. The letter reads: I MISS YOU AND I LOVE YOU.

> WOMAN (V.O.)
> ...I asked my best friend at age
> twelve, and she told me if you kiss a
> boy you can have a baby. So I avoided
> kissing them...

INT. KINSEY HOUSE - FRONT HALLWAY - DAY (1944)

Moving down the letter: AND I WILL SPEND MORE TIME AT HOME SOON. I PROMISE.

> ANOTHER WOMAN (V.O.)
> ...I went to my mother and said, is
> this true? Do men really put their
> thing in women?

Clara finishes reading and drops the letter on a table. She steps into the empty house.

BLACK & WHITE FILM (EXISTING FOOTAGE)

Period footage of CROWDS at dance clubs, train stations, busy city streets, as the team makes its way from San Francisco to New York.

INT. KINSEY HOUSE - DINING ROOM - NIGHT (1944)

Moving past Clara as she finishes typing a page, then attaches it to a small notebook. She reaches for the next diary.

MORE FACES

emerge, in quick succession now:

> OLD WOMAN
> ...if you weren't a virgin you were a
> fallen woman. Nobody would want you...

> RADIO REPAIRMAN
> ...they also tested us for masculine
> and feminine traits...

                    BELLHOP
          ...they were on the couch. They were both
          naked...

                    MALE IMPERSONATOR
          ...it was right there. It was part of me...

                    BALLET TEACHER
          ...I took off all my clothes...

The faces speed up until they seem to merge into one. We pull back
to reveal the map of America, covered by a spider's web of lines
reflecting the team's progress. We zoom back into Bloomington:

EXT. KINSEY HOUSE - GARDEN - DAY (1945)

An intimate wedding ceremony. Clyde Martin and his bride ALICE
kiss, having just taken their vows from a Justice of the Peace.
Kinsey watches proudly while Clara wipes away a tear.

EXT. KINSEY HOUSE - GARDEN - DAY (LATER)

The team poses for a photograph with their wives. Gebhard's wife
AGNES is a Radcliffe graduate, tall, elegant, and sharp-witted.
MARTHA POMEROY is more suburban, but just as fun and irreverent as
her husband.

                    ALICE
          Did you hear? Professor Kinsey found
          us a place to live.

                    AGNES
          Let me guess. It's just a few blocks
          from here.

                    ALICE
          How did you know?

                    AGNES
          He likes to keep the troops in one place.

                    MARTHA
          At least you passed the test.

                    ALICE
          What do you mean?

                    MARTHA
          He took your sex history, didn't he?

Alice nods.

                    MARTHA
         Well he wouldn't have let Clyde marry
         you unless he thought you'd fit in.

                    GEBHARD
         Didn't Clyde mention the calendars?

Alice turns to Martin, who nervously explains:

                    MARTIN
         Prok likes us to keep a record of our
         sexual activity.

                    AGNES
         Buddy, tell them about that dream you
         had the other night.

                    GEBHARD
         I was in the middle of a very intense
         erotic encounter...

                    AGNES
         He wouldn't say who with.

                    GEBHARD
         ...when the door flew open and Prok
         appeared, staring at me with that stern
         look of his. "Gebhard, hurry up.
         You're wasting countless thousands of
         hours of project time." Needless to
         say, the mood was broken.

                    AGNES
         So he woke up and I had to take over.
         It was the quickest orgasm he ever had.

                    GEBHARD
         We're trying to get pregnant again, so
         there was no raincoat to dull the
         sensation.

Alice's eyes widen, hardly able to believe the conversation.

                    ALICE
         Do the Kinseys know you talk like this?

They glance across the yard, where Kinsey and Clara are playing tug-
of-war with the Pomeroy and Gebhard children.

                        MARTHA
          Call me when you get back from the
          honeymoon. We'll have a nice long
          lunch.

INT. ZOOLOGY DEPARTMENT OFFICES - DAY (1945)

The staff has grown to over a dozen now. An OFFICE MANAGER moves
past the staff secretary, who is breaking in a new RECRUIT.

                    STAFF SECRETARY
          You can have either Thanksgiving or
          Christmas off. Your choice entirely.

We follow the office manager into the mailroom, where a MIDDLE-AGED
FEMALE VOLUNTEER opens boxes of erotic material. The manager picks
up a stack of letters and heads through the library, where erotica
fills every available space. He drops some mail in the statistics
room, where TECHNICIANS transfer information from sex histories onto
punch cards. Then he passes a small photography area, where the
STAFF PHOTOGRAPHER has set an animal cage on sawhorses, surrounded
by lights and a camera. He moves through the bullpen, where
Gebhard, Martin and Pomeroy work on a manuscript.

                        GEBHARD
          What's the point? He'll rewrite it
          anyway.

He tears a piece of paper from the typewriter and hands it to an
AIDE, who drops it into a can full of discarded pages. The aide
lights a match and sets them on fire.

The office manager meets up with the staff secretary again in the
hallway. He hands her the large stack of letters, which she carries
to Kinsey's office. She knocks.

                        KINSEY (O.S.)
          Enter.

INT. KINSEY'S OFFICE - DAY (1945)

Kinsey looks up, his face haggard and drawn.

                    STAFF SECRETARY
          Do you need anything before I go?

                        KINSEY
          We'll never get this book done if
          people start leaving early.

She hands him the pile of letters.

                    STAFF SECRETARY
          I wish you'd let me help you with
          these. You don't have the time to
          answer each one personally.

                    KINSEY
          These people take the trouble to write.
          It's the least I can do.

                    STAFF SECRETARY
          Mrs. Kinsey said to remind you to come home
          to eat. And your father phoned again.

She leaves. He sighs, stares at the phone.

INT. KINSEY CHILDHOOD HOUSE - FOYER/PARLOR - DAY (1945)

A black wreath on the front door, which opens to reveal a reception
for family and friends of the deceased. MILDRED, 45, welcomes an
elderly NEIGHBOR.

                    MILDRED
          Mr. Morrissey. Come say hello to father.

She leads him into the parlor, where Kinsey Sr. sits on the sofa
with his son Robert and his family.

                    NEIGHBOR
          I'm very sad for you, Alfred.

                    KINSEY SR.
          It's not as though I'll be alone. My
          daughter's too fat to find a husband,
          and my son's lost his business and
          moved back home.

Robert smiles uncomfortably. Kinsey Sr. looks across at Kinsey
coming down the stairs.

                    KINSEY SR.
          The only one I got rid of is the big
          scientist. Now he's working on some
          secret project. He's always been the
          secretive kind.

                    KINSEY
          Would you like to know what I'm
          studying, father?

                         KINSEY SR.
          Oh he's going to let me in on his
          secret.

                         KINSEY
          It's really not a secret at all. I'm
          trying to find out what people do
          sexually.

Kinsey Sr. turns to Robert, confused.

                         KINSEY
          You heard right, father. It's a sex
          study.

Kinsey Sr. lets out a loud grunt.

                         KINSEY SR.
          What do you expect me to do, applaud?

                         KINSEY
          No. But I would like you to contribute
          to the project.

Kinsey Sr. looks up, surprised by the invitation.

INT. KINSEY CHILDHOOD HOUSE - STUDY - DUSK (LATER) (1945)

The two men sit in semi-darkness.

                         KINSEY
          And you first moved to Hoboken at what
          age?

                         KINSEY SR.
          Sixteen.

His palsied hand trembles as he lights up a cigar.

                         KINSEY SR.
          You could have done this interview
          without me, Al. I haven't told you a
          damn thing you didn't already know.

                         KINSEY
          Let's move on then.

He looks down at the survey sheet.

                    KINSEY
          How young were you when you first
          masturbated?

                    KINSEY SR.
          What?

                    KINSEY
          Touched yourself.

Kinsey Sr. answers without hesitation.

                    KINSEY SR.
          I never did that.

                    KINSEY
          This only works if you tell the truth.

                    KINSEY SR.
          I always tell the truth.

                    KINSEY
          One of the things I've discovered is
          that the male without a history of
          masturbation is almost non-existent.

                    KINSEY SR.
          Well he exists, Al, and you're looking
          at him.

                    KINSEY
          This isn't going to work. I don't know
          why I bothered.

Kinsey folds the piece of paper and caps his pen. His father speaks
softly:

                    KINSEY SR.
          Stay where you are, son. I'll try again.

                    KINSEY
          How often did your masturbation occur
          as an adolescent?

                    KINSEY SR.
          There was a problem. A chronic
          condition, the doctors called it.

                    KINSEY
          How long did this continue?

                         KINSEY SR.
          I was outfitted with a tight strap that
          I wore at all times. It kept me from
          coming into contact with my genitals.

In the darkness, Kinsey flinches slightly.

                         KINSEY SR.
          It was a highly embarrassing remedy,
          but after it proved effective. The
          condition was cured.

                         KINSEY
          How old were you?

                         KINSEY SR.
          I was ten.

                         KINSEY
          I'm so sorry, father.

                         KINSEY SR.
          I'm feeling a little tired now.

The old man snuffs out his cigar and gets to his feet.

                         KINSEY SR.
          Sounds to me like you're wasting your
          time, Al. Nobody wants to know about
          these things.

Kinsey watches the shrunken old man shuffle out of the room, as we
FADE OUT.

EXT. INDIANA UNIVERSITY - DAY (1947)

A busload of national press descends on the campus. REPORTERS run
up to a middle-aged professor.

                         REPORTERS
                    (in unison)
          Dr. Kinsey! Dr. Kinsey!

The man turns. It is Thurman Rice.

                         RICE
          My name is Dr. Thurman Rice and I'd be
          happy to talk to you about Dr. Kinsey's
          repugnant book...

But the reporters are already moving on.

INT. LECTURE HALL - DAY (1947)

The journalists wait hungrily as the staff hands out pre-publication proofs.

> MARTIN
> You're free to read and make notes, but
> the book can't leave the room.

INT. UNIVERSITY CONFERENCE ROOM - DAY (1947)

Herman Wells gives an eve-of-battle speech to the trustees.

> WELLS
> I won't deny that the going might get
> rough. Dr. Kinsey's findings are
> surprising, sometimes even shocking.
> For example, marital sex, which is
> really the only kind everyone agrees
> on, is only one of nine means by which
> American males achieve orgasm.
> Premarital sex, extramarital sex,
> masturbation, and homosexuality are
> much more prevalent than anyone has
> ever imagined before.

There's a clear split in the room, some trustees nodding approvingly, others uncomfortable.

> WELLS
> I can assure you that Dr. Kinsey has
> done everything in his power to present
> the book tastefully. So I thought this
> might be a good time to ask for a
> formal show of support. Those in
> favor?

A few hands shoot up. The others follow more slowly, leaving one elderly DOWAGER, who finally puts a tiny finger in the air.

> DOWAGER
> I just hope it doesn't bring too much
> publicity.

> WELLS
> With any luck, the general public won't
> even notice.

The woman smiles in relief, as we hear the sound of a bomb exploding. We CUT TO:

CLIP (EXISTING FOOTAGE)

An atomic bomb explodes.

A NEWSPAPER CARTOON (EXISTING)

which compares the book's publication to a nuclear detonation. A
caption inside the mushroom cloud screams: "It's K-Day in the
U.S.A."

STILLS (1948)
America reacts to the Male Volume. A "New York Times" headline
compares Kinsey to Copernicus and Darwin. A "Daily News" headline
reads: "DR. SEX SAYS 50% OF MEN UNFAITHFUL. Another calls the book
one of the most important scientific documents of the century. A
"New York Post" article reports: "GALLUP POLL: 78% APPROVE REPORT,
10% DISAPPROVE."

INT. BOOKSTORE - DAY (1948)

CLOSE on a stack of books. A CLERK rings up a sale.

                         CLERK
              That'll be sex fifty, please.

We move past the clerk to reveal:

STILL (1948)

A photo shows Kinsey lecturing to a crowd of 10,000 in the gymnasium
at UC Berkeley.

INT. TYPICAL LIVING ROOM - DAY (1948)

An average American HOUSEWIFE tries to read the 804-page book, but
she's quickly bored by all the graphs and charts. She closes the
book and picks up the illustrated synopsis in "Good Housekeeping"
instead.

STILLS & CLIPS (EXISTING)

Kinsey gets the cover of every major magazine: Time, Newsweek,
Collier's, Look, Life. A New Yorker cartoon shows a woman looking
up from her copy of the book, asking: "Is there a Mrs. Kinsey?" We
move past to once again reveal:

INT. RADIO STATION - SOUND BOOTH - DAY (1948)

Thurman Rice intones into a microphone.

                              RICE
          Mark my words — once the publicity dies
          down, the American public will greet
          this book with the thundering silence
          it deserves.

INT. GRAND CENTRAL STATION - NEW YORK - DAY (1948)

Kinsey and Clara head across the concourse, followed by REPORTERS.
With his wool suit and bowtie, and her plaid coat and oversized
pocketbook, they're an older, dowdier version of Ozzie and Harriet.

                         REPORTER # 1
          What brings you to New York, Dr.
          Kinsey?

                           KINSEY
          We'll be taking the sex histories of
          artists, writers, and actors, including
          the entire cast of "A Streetcar Named
          Desire." And of course meeting with
          our benefactors at the Rockefeller
          Foundation.

                         REPORTER #2
          Are you surprised by the book's success?

                           KINSEY
          No. It shows that the world has wanted
          this thing done.

                         REPORTER #3
          Any plans for a Hollywood picture based
          on your book?

                           KINSEY
          I can't think of anything more
          pointless.

                         REPORTER # 1
          How about you, Mrs. Kinsey? Has your
          life changed much?

                           CLARA
          My husband's busier than ever. I
          hardly ever see him since he took up
          sex.

The reporters laugh at the risque joke. Kinsey stops, holds up his
hands.

                         KINSEY
              Gentlemen, if you want to write about
              something useful, I suggest you look
              into the current sex offender codes.

Clara turns, surprised by this sudden detour.

                         KINSEY
              95% of sex offenders in prison have
              nothing in their histories different
              from the rest of the population. Their
              only crime is being too poor to hire a
              lawyer. This is unfair. Everybody's
              sin is nobody's sin. And everybody's
              crime is no crime at all.

                         GREGG (V.O.)
              I must say, it took us a bit by
              surprise.

INT. GREGG'S OFFICE - ROCKEFELLER FOUNDATION - DAY (1948)

A impressive office filled with modern art. Gregg holds up the
morning "Herald-Tribune," with the headline: "KINSEY SAYS RAPISTS
ARE VICTIMS."

                         KINSEY
              That wasn't my point at all. The
              newspapers lift things out of context
              to make sensational reading.

                         GREGG
              Still, it's hardly your place to offer
              moral prescriptions. You're sounding
              more like a preacher than a scientist.

Kinsey smiles, caught off guard.

                         KINSEY
              My father always hoped I'd become a
              preacher.

                         GREGG
              And why do you insist on flaunting your
              association with the foundation?

                         KINSEY
              Haven't I just given you the best-selling
              scientific volume ever published? Not only
              here but across the globe?

                    GREGG
          Yes, and it's casting a bright light on
          every aspect of the project.
          Especially some of your latest
          methodology.

Kinsey's eyes narrow.

                    KINSEY
          Who have you been talking to?

                    GREGG
          Does it matter?

                    KINSEY
          Tell me what you've heard.

                    GREGG
          I assume most of it's gossip.

                    KINSEY
          Alan.

                    GREGG
          It's been said that you've taken to
          observing women.

                    KINSEY
          Go on.

                    GREGG
          In a heightened state of arousal.

Kinsey runs his hand across his face.

                    GREGG
          So it's true.

                    KINSEY
          Yes, and do you know why? We went to
          the leading gynecologists and asked for
          physical measurements and they barely
          knew what we were talking about! When
          it comes to female sex organs, we're
          all tragically ignorant.

                    GREGG
          Who are these women?

                    KINSEY
          Volunteers. Friends of the project.

                    GREGG
          Prostitutes.

                    KINSEY
          No, prostitutes are useless. They fake
          their orgasms.

                    GREGG
          Jesus.

                    KINSEY
          Alan, the sex histories we have are
          invaluable but everyone knows true
          science lies in direct observation.
          Nothing can replace what the eye can
          see directly, or the camera...

                    GREGG
          Camera? Don't tell me you're making
          movies.

                    KINSEY
          Well...just some photographic studies
          of mammalian behavior.

                    GREGG
          Oh. Nature films. Animals.

                    KINSEY
          Yes. If you like.

A blinding LIGHT switches on. We CUT TO:

INT. KINSEY HOUSE - ATTIC - DAY (1950)

An attic with a pine-board floor and a mattress, bathed in the
powerful cone of light. Clara steps into the shot to change the
sheets, while Kinsey paces in front of her.

                    KINSEY
          Gentlemen, you're about to meet a truly
          rare creature. Even the most casual
          contact arouses a sexual response in
          her.

The team stands in the corner, next to the staff photographer who sets the focus on a 16mm. camera.

> KINSEY
> In intercourse, her first orgasm occurs within two to five seconds after entry.

From the hall, we hear the woman cough shyly.

> KINSEY
> All set there, Barbara?

> WOMAN (O.S.)
> I think so.

> KINSEY
> Come on in.

BARBARA MERKLE steps into the shot, wearing a terry-cloth bathrobe. She is in her late 60s, very thin, a typical grandmother.

> KINSEY
> Did I mention that Barbara didn't have her first orgasm until she was forty?

Barbara smiles, revealing big uneven teeth.

INT. KINSEY HOUSE - BASEMENT - NIGHT (1950)

Kinsey and the staff watch the black-and-white film of Barbara Merkle masturbating. Kinsey stands inches from the screen.

> KINSEY
> Notice how she gently strokes the inner lips and the clitoris. 84% of our sample stimulate themselves in this way.

> GEBHARD
> What about the vagina?

> KINSEY
> For all but a small minority of women, the vaginal tube is a dead cavity, practically devoid of nerve endings.

Onscreen, we switch to a different film. A tight angle of Barbara having intercourse.

                         KINSEY
          As you can see, the introduction of the
          penis does nothing to relocate the
          source of stimulation. Even with as
          skillful a partner as Pomeroy.

He squints at the screen.

                         KINSEY
              That is you, isn't it?

                        POMEROY
              Last time I looked.

Kinsey turns to the team. Behind him, Barbara is experiencing
machine gun orgasms.

                         KINSEY
          For years, women have been told that a
          clitoral orgasm is immature, neurotic.
          So they've struggled, with great
          anxiety, to relocate the orgasm in the
          vagina, when for many it's a biologic
          impossibility.

He steps in front of the screen, the images playing on his clothes.

                         KINSEY
          According to the psychoanalysts, this
          woman is frigid.

EXT. KINSEY HOUSE - GARDEN - NIGHT (1950)

A small gathering of the extended team, including the photographer
and a few other FRIENDS of the project. Kinsey holds Clara's hand
as he addresses the group.

                         KINSEY
          Good news, everyone. The Rockefeller
          Foundation announced its annual grants
          today. We've received $40,000 for the
          next year, the largest grant they've
          ever bestowed on a scientific project.

Whoops and screams of amazement from the group.

                              KINSEY
              They've also agreed to underwrite a new
              corporation, making us future employees
              of the Institute for Sex Research!

                              GEBHARD
                  To Dr. Kinsey!

The group lifts their glasses of grape juice in a toast.

                              MARTIN
                  To Mrs. Kinsey!

                              MARTHA
              And to our husbands, the Fuller Brush
              men of sex!

The others clap. Pomeroy grabs Martha.

                              POMEROY
              Come here, my little prick nibbler.

Alice Martin, a little unnerved, turns to find Gebhard standing next
to her. He spikes her drink with whiskey from a flask.

                              GEBHARD
              You don't look happy.

                              ALICE
              No, I am, really. It's just that Clyde's
              going to be away so long this time.

                              GEBHARD
              Don't worry. I'll keep an eye on him.

                              ALICE
              A lot of good that'll do.

                              GEBHARD
              What are you trying to say, Mrs.
              Martin?

Alice blushes.

                              GEBHARD
              God, you're pretty.

He nips her neck with a kiss.

                    KINSEY
        Drink your grape juice, gentlemen. We only
        have 9,300 histories and the Female volume
        to complete. Starting tomorrow, we need to
        triple our efforts.

                    POMEROY
        Well it's still tonight and since my
        third leg keeps hitting me in the face
        I think it's time for a tumble.

Pomeroy and Martha exchange a look, which they share with Kinsey and
Clara.

                 KINSEY (V.O.)
        In the Bonobo chimpanzee, our nearest
        primate relations, sex is the glue of
        social cohesion and peace.

Agnes smiles at Martin, who in turn lifts his glass to Gebhard and
Alice. They return the toast.

                 KINSEY (V.O.)
        Cleared of notions like romantic love,
        or religion, or morality, their
        society's behavior hangs together as a
        coherent unit of biology and
        conditioning.

INT. KINSEY'S OFFICE - NIGHT (1951)

Kinsey speaks into a dictaphone.

                    KINSEY
        Based on the experiences of females who
        have contributed to our histories, we
        have observed a wide range of
        motivations for extramarital coitus.
        At times it is a conscious or
        unconscious attempt to acquire social
        status. In other instances, it gives
        them a variety of experiences with new
        sexual partners who are sometimes
        superior to their marriage partner.

BLACK & WHITE FILM (1951)

Bodies and faces reach orgasm, as captured in more of the 16 mm.
attic films. We catch tiny glimpses, almost subliminal, of familiar
faces — Pomeroy; Gebhard; their wives, Martha and Agnes; Clyde
Martin; Kinsey; Clara.

86.

                              KINSEY (V.O.)
                    There are occasions when it is done in
                    retaliation for the partner's
                    extramarital activity, or for some sort
                    of non-sexual mistreatment.

INT. KINSEY HOUSE - DINING ROOM - NIGHT (1951)

Clara types as Kinsey's voice plays on the dictaphone.

                              KINSEY'S VOICE ON DICTAPHONE
                    Some females discover new sources of
                    emotional satisfaction, while others
                    find it impossible to share such an
                    intimate relationship with more than
                    one partner.

She glances over at Kinsey, who looks up from his reading.

BLACK & WHITE FILM (1951)

Moving up the bodies of a man and woman having intercourse.

                              KINSEY (V.O.)
                    We have also encountered a considerable
                    group of cases in which husbands
                    encourage their wives to engage in
                    extramarital activities, in an honest
                    attempt to give them the opportunity
                    for additional sexual satisfaction.

We reveal Alice Martin and Paul Gebhard, in the throes of extreme
sexual pleasure. And something more, a visible emotional
connection.

INT. KINSEY HOUSE - BASEMENT - NIGHT (1951)

The team watches the film, Kinsey's face registering disapproval.
He glances sympathetically at Martin, whose expression remains
impenetrable, as we FADE OUT.

EXT. CHICAGO HOTEL - DAY (1952)

Moving in on a grid of identical windows.

                              KINSEY (V.O.)
                    I've waited ten years for this day,
                    Pomeroy. This man has amassed a
                    lifetime of data.

INT. HOTEL ROOM - CHICAGO - DAY (LATER) (1952)

Kenneth Braun, 60, soft-spoken, serves soft drinks to Kinsey and Pomeroy.

> BRAUN
> Working for the forestry department has involved a lot of travelling, so I've met a wide array of people. By the way, my name is...

> KINSEY
> Please, there's no need.

> BRAUN
> Kenneth Braun. Don't worry, Dr. Kinsey. I trust you.

Braun sits. There's an unsettling combination of coyness and menace in his manner.

> BRAUN
> We're actually a lot alike, you know.

> KINSEY
> How so?

> BRAUN
> As you know, I record everything too. The depth of every vagina I've encountered, the length and circumference of every penis. The time to reach orgasm, the volume of semen, the distance of ejaculation. I've written it all down.

He reaches for an enormous leather-bound book.

> BRAUN
> A record of my life's real work. I find recording is a way of experiencing things a second time. Don't you?

Kinsey doesn't rise to the bait.

> BRAUN
> I also have certain rare abilities. From a completely flaccid start, I can become erect and ejaculate in ten seconds flat.

                         POMEROY
             I'd say that's pretty much
             physiologically impossible. Why the
             rush of blood alone...

Before Pomeroy can finish, Braun stands and opens his fly. We hold
on Pomeroy's astonished look as Braun demonstrates his particular
talent.

                         KINSEY
             Shall we get started?

INT. HOTEL ROOM - CHICAGO - DAY/NIGHT (LATER)

A series of DISSOLVES cover Braun's responses, as day turns to
night.

                         BRAUN
             My grandmother introduced me to sexual
             intercourse when I was 10.

                         BRAUN
             My first homosexual act was with my
             father. I was 11.

                         BRAUN
             Of the 33 members of my extended
             family, I've had sex with 17 of them.

                       (a proud smile)
             5 generations now. I suppose I'm what
             you'd call an omniphile.

                         BRAUN
             My penis is 8.24 inches long, with a
             diameter of 3.8 inches when erect.

                         BRAUN
             In my youth, I averaged 8 ccs of semen
             per ejaculation. By the age of 50, it
             was down to 5.

                         BRAUN
             I've had intercourse with 22 separate
             species of animal.

                         BRAUN
             I've had intercourse with 9,412 people.

                         BRAUN
          I've had sexual relations with 605 pre-
          adolescent males and 231 pre-adolescent
          females.

Pomeroy stops writing. Kinsey remains stone-faced.

                         BRAUN
          Have you ever seen a boy orgasm?

Kinsey doesn't respond.

                         BRAUN
          No, that was a real gap in your book.
          I guess that's why I'm such a catch.
          It's physiologically almost identical
          with adult orgasm...

                         POMEROY
          Screw this.

He throws down the interview sheet.

                         POMEROY
          I'll see you down in the bar.

Pomeroy leaves, slamming the door on the way out.

                         BRAUN
          I thought you trained them to be
          impartial.

                         KINSEY
          Sometimes it's difficult.

                         BRAUN
          I suppose someone like me really puts
          your beliefs to the test.

                         KINSEY
          How so?

                         BRAUN
          Oh you know. "Everybody should do what
          they want."

                         KINSEY
          I've never said that. No one should be
          forced to do anything against their
          will. No one should ever be hurt.

Braun's smile fades.

> BRAUN
> You're a lot more square than I thought
> you'd be.

> KINSEY
> Let's get on with it.

INT. INDIANAPOLIS CUSTOMS BOARD OFFICE - DAY (1952)

A small box is carried like a time bomb through the customs office.
The box, which is addressed to "DR. KINSEY c/o INSTITUTE FOR SEX
RESEARCH," is set on a table, where it is scrutinized by half a
dozen CUSTOMS OFFICIALS and LAWYERS. A FEDERAL AGENT rips open the
box and dumps out some porcelain dildos from China, as well as a set
of erotic scrolls and black-and-white photographs.

INT. WELLS OFFICE - DAY (1952)

Kinsey paces as Herman Wells argues on the phone with the Governor.
He glances at the Indianapolis Times headline: 'SCIENCE' SAYS
KINSEY, 'DIRTY STUFF' SAYS U.S.

> WELLS
> ...Governor, you're so mad I can't
> reason with you. When you calm down,
> we'll discuss it.

He puts down the receiver, turns to Kinsey:

> WELLS
> It seems the Archbishop of Fort Wayne
> tipped off the Customs Board.

> KINSEY
> What's wrong with these people?
> They're simply depictions of man in his
> natural state.

> WELLS
> I don't know much about natural states,
> but here in the state of Indiana we've
> got a problem.

> KINSEY
> We'll just have to take the Customs
> Office to court.

                    WELLS
          Who's going to pay for that, the
          Rockefeller Foundation? You're an inch
          away from losing your grant as it is.

                    KINSEY
          That's not true. What do you mean?

                    WELLS
          Gregg has got the F.B.I. breathing down
          his neck. Hoover's still mad that you
          won't help him find homosexuals in the
          State Department. It's rumored he's
          compiling dossiers on you and the rest
          of the staff.

Kinsey can't disguise his surprise, and concern.

                    WELLS
          And people have been complaining about
          your statistical methods.

                    KINSEY
          Trumped up nonsense! Nothing but
          disguised prudery.

Wells throws him a skeptical look.

                    KINSEY
          Maybe there were small mistakes made in
          the Male study, but we've corrected
          them in the Female volume. It will be
          a very great book, much better than the
          first.

                    WELLS
          Let's hope so.

LIFE MAGAZINE (EXISTING)

runs a picture of Kinsey that makes him look sinister.

                    KINSEY (V.O.)
          "Self-appointed messiah of the sexually
          despised."

INT. KINSEY HOUSE - KITCHEN - DAY (1953)

Kinsey reads aloud from the "Life" review. His eyes are watery and
red-rimmed from lack of sleep.

                              KINSEY
              "Having had his way with the male of
              the species, Kinsey now insecticizes
              American womanhood." How many years do
              I have to study human behavior before
              I'm no longer an entomologist?

                              CLARA
              Why do you read them, Prok?

                              KINSEY
              I'm trying to understand why people
              hate this book so.

                              CLARA
              You told them their grandmothers and
              daughters are masturbating, having
              extramarital sex, sex with each other.
              What did you expect?

                              KINSEY
                         (an explosion)
              Some respect!

He sweeps the pile of newspapers and magazines onto the floor. The
phone rings.

                              CLARA
              Don't answer it.

Kinsey grabs the phone. No voice on the other end, just some
clicking sounds. Kinsey carefully puts down the receiver.

                              KINSEY
              We're in trouble.

He pops two pills into his mouth and downs them with a splash of
Coke.

INT. KINSEY'S OFFICE - DAY (1954)

Pomeroy stands over Kinsey's shoulder as he examines a budget sheet.

                              KINSEY
              The cost of film stock is astronomical.
              Shouldn't our non-profit status get us
              a discount, or at least —

There is a thump on the door, followed by screaming.

                         KINSEY
              What in heaven's name?

He jumps up and opens the door. In the hall, Gebhard and Martin are
engaged in an awkward fistfight. Martin lands a blow, sending
Gebhard tumbling to the floor.

                         KINSEY
              Stop this! Stop it at once!

Kinsey grabs Martin by the shoulder and pushes him into the office.

                         KINSEY
              Gebhard! Get in here.

Gebhard stumbles to his feet. Kinsey turns to the staff.

                         KINSEY
              Everyone back to work.

Kinsey slams the door.

                         KINSEY
              Do you have any idea what a delicate
              time this is? Our enemies are watching
              everything we do. We can't afford a
              single slip-up.

                         MARTIN
              This isn't about the project.

                         KINSEY
              Everything is about the project.

                         GEBHARD
              It's just a misunderstanding.

                         KINSEY
              No it's not. You let things get out of
              hand with Martin's wife and now she wants
              to leave him. Is that right, Martin?

Martin nods.

                         KINSEY
              What about you, Gebhard? Are you
              planning to leave Agnes and the kids?

                         GEBHARD
              Of course not.

                        KINSEY
          Then end it.

                        GEBHARD
          I've tried.

                        KINSEY
          It's not difficult. Just tell her it's
          over. No explanation necessary.

                        GEBHARD
          All right.

                        KINSEY
          Do it today.

He opens the door. Gebhard turns to Martin.

                        GEBHARD
          Clyde, I'm sorry about this.

Martin clenches his jaw, looks away. Gebhard leaves.

                        KINSEY
          I saw this coming. Gebhard should have
          nipped it in the bud.

                        MARTIN
          You are so full of shit.

Kinsey turns with a startled look.

                        MARTIN
          What are we to you, laboratory rats?
          Was this just another part of the
          project? Prove that sex...sorry,
          fucking...is nothing but friction and
          harmless fun? Well let me tell you,
          that's a risky game, because fucking
          isn't just something, it's the whole
          thing. And if you're not careful it'll
          crack you wide open.

                        KINSEY
          Go home to your wife, Martin. She's
          going to need you.

Martin storms out. Kinsey turns to Pomeroy.

                         KINSEY
          I thought the rules were clear. No
          intense romantic entanglements. They
          only make people's lives unstable.

                         POMEROY
                      (pointedly)
          I guess we can't all be as disciplined
          as you are, Prok.

He leaves. Kinsey stands by the window.

INT. UNIVERSITY THEATER - DAY (1954)

Moving past busts of classical figures:

                         KINSEY
          The question of marital infidelity
          remains one of the most complicated
          issues facing our society today.

Kinsey reads from a stack of file cards.

                         KINSEY
          The reconciliation of the married
          individual's desire for a variety of
          sexual partners, and the maintenance of
          a stable marriage, presents a problem
          which has not been satisfactorily
          resolved in our culture.

Less than half the seats are filled. A man and woman in the front
row stand and head up the aisle.

                         KINSEY
          It is not likely to be resolved until
          man moves completely away from his
          mammalian ancestry. The fact is,
          America is awash in sexual activity,
          only a small portion of which is
          sanctioned by society. At any moment,
          public opinion is a chaos of
          superstition, misinformation, and
          prejudice. Sexual morality needs to be
          reformed, and science will show the
          way.

Kinsey watches the couple leave. He notices the silhouette of a
TALL MAN standing in back.

                    KINSEY
          Sometimes I wonder what this country would
          look like if the Puritans had stayed at
          home. What if all the rogues and libertines
          had crossed the Atlantic instead?

Kinsey stares at the tall man, who bears a resemblance to his
father. Kinsey closes his eyes and steadies himself.

                    KINSEY
          But the enforcers of chastity are
          massing once again, to dissuade the
          scientist, intimidate him, convince him
          to cease research...

Kinsey lurches forward.

INT. HOSPITAL - DAY (1954)

Moving with Martin down a corridor. He sees Clara by a nurse's
station.

                    MARTIN
          Mac.

She turns to him, panicked.

                    CLARA
          He's killing himself. You've got to
          help me stop him.

INT. HOSPITAL - KINSEY'S ROOM - DAY (LATER) (1954)

Kinsey's eyes flutter open as Martin approaches.

                    KINSEY
          Come to see if the rumors are true?

Martin smiles, sits on the corner of the bed.

                    KINSEY
          The doctors say my heart sounds like a
          cement mixer.

                    MARTIN
          At least they found one.

                    KINSEY
          Seems I've developed a dependence on
          barbiturates. If I've been a little
          harsh lately...

Martin nods, acknowledging Kinsey's stab at an apology.

                    KINSEY
          How is Alice?

                    MARTIN
          She's fine. We're fine. Why don't you
          get some sleep now?

                    KINSEY
          Maybe I should.

Martin stands. Kinsey grabs hold of his hand, with surprising
strength.

                    KINSEY
          It's always been my biggest fear, you
          know. Dying before I finish this work.

He closes his eyes. Martin runs his hand along Kinsey's cheek, as
we FADE OUT.

INT. CONGRESSIONAL HEARING ROOM - DAY (1954)

B. CARROLL REECE, Republican of Tennessee, plays to the cheap seats.

                    REECE
          In the course of these hearings on tax-
          exempt foundations, we intend to show how
          Communists are financed in the United
          States.

INT. KINSEY HOUSE - PARLOR - DAY (1954)

Kinsey sits in a robe, still convalescing. Clara serves him soup on
a TV tray. On the black-and-white console:

                    REECE
          There is a diabolical conspiracy in
          back of all this, and its aim is the
          furtherance of socialism in America.

INT. ZOOLOGY DEPARTMENT OFFICES - DAY (1954)

A little later. Work has come to a standstill, as the entire office
watches Reece grill Dr. Alan Gregg.

                    REECE
          Do you agree that Kinsey's research
          aids the Communistic aim to weaken and
          destroy the youth of our country?

GREGG
I do not agree, sir.

Martin turns to Pomeroy, encouraged. On TV, Reece lowers his glasses to stare down at Gregg.

REECE
Tell me, Dr. Gregg. Does the Rockefeller Foundation really believe it belongs in the business of sex research?

Gregg takes what seems like an endless pause. Martin, Pomeroy and Gebhard stare anxiously at the TV.

INT. KINSEY HOUSE - PARLOR - DAY (1954)

Kinsey and Clara wait as Gregg takes a sip of water.

GREGG
I think it's probably something the foundation shouldn't have anything to do with.

Kinsey closes his eyes.

GREGG
Dr. Kinsey's project is now in a position to obtain support from other sources.

Kinsey leans forward and flicks off the TV. He stands and moves heavily out of the room.

INT. UNIVERSITY CONFERENCE ROOM - DAY (1955)

A meeting of the Board of Trustees. Wells speaks loudly enough to be heard above the creak of an old portable fan.

WELLS
With the loss of support from the Rockefeller Foundation, Dr. Kinsey's project will need other funding if it's to survive.

We recognize most of the trustees from the earlier meeting.

INT. KINSEY HOUSE - KITCHEN - DAY (1955)

Sibelius wafts through the empty rooms. Clara puts down the packages.

                         CLARA
          Prok?

INT. UNIVERSITY CONFERENCE ROOM - DAY (1955)

Wells dries his face with a handkerchief, fighting the stifling heat
of an Indiana summer.

                         WELLS
              We're running a budget surplus due to
              higher enrollments, which are a direct
              result of Dr. Kinsey's success and
              fame. A small portion of this money
              would be enough to keep the project
              afloat.

INT. KINSEY HOUSE - PARLOR - DAY (1955)

Clara is startled to see dozens of albums strewn across the sofa and
floor. She lifts the needle on the album.

                         CLARA
          Prok? Are you home?

INT. UNIVERSITY CONFERENCE ROOM - DAY (1955)

                         WELLS
              Why don't we put it to a vote? All
              those in favor of increasing Dr.
              Kinsey's grant...

We move across the room. The first trustees keep their hands at
their sides.

INT. KINSEY HOUSE - PARLOR - DAY (1955)

Clara climbs the stairs, more frantic now. She stops when she hears
water running in the bathroom.

INT. UNIVERSITY CONFERENCE ROOM - DAY (1955)

Wells watches sadly as the vote continues to go against Kinsey.

INT. KINSEY HOUSE - BATHROOM - DAY (1955)

Clara knocks a few times, then pushes the door open. Kinsey sits on
the edge of the bathtub, holding a stack of letters.

                         CLARA
          Prok...

INT. UNIVERSITY CONFERENCE ROOM - DAY (1955)

The final voter is the newest trustee, Dr. Thurman Rice. He shakes
his head firmly, making the vote against Kinsey unanimous.

>   WELLS
>   That's it then.

INT. KINSEY HOUSE - BATHROOM - DAY (1955)

Kinsey reads from a letter.

>   KINSEY
>   This woman was beaten by her father
>   when she first menstruated. Now she's
>   incapable of physical intimacy of any
>   kind. And this man...

As he switches to another letter, Clara notices a drop of blood
which falls from between his legs. She rushes over, sees bloody
water swirling in the tub.

>   CLARA
>   Where did that blood come from?

>   KINSEY
>   I punctured my foreskin. I wanted to
>   understand different...different kinds
>   of sensation.

He gazes up, glassy-eyed.

>   KINSEY
>   It didn't give me any pleasure, and
>   there was hardly any...

>   (his voice catches)
>   Pain.

He breaks into sobs. The letters drop from his hand.

>   KINSEY
>   I couldn't help them, Mac. I couldn't
>   figure it out. Now I've ruined it for
>   everyone.

Clara reaches over and tries to hold him, as we FADE OUT.

INT. HOTEL ROOM - NEW YORK - DUSK (1956)

Clara helps Kinsey with his bowtie.

                    KINSEY
          This is an exercise in futility.

                    CLARA
          Huntington Hartford is heir to the A&P
          fortune. He could solve your financial
          problems with the stroke of a pen.

Kinsey stares at his ashen complexion in the mirror.

                    KINSEY
          I can't beg, Mac. I can't beg.

Clara holds up his jacket, breaking him out of his reverie.

INT. HUNTINGTON HARTFORD'S APARTMENT - NIGHT (1956)

New York society has turned out in force to meet the famous sex
doctor. Kinsey sits between HUNTINGTON HARTFORD and his current
wife, MARJORIE. Huntington is blowing cigar smoke in Kinsey's
direction, clearly bored.

                    KINSEY
          ... Ohio deplores fellatio but tolerates
          cunnilingus, whereas in my home state of
          Indiana, all forms of oral sex are illegal,
          even within marriage. The current sex laws
          are completely out of touch with the real
          world.

                    HARTFORD
          I've had four wives. Some people say
          that makes me a sex offender.

A sprinkling of laughter among the guests.

                    MARJORIE
          Well, Hunt, if you keep interrupting
          Dr. Kinsey, you're going to have to
          find a fifth.

                    (to Kinsey)
          Please, go on.

Kinsey shifts uneasily as a servant leans over his shoulder to
refill his wine glass.

                         KINSEY
              Even now, 43 states will punish a
              single act of adulterous intercourse.
              In no other Western society is
              fornication a criminal offense...

                         HARTFORD
              I'm thinking of building a museum.
              What's your opinion of modern art, Dr.
              Kinsey?

                         KINSEY
              It's not my area of expertise. I
              really don't consider myself qualified
              to discuss it.

                         HARTFORD
              Why not? Just because I own
              supermarkets, that doesn't mean I'm
              only capable of talking about
              groceries.

Hartford turns to the woman sitting next to him.

                         HARTFORD
              Do you hate modern art as much as I do?
              Blank canvases, squiggly lines, white
              on white...

Kinsey downs a glass of wine, stung by the rejection. Marjorie
rests her hand on his arm.

                         MARJORIE
              So the next book will deal with sex
              offenders?

Kinsey wipes his hand over his face, from the forehead down, as if
to shake off his weariness.

                         KINSEY
              We need money, Mrs. Hartford.

He turns back to Hartford.

                         KINSEY
              We need someone to give us money.

A heavy silence settles over the room. Clara watches helplessly
from across the table.

                          KINSEY
          You have no idea what I've had to
          endure, just to obtain the same rights
          other scientists take for granted. My
          funding has been slashed...this customs
          case has drained our reserves...and my
          name has been dragged through the mud
          in every newspaper and magazine across
          this country...

A servant leans down to pick up Kinsey's napkin, while another tries
to refill his wine glass.

                          KINSEY
                    (sharply)
          Leave me alone.

The servants retreat.

                          KINSEY
          Every dollar I've ever made has gone
          back into the project. But fighting
          this customs case has cost us an
          appalling amount. We're broke.

                          CLARA
          Prok, don't.

                          HARTFORD
          Dr. Kinsey...

                          KINSEY
          Please. I'm not even sure how much
          time I have left. Help me. I have to
          get it all on the record.

                          HARTFORD
          I'm very sorry, but any support I'd
          give might be misconstrued as an
          endorsement of sex. I can't afford
          that kind of exposure.

                          KINSEY
          I see.

                          HARTFORD
          But I'm sure something will come
          through.

Kinsey stares down at his plate, his face slack with humiliation.

INT. HUNTINGTON HARTFORD'S APARTMENT - NIGHT (LATER)

Kinsey sits alone on a sofa, breathing heavily. Clara arrives with
a glass of water and a nitroglycerin pill, which she places on his
tongue.

                    CLARA
          You're right, rich people do have lazy
          minds. It took them five minutes to
          find a water glass.

He gasps for breath.

                    CLARA
          I'm taking you to the hospital.

                    KINSEY
          No, I can't lie in any more beds. I
          spent my whole childhood lying in bed.

His face is more blue-gray than flesh-like.

                    KINSEY
          Let's go back to the hotel, Mac.

Clara helps him to his feet.

                    KINSEY
          I want to pick up a few histories in
          the morning.

INT. NEW YORK APARTMENT - DAY (1956)

A fine-boned WOMAN, late 50s, perches on a settee in her well-
appointed living room. Kinsey sits opposite her, taking her sex
history.

                    WOMAN
          ...we'd been married for twenty-three
          years, with three marvelous children.
          As soon as my youngest left for
          college, I took a job at an arts
          foundation.

Kinsey smiles patiently.

                        WOMAN
          I met a woman there, a secretary in the
          grants office. We became fast friends,
          and before long I fell in love with
          her. This came as quite a shock, as
          you might imagine. The more I tried to
          ignore it, the more powerful it became.
          You have no idea what it's like to have
          your own thoughts turn against you like
          that.

Kinsey nods sympathetically, more fatigued than moved by the story.

                        WOMAN
          I couldn't talk to anyone about my
          situation, so I found other ways to
          cope. I took up drinking. Eventually
          my husband left me, and even my
          children fell away. I came very close
          to ending it all.

                        KINSEY
          It's just another reminder of how
          little things have changed in our
          society.

                        WOMAN
          What are you talking about?

The woman breaks into a bright smile.

                        WOMAN
          Things have gotten much better.

                        KINSEY
          Really? What happened?

                        WOMAN
          Why you did, of course. After I read
          your book, I realized how many other
          women were in the same situation. I
          mustered the courage to talk to my
          friend, and she told me, to my great
          surprise, that the feelings were
          mutual. We've been together for three
          happy years now.

The woman stands and moves across to Kinsey. She puts out her hand.

                              WOMAN
                    You saved my life, sir.

Kinsey's thick fingers wipe a tear from his cheek.

                         MARTIN   (V.O.)
                    Good, we're almost through. Just one
                    more question.

INT. LAB ROOM - DAY (1942)

Back to the opening of the film, black-and-white footage of Kinsey
teaching Martin to take a sex history.

                              MARTIN
                    You've just told me your entire
                    history. Childhood, family, career.
                    Every person you've ever had sex with.
                    But there hasn't been a single mention
                    of love.

                              KINSEY
                    That's because it's impossible to
                    measure love. And without measurements
                    there can be no science. But I've been
                    thinking a lot about the problem
                    lately.

                              MARTIN
                    Problem?

                              KINSEY
                    When it comes to love, we're all in the
                    dark.

Kinsey falls silent.

                         MARTIN (O.S.)
                    So you do think it matters?

INT. TAXICAB - DAY (1956)

Clara stares out the cab window. Kinsey smiles at his wife.

                              KINSEY
                    What time's our flight, Mac?

                         CLARA
              Not for a few hours.

                         KINSEY
              Let's stop in the woods.

She turns to Kinsey, a bit surprised.

EXT. MUIR WOODS - DAY (1956)

Kinsey and Clara walk at a slow pace among the towering redwoods.
They take in the glorious floods of light, the white beams streaming
through wind-swept branches.

Kinsey glances around, his powers of observation as keen as ever.
Some deer. An owl. He takes a deep breath and shuts his eyes, as
close to reverence as we have seen him.

When he opens his eyes, Clara is gone. Kinsey scans the forest, in
a momentary panic.

                         KINSEY
              Mac?

                         CLARA
              I'm right here, Prok.

Clara emerges from behind an ancient trunk.

                         CLARA
              Just imagine. This tree is over a
              thousand years old.

                         KINSEY
              Hence the name. 'Sequoia
              Sempervirens.' Always green. Always
              alive.

Clara's face clouds over at this sudden mention of mortality. She
tries to cover but Kinsey can read her thoughts.

                         KINSEY
              Mac, have I ever told you about the
              Mbeere? They're an ancient tribe of
              East Africa.

                         CLARA
              No, not that I recall.

Kinsey moves toward her.

                              KINSEY
          They believe that trees are imperfect
          men, eternally bemoaning their
          imprisonment — the roots that keep them
          stuck in one place.

He reaches Clara.

                              KINSEY
          But I've never seen a discontented
          tree. Look at this one. The way it's
          gripping the ground — I believe it
          really loves it.

Kinsey slips his fingers through hers.

                              KINSEY
          Come on, Mac.

                              CLARA
          What's the hurry?

                              KINSEY
          There's a lot of work to do.

Kinsey lets go of her hand and strides off, cheeks flushed,
physically renewed by this brief encounter with nature.

Clara hangs back a moment. She watches Kinsey head toward the cab,
his huge old body dwarfed by the cathedral-like setting. She starts
after him, as we FADE OUT.

Cast and Crew Credits

FOX SEARCHLIGHT PICTURES Presents
In Association with QWERTY FILMS
A N1 EUROPEAN FILM PRODUKTIONS/
AMERICAN ZOETROPE/
PRETTY PICTURES Production

LIAM NEESON
LAURA LINNEY

KINSEY

CHRIS O'DONNELL
PETER SARSGAARD
TIMOTHY HUTTON
JOHN LITHGOW
TIM CURRY
OLIVER PLATT
DYLAN BAKER

Music by .... CARTER BURWELL
Co-Producer .... RICHARD GUAY
Costume Designer .... BRUCE FINLAYSON
Film Editor .... VIRGINIA KATZ
Production Designed by ..... RICHARD SHERMAN
Director of Photography FREDERICK ELMES, A.S.C.
Executive Producers .... MICHAEL KUHN
FRANCIS FORD COPPOLA
BOBBY ROCK
KIRK D'AMICO
Produced by .... GAIL MUTRUX
Written and Directed by .... BILL CONDON

CAST

ALFRED KINSEY .... LIAM NEESON
CLARA MCMILLEN .... LAURA LINNEY
WARDELL POMEROY ...... CHRIS O'DONNELL
CLYDE MARTIN .... PETER SARSGAARD
PAUL GEBHARD .... TIMOTHY HUTTON
ALFRED SEGUINE KINSEY .... JOHN LITHGOW
THURMAN RICE .... TIM CURRY
HERMAN WELLS .... OLIVER PLATT
ALAN GREGG .... DYLAN BAKER
ALICE MARTIN .... JULIANNE NICHOLSON
KENNETH BRAUN .... WILLIAM SADLER
HUNTINGTON HARTFORD .. JOHN MCMARTIN
SARA KINSEY .... VERONICA CARTWRIGHT
BARBARA MERKLE ..... KATHLEEN CHALFANT
MARTHA POMEROY .. HEATHER GOLDENHERSH
AGNES GEBHARD ..... DAGMARA DOMINCZYK

YOUNG MAN IN GAY BAR ...... HARLEY CROSS
STAFF SECRETARY .... SUSAN BLOMMAERT
KINSEY AT 19 .... BENJAMIN WALKER
KINSEY AT 14 .... MATTHEW FAHEY
KINSEY AT 10 .... WILL DENTON
BEN .... JOHN KRASINSKI
EMILY .... ARDEN MYRIN
REP. B. CARROLL REECE .... ROMULUS LINNEY
MRS. SPAULDING .... KATHARINE HOUGHTON
ROBERT KINSEY .... DAVID HARBOUR
MILDRED KINSEY .... JUDITH J.K. POLSON
ANNE KINSEY .... LEIGH SPOFFORD
JOAN KINSEY .... JENNA GAVIGAN
BRUCE KINSEY .... LUKE MACFARLANE
KENNETH HAND .... MIKE THURSTLIC
GROCER .... JARLATH CONROY
DR. THOMAS LATTIMORE .... BILL BUELL
GALL WASP CLASS COED .. MICHELE FEDERER
BLACK STUDENT .... ALVIN KEITH
MARRIAGE CLASS COED .... AMY WILSON
FEMALE ASSISTANT
PROFESSOR .... MARYELLEN OWENS
CLERICAL WORKER .... RODERICK HILL
RETIRED TEACHER .... PEG SMALL
MIDDLE-AGED BUSINESSMAN .... DON SPARKS
JANITOR .... JOE ZALOOM
FEMALE STUDENT #1 .... KATE REINDERS
FEMALE STUDENT #2 .... MARA HOBEL
FEMALE STUDENT #3 ..... LINDSAY SCHMIDT
MALE STUDENT #1 ....JASON PATRICK SANDS
MALE STUDENT #2 .... MARCEL SIMONEAU
MALE STUDENT #3 .... BOBBY STEGGERT
MALE STUDENT #4 .... JOHNNY PRUITT
EFFETE MAN IN GAY BAR ..... JOHN EPPERSON
EFFETE MAN'S FRIEND ...... JEFFERSON MAYS
SLAVIC MAN .... MARK MINEART
BARTENDER .... MARTIN MURPHY
MARJORIE HARTFORD .. KATE JENNINGS GRANT
IU REPORTER #1 .... BARRY DEL SHERMAN
IU REPORTER #2 .... FRED BURRELL
NYC REPORTER #1 .... MICHAEL ARKIN
NYC REPORTER #2 .... DANIEL ZISKIE
NYC REPORTER #3 .... TUCK MILLIGAN
MR. MORRISSEY .... EDWIN MCDONOUGH
BOOKSTORE CLERK .. JOHN ELLISON CONLEE
SHARECROPPER .... ARTHUR FRENCH
PRISON INMATE .... CHANDLER WILLIAMS
HISPANIC MAN .... JAIME ROMAN TIRELLI
BALLET TEACHER .... DRAPER SHREEVE
BELLHOP .... PHILLIP KUSHNER
RADIO REPAIRMAN .... JOE BADALUCCO
POET .... HENRIETTA MANTOOTH
OLD WOMAN .... DORIS SMITH

MALE IMPERSONATOR .... RENO
YOUNG BLACK WOMAN .... PASCALE ARMAND
STAFF PHOTOGRAPHER .... SEAN SKELTON
REVEREND STEVEN .... EDWARD HART
PROFESSOR SMITHSON ..... CLIFFORD DAVID
STUDENT .... RANDY REDD
AND
FINAL INTERVIEW SUBJECT ... LYNN REDGRAVE

UNIT PRODUCTION
MANAGER .... DIANA SCHMIDT
FIRST ASSISTANT DIRECTOR .. JUDE GORJANC
SECOND ASSISTANT
DIRECTOR .... LINDA PERKINS
PRODUCTION EXECUTIVES FOR N1
AND QWERTY FILMS .... JILL TANDY
MALCOLM RITCHIE
FOR N1 .... PETER LÜKE
EXECUTIVE IN CHARGE OF PRODUCTION
FOR N1 .... MARK WOLFE
ASSOCIATE PRODUCERS .... VALERIE DEAN
ADAM SHULMAN

ANIMAL FOOTAGE COURTESY OF
THE KINSEY INSTITUTE

ART DIRECTOR .... NICHOLAS LUNDY
SET DECORATOR .... ANDREW BASEMAN
LOCATION MANAGER .... KATHY CIRIC
SCRIPT SUPERVISOR .... MARY CYBULSKI
ASSISTANT EDITORS .... JIM BRUCE
LAURA CONGLETON
GAFFER .... JONATHAN LUMLEY
KEY GRIP .... ROBERT A. ANDRES
CAMERA OPERATOR .... PATRICK CAPONE
FIRST ASSISTANT CAMERA .. CARLOS GUERRA
SOUND MIXER .... T.J. O'MARA
BOOM PERSON............. MICHAEL SCOTT
STILL PHOTOGRAPHER .... KEN REGAN
MUSIC SUPERVISOR .... FRANKIE PINE
POST PRODUCTION
SUPERVISORS .... STEVEN KAMINSKY
TIM PEDEGANA
MUSIC EDITORS .... TODD KASOW
BARBARA MCDERMOTT
VISUAL EFFECTS SUPERVISOR ... MARLO PABON
GRAPHIC ARTIST .... ELTON GARCIA
LEADMAN .... RICHARD J. TICE
SET DRESSERS .... JOANN ATWOOD
JONI FINLAY
SECOND SECOND ASSISTANT
DIRECTOR .... AMANDA TAYLOR

SECOND ASSISTANT
CAMERA .... BRADEN BELMONTE
LOADER .... ANGELA BELLISIO
STEADICAM
OPERATORS .... STEPHEN CONSENTINO
TOM LOHMANN
CABLE PERSONS .... DANIEL PAIKIN
KIM MAITLAND
VIDEO PLAYBACK .... DENNIS GREEN
PROPERTY MASTER .... ANTHONY DIMEO
ASSISTANT PROPERTY
MASTERS .... JOE BADALUCCO
JUSTINE DOLAN-COTE
BEST BOY ...... ELECTRIC RALPH CROWLEY
RIGGING GAFFER .... WILLIAM ALMEIDA
RIGGING BEST BOYS .. MICHAEL PAPADOPOULOS
MARK VAN ROSSEN
GENNY OPERATORS .... CLAY LIVERSIDGE
JAMIE GALLAGHER
COMPANY ELECTRICS .... TOM SHINN
SAM FRIEDMAN
CHRIS LISCINSKY
SCOTT KINCAID
BEST BOY GRIP .... ALISON BARTON
DOLLY GRIP .... TONY CAMPENNI
RIGGING GRIP .... CHRIS SKUTCH
COMPANY GRIPS .... KEITH BUNTING, JR.
LAMONT CRAWFORD
MEL CANNON
PAT TAISTRA
PETER DONAHUE
ASSISTANT COSTUME
DESIGNER .... HILARY NIEDERER
MEN'S COSTUME
SUPERVISOR .... J. KEVIN DRAVES
WOMEN'S COSTUME
SUPERVISOR .... DEIRDRE WILLIAMS
SET COSTUMER .... KELLY LEE GREGSON
MAKEUP FOR MR. NEESON ... MICHAEL LAUDATI
MAKEUP FOR MS. LINNEY .... MINDY HALL
KEY MAKEUP ARTIST .... CARLA WHITE
ADDITIONAL MAKEUP
ARTIST .... JAMES SARZOTTI
SPECIAL EFFECTS
MAKEUP ARTIST .... TODD KLEITSCH
KEY HAIRSTYLISTS .... JEFFREY SACINO
ROY BRYSON
HAIRSTYLIST .... WAYNE HERNDON
PRODUCTION
COORDINATOR .... MONTEZ A. MONROE
ASSISTANT PRODUCTION
COORDINATOR .... JEN CRAMMER
SPECIAL EFFECTS .... CONNIE BRINK, SR.

ART DEPARTMENT
COORDINATOR . . . . JENNIFER SANTUCCI
CONSTRUCTION
COORDINATOR . . . . RICHARD HEBRANK
CONSTRUCTION FOREMAN . . . PETER BUNDRICK
GREENSPERSON . . . . AMY SAFHAY
SCENIC FOREMEN . . . . JON RINGBOM
FRANCESCO SCIARRONE
SET SCENIC . . . . STEVEN SHELLOOE
ASSISTANT TO MR. CONDON . . . . . ADAM COOK
ASSISTANTS TO
MS. MUTRUX . . . . GUADALUPE RILOVA
STEVEN JACOBSON
ASSISTANT TO MR. GUAY. . CARA ROSENBLOOM
STUNT COORDINATORS . . . GEORGE AGUILAR
BLAISE CORRIGAN
PRODUCTION ACCOUNTANT . . J.R. CRAIGMILE
FIRST ACCOUNTANT . . . . HILLARY MEYER
PAYROLL ACCOUNTANT . . . . FELIX CHEN
POST PRODUCTION
ACCOUNTANT . . . . JULIE HANSEN
FILM AUDITORS, INC.
PRODUCTION SECRETARY . . . CAITLIN MCGINTY
PRODUCTION ASSISTANTS . . . . . . HENRI SANN
MELISSA MUGAVERO
CIARA BRESNIHAN
NICHOLAS VANDERPOOL
BRUNO MICHELS
THOMAS AHLERS
JON BERNIER
MOLLIE SMITH
LAURA LIM
ANDY CESANA
NINA FIORE
EMRE OZPIRINCCI
INTERNS . . . . ANNABEL CLARK
KRISTEN VON HOFFMAN
JUSTIN M. PANDOLFINO
ELI LICHTER-MARCK
DIALECT COACH . . . . DEBORAH HECHT
EXTRAS
CASTING . . . MEREDITH JACOBSON MARCIANO
CASTING ASSISTANTS . . . . LAURA CASS
MATT SCHREIBER
UNIT PUBLICIST . . . . ROBERT LEVINE
TRANSPORTATION CAPTAIN . . . . KEVIN KEEFE
TRANSPORTATION
CO-CAPTAIN . . . . MAURICE FITZGERALD
CATERING . . . . . . COAST TO COAST CATERING
CRAFT SERVICE . . . . . BY DAWN'S EARLY LIGHT
EDITORIAL PRODUCTION
ASSISTANTS . . . . . . TODD DANIEL SCHECHTER
AINA ABIODUN

SUPERVISING SOUND
EDITORS . . . . RICHARD E. YAWN, M.P.S.E.
ERIC WARREN LINDEMANN
RERECORDING MIXERS . . STEPHEN PEDERSON
LANCE BROWN
RECORDIST . . . . GARY RITCHIE
FIRST ASSISTANT SOUND
EDITOR . . . . NANCY BARKER, M.P.S.E.
APPRENTICE EDITOR . . NATHAN WHITEHEAD
SOUND DESIGN &
EDITORIAL . . . . DANETRACKS, INC.
SUPERVISING ADR & DIALOGUE
EDITOR . . . . . . KIMBERLY LOWE VOIGT, M.P.S.E.
DIALOGUE EDITOR . . . . PAUL HACKNER
FOLEY SUPERVISOR . . . . MICHAEL GEISLER
FOLEY ARTIST . . . . GREGG BARBANELL
FOLEY MIXER . . . . JASON PIATT
FOLEY EDITOR . . . . DAVID LOTT
ADR EDITORS –
NEW YORK . . . . HARRIET FIDLOW
KENTON JAKUB
ORCHESTRATED AND
CONDUCTED BY . . . . CARTER BURWELL
MUSIC SCORING MIXER . . . MICHAEL FARROW
SCORE RECORDED BY . . . . . ALAN SILVERMAN
SCORE RECORDED AT . . . . RIGHT TRACK
RECORDING, NEW YORK
MUSICIAN CONTRACTOR . . . . . . SANDRA PARK
MUSIC PREPARED BY . . . . TONY FINNO
SCORE PRODUCTION
MANAGER . . . . DEAN PARKER
MUSICIANS . . . . SHARON YAMADA LISA KIM
ROBERT RINEHART
ALAN STEPANSKY
JOHN PATITUCCI
JON MANASSE
TOM SEVCOFIC
SHELLY WOODWORTH
NADINE ASIN
KEN BICHEL
STACEY SHAMES
MUSIC CLEARANCES . . . . BRIAN GODSHALL
ADR MIXER – L.A. . . . . ANN HADSELL
ADR RECORDIST – L.A. . . . . CHRIS NAVARRO
ADR STAGE – L.A. . . . . WILSHIRE STAGES
ADR MIXER – NEW YORK . . . . . . PAUL J. ZYDEL
ADR RECORDIST – NEW YORK . . . . ALEX RASPA
ADR STAGE – NEW YORK . . . . SOUNDONE
VOICE CASTING . . . . BARBARA HARRIS
FILM RESEARCHERS . . . . KATI MEISTER
DEBORAH RICKETTS
ANIMAL TRAINERS . . . . STEVE MCAULIFF
KIM KRAFSKY

ANIMALS SUPPLIED BY ...... ANIMAL ACTORS
INTERNATIONAL, INC.
NEGATIVE CUTTER .... MO HENRY
D. BASSETT & ASSOC.
COLOR TIMER .... KENNY BECKER
COLOR PRINTS BY ... DELUXE LABORATORIES
FILM DAILIES BY .... DUART
DIGITAL VISUAL EFFECTS
AND TITLES BY .... TITLE HOUSE DIGITAL
VISUAL EFFECTS PRODUCER .... JOSH COMEN
SENIOR DIGITAL
COMPOSITOR .... MIKE ADKISSON
DIGITAL COMPOSITORS .... ROBB ENGLIN
MIKE OCOBOC
DIGITAL EDITORS .... CLAY SPARKS
MARTIN AVITIA

FOR QWERTY FILMS
HEAD OF COMMERCIAL AND BUSINESS
AFFAIRS .... ANDREW HILDEBRAND
HEAD OF LEGAL AFFAIRS .... KATHRYN CRAIG
CHIEF FINANCIAL OFFICER .. MARK WOOLLEY
PRODUCTION
COORDINATOR .... SARAH NUTTALL
ASSISTANT TO
MR. KUHN .... ALEXANDRA ARLANGO
PRODUCTION LEGAL
COUNSEL .... ANDREA CANNISTRACI
SARA CURRAN
SUE BODINE
PRE AND POST PRODUCTION CONSULTANT
ON BEHALF OF N1 .... STEVE HARROW
COLLECTION ACCOUNT
MANAGEMENT .... FINTAGE HOUSE

STOCK FOOTAGE PROVIDED BY

GETTY IMAGES, STREAMLINE FILMS,
THE WPA FILM LIBRARY, FOOTAGEBANK,

CORBIS MOTION, UNIVERSAL CITY STUDIOS,
JOHN E. ALLEN, INC.,

PRODUCERS LIBRARY SERVICE,
HISTORIC FILMS ARCHIVE

TIME MAGAZINE © TIME INC.
REPRINTED BY PERMISSION

THE INDIANAPOLIS STAR
REPRINTED BY PERMISSION

"PORTRAIT OF FAY BAINTER"
BY ROBERT HENRI
COURTESY OF BRIGHAM YOUNG UNIVERSITY
MUSEUM OF ART

"THE NAKED AND THE DEAD"
BY NORMAN MAILER
COURTESY OF HENRY HOLT AND COMPANY,
LLC

"IS THERE A MRS. KINSEY?"
© THE NEW YORKER COLLECTION 1948
PETER ARNO
FROM CARTOONBANK.COM, ALL RIGHTS
RESERVED

© COPYRIGHT N1 EUROPEAN FILM
PRODUKTIONS-GMBH & CO. KG 2004

ALL RIGHTS RESERVED

N1 EUROPEAN FILM PRODUKTIONS-
GMBH & CO. KG
IS THE AUTHOR OF THIS MOTION PICTURE
FOR PURPOSES
OF COPYRIGHT AND OTHER LAWS.

"ETUDES, OPUS 25"
WRITTEN BY FRYDERYK CHOPIN
PERFORMED BY IDIL BIRET
COURTESY OF NAXOS OF NORTH AMERICA, INC.

"STRING QUARTET IN G MAJOR,
K.80 ALLEGRO"
WRITTEN BY WOLFGANG AMADEUS MOZART
PERFORMED BY EDER QUARTET
COURTESY OF NAXOS OF NORTH AMERICA, INC.

"TOO DARN HOT"
WRITTEN BY COLE PORTER
PERFORMED BY ELLA FITZGERALD
PUBLISHED BY CHAPPELL & CO (ASCAP)
COURTESY OF POLYGRAM RECORDS, INC./
UNIVERSAL MUSIC ENTERPRISES

"FEVER"
WRITTEN BY JOHN DAVENPORT
AND EDDIE COOLEY
PERFORMED BY LITTLE WILLIE JOHN
PUBLISHED BY FORT KNOX MUSIC, INC. (BMI)
AND WINDSWEPT PACIFIC
COURTESY OF KING RECORDS

"DIXIE SWING"
WRITTEN BY STEPHEN LANG, JAMIE DUNLAP
AND SCOTT NICKOLEY
PERFORMED BY MOLLY PASUTTI
PUBLISHED BY REVISION WEST (BMI)
AND RED ENGINE MUSIC (ASCAP)
COURTESY OF MARC FERRARI/MASTER-
SOURCE

"TOP OF THE PLAZA"
WRITTEN AND PERFORMED BY DANIEL MAY
PUBLISHED BY REVISION WEST (BMI)
COURTESY OF MARC FERRARI/MASTERSOURCE

"I'M TIRED OF YOU"
WRITTEN AND PERFORMED BY
MARTIN BLASICK
PUBLISHED BY LAVISH MUSIC (BMI)

"VIOLIN CONCERTO IN D MINOR,
OPUS 47 ALLEGRO MODERATO"
WRITTEN BY JEAN SIBELIUS
PERFORMED BY LAHTI SYMPHONY
ORCHESTRA/
LEONIDAS KAVAKOS, VIOLIN/
CONDUCTED BY OSMO VANSKA
PUBLISHED BY ZIMMERMAN PUBLISHERS
COURTESY OF BIS RECORDS AB

"VIOLIN CONCERTO #3,
D MINOR, OPUS 58"
WRITTEN BY MAX BRUCH
PERFORMED BY JAMES EHNES/
MONTREAL SYMPHONY
COURTESY OF CBC RECORDS/LES DISQUES SRC

"LINDY HOP"
WRITTEN BY LINDA MARTINEZ
COURTESY OF 5 ALARM MUSIC

"BETTER THINGS TO DO"
WRITTEN BY STEPHEN LANG, JAMIE DUNLAP
AND SCOTT NICKOLEY
PERFORMED BY KACEE CLANTON
PUBLISHED BY REVISION WEST (BMI)
AND RED ENGINE MUSIC (ASCAP)
COURTESY OF MARC FERRARI/MASTERSOURCE

"I LOVE PENNY SUE"
WRITTEN AND PERFORMED BY DANIEL MAY
PUBLISHED BY REVISION WEST (BMI)
COURTESY OF MARC FERRARI/MASTERSOURCE

THE PRODUCERS WISH TO THANK

JONATHAN GATHORNE-HARDY
"KINSEY: SEX THE MEASURE OF ALL THINGS"
BART WALKER
L. WAYNE ALEXANDER
KEITH CLARK
JACK MORRISSEY
RICHARD PHILIPPS
CHARLES MOORE
ALAN BRUNSWICK
MAUREEN DUFFY

GREG TRATTNER
DIANE WARD
INDIANA UNIVERSITY
THE KINSEY INSTITUTE FOR RESEARCH IN
SEX, GENDER AND REPRODUCTION
LOCAL 817
NEW YORK CITY MAYOR'S OFFICE OF FILM,
BROADCAST AND THEATER
NEW JERSEY FILM COMMISSION
DAVID SHONER, NYPD
THE TV/MOVIE UNIT CITY OF PLAINFIELD,
NEW JERSEY
BRONX COMMUNITY COLLEGE
FORDHAM UNIVERSITY

ANAMORPHIC LENSES PROVIDED BY
JOE DUNTON CAMERAS
No. 40544

THIS MOTION PICTURE IS INSPIRED BY
ACTUAL HISTORICAL EVENTS.
HOWEVER, CERTAIN OF THE CHARACTERS,
EVENTS AND DIALOGUE PORTRAYED
IN THIS MOTION PICTURE WERE CREATED
FOR THE PURPOSE OF FICTITIOUS
DRAMATIZATION, AND ANY SIMILARITY TO
ANY PERSON LIVING TODAY
IS PURELY COINCIDENTAL AND
UNINTENTIONAL.
AMERICAN HUMANE ASSOCIATION
MONITORED THE ANIMAL ACTION.
NO ANIMAL WAS HARMED IN THE MAKING OF
THIS FILM. (AHA 00528)
OWNERSHIP OF THIS MOTION PICTURE IS
PROTECTED BY COPYRIGHT
AND OTHER APPLICABLE LAWS, AND ANY
UNAUTHORIZED DUPLICATION,
DISTRIBUTION OR EXHIBITION OF THIS
MOTION PICTURE COULD
RESULT IN CRIMINAL PROSECUTION AS WELL
AS CIVIL LIABILITY.

RELEASED BY
TWENTIETH CENTURY FOX

*Above: The
original staff of
the Institute for
Sex Research,
1948.*

*Below: Richard
Sherman (produc-
tion designer),
Bill Condon, Gail
Mutrux and
Liam Neeson.*

About the Filmmakers

BILL CONDON (Writer/Director)

Bill Condon's previous directing effort, *Gods and Monsters*, was named Best Picture by the National Board of Review, and earned Condon the Academy Award for Best Adapted Screenplay. A poetic meditation on the final days of film director James Whale, *Gods and Monsters* starred Ian McKellen, Brendan Fraser and Lynn Redgrave.

Most recently, Condon wrote the screenplay for the critically acclaimed box-office hit *Chicago*. The film, which won six Academy Awards, including Best Picture, also garnered Condon a nomination for Best Adapted Screenplay.

Condon began his career as a film journalist. An analytical piece in *Millimeter* magazine brought him to the attention of producer Michael Laughlin. He subsequently co-wrote the feature film *Strange Behavior* with Laughlin, who also directed the film. The film became a cult hit, leading to an unofficial sequel, *Strange Invaders*. Condon made his directorial debut with *Sister, Sister*, which starred Jennifer Jason Leigh, Judith Ivey and Eric Stoltz.

Condon was born in New York City. He attended Regis High School and Columbia University, where he graduated with a degree in philosophy. He currently serves on the board of IFP/Los Angeles, as well as the recently formed Independent Writers Steering Committee of the Writers Guild of America.

GAIL MUTRUX (Producer)

Gail Mutrux is partnered with filmmaker Neil LaBute in Pretty Pictures, a production company at Focus Features. Last year she produced LaBute's *The Shape of Things*, which he adapted from his stage play and directed. In 2000, Mutrux produced *Nurse Betty*, directed by LaBute, and starring Renée Zellweger and Morgan Freeman. The film won the Best Screenplay Award at the Cannes Film Festival and earned Zellweger a Golden Globe for Best Actress in a Comedy/Musical.

Mutrux studied art history at UCLA and, upon graduating, began her career in the film business. She served as associate producer on two films for director Ulu Grosbard: *Straight Time,* starring Dustin Hoffman, and *True Confessions.* Hoffman then recruited Mutrux to associate produce Barry Levinson's multi-Academy Award-winning *Rain Man,* after which she joined Levinson's production company Baltimore Pictures.

At Baltimore, Mutrux developed and co-produced Robert Redford's Academy Award-nominated *Quiz Show* and Mike Newell's acclaimed *Donnie Brasco.* There, she also developed and produced the Peabody Award-winning television series *Homicide: Life on the Street,* which ran for seven seasons on NBC. Mutrux is a board member of IFP/Los Angeles.

About the Contributors

LINDA WOLFE is a journalist, essayist and fiction writer. She has published ten books, including *Wasted: The Preppie Murder,* for which she received an Edgar Award nomination and which was a *New York Times* "Notable Book of the Year." A longtime contributing editor of *New York Magazine,* her articles and essays—many of which discuss sexual research, therapy and behavior—have also appeared in the *New York Times, Vanity Fair, Playboy,* and other publications. She is also the author of the highly regarded 1981 book *The Cosmo Report,* an analysis of a detailed sex survey of 106,000 women sponsored by *Cosmopolitan* magazine.

JONATHAN GATHORNE-HARDY served as a consultant during the filming of the motion picture *Kinsey.* In addition to *Kinsey: Sex the Measure of All Things,* he is the author of *The Rise and Fall of the British Nanny* and *The Public School Phenomenon.* He has also written a biography of Gerald Brenan, *The Interior Castle.*

Acknowledgments of Permissions

We are grateful to the publishers and copyright holders named below for permission to reprint artwork and excerpts from these previously published works. Excerpts and artwork appear on the pages listed.

Special thanks to The Kinsey Institute for Research in Sex, Gender, and Reproduction, Inc. and the staff for their tremendous contribution to the archival materials in this book.

ARCHIVAL IMAGES: **16:** Photo by George Platt Lynes. © Copyright the Estate of George Platt Lynes. **19:** Photo by Keystone Features/Getty Images. **20:** Reproduced courtesy of The Kinsey Institute for Research in Sex, Gender, and Reproduction, Inc. (KI) **22 (top):** Photographer unknown. Courtesy of KI. **22 (bottom):** Photographer unknown. Courtesy of KI. **24:** Photographer unknown. Courtesy of KI. **27:** Photographer unknown. Courtesy of KI. **27:** Photographer unknown. Courtesy of KI. **28:** Photographer unknown. Courtesy of KI. **29:** Photographer unknown. Courtesy of KI. **32 (top):** Photographer unknown. Courtesy of KI. **32 (bottom):** Photographer unknown. Courtesy of KI. **36:** Photographer unknown. Courtesy of KI. **38:** Photographer unknown. Courtesy of KI. **40:** Photographer unknown. Courtesy of KI. **42:** Photographer unknown. Courtesy of KI. **44 (top):** Photo by the Kinsey Institute's staff photographer, William Dellenback. Courtesy of KI. **44 (bottom):** Photographer unknown. Courtesy of KI. **47:** Photographer unknown. Courtesy of KI. **49:** Photo by William Dellenback. Courtesy of KI. **50 (top):** Engraving by William Hogarth, 1736. Courtesy of KI. **50 (bottom):** Artist unknown. Courtesy of KI. **53:** Photographer unknown. Courtesy of KI. **54:** Artist unknown. Courtesy of KI. **55:** Photo by William Dellenback. Courtesy of KI. **56 (top left):** Photo by Arthur Siegel/Time Life Pictures/Getty Images. **56 (top right):** Photographer unknown. Courtesy of KI. **56 (bottom):** Photo by William Dellenback. Courtesy of KI. **59:** Unidentified comic. Courtesy of KI. **64:** Photo by Wallace Kirkland/Time Life Pictures/Getty Images. **65:** Photo by Loomis Dean/Time Life Pictures/Getty Images. **68:** Artist unknown. Courtesy of KI. **69:** Photo by William Dellenback. Courtesy of KI. **71:** Photo by William Dellenback. Courtesy of KI. **75:** Courtesy of *Playboy Magazine*. **76:** Photo by Leonard McCombe/Time Life Pictures/Getty Images. **77:** Photo by Hulton Archive/Getty Images. **79:** Photographer unknown. Courtesy of KI. **82:** Photo by Clarence Tripp. Courtesy of KI. **91:** Photo by David Weissman. Photo manipulation by David Gan. Courtesy of The Kinsey Sicks, America's Favorite Dragapella Beautyshop Quartet, www.kinseysicks.com. **92:** Photo by William Dellenback. Courtesy of KI. **97:** Photo by Museum of the City of New York/Getty Images. **102:** Photographer unknown. Courtesy of KI. **111:** Photo by Metronome/Getty Images. **112:** Photo by Arthur Siegel/Time Life Pictures/Getty Images. **118:** Photo by William Dellenback. Courtesy of KI. **121:** Photo by William Dellenback. Courtesy of KI. **122:** Photo by William Dellenback. Courtesy of KI. **127:** Photo by Loomis Dean/Time Life Pictures/Getty Images. **128-129:** From Oh! Dr. Kinsey! A Photographic Reaction to the Kinsey Report, by Lawrence Lariar, Cartwrite Publishing Co., New York, 1953. Courtesy of KI. **133:** TIME Magazine © 1953 Time Inc. Reprinted by permission. **140 (clockwise from top-left):** All courtesy of KI. Cartoon by Wesley Thompson; cartoon by John Adams, *Medical Economics,* October 1950; cartoon by Peter Arno, *The New Yorker,* September 26, 1953; and cartoon by Franklin Folger, *The Indianapolis Star,* September 25, 1954. **144:** Photographer unknown. Courtesy of

KI. **151 (top left):** Photo by Anonymous. Courtesy of KI. **151: (top right):** Untitled, 1939, by John Alexander Scott Coutts, a.k.a. John Willie. Courtesy of KI. **151 (bottom):** Photo by Anonymous. Courtesy of KI. **157:** Photographer unknown. Courtesy of KI. **162:** Photographer unknown. Courtesy of KI. **173:** Photographer unknown. Courtesy of KI. **346:** Photographer unknown. Courtesy of KI.

EXCERPTS:

20: By permission of Janice M. Epp, Ph.D. **25:** By permission of William Yarber. **30:** By permission of Ronald Moglia. **34:** By permission of The Reverend Debra W. Haffner. **34:** By permission of Milton Diamond. **39:** By permission of Stephanie A. Sanders. **43:** By permission of Pepper Schwartz. **46:** Courtesy of KI. **54:** By permission of Dr. Judy Kuriansky. **60:** By permission of David McWhirter. **63:** By permission of Vern L. Bullough. **72:** By permission of Andrew Mattison. **77:** By permission of David Fleming. **83:** From *The Fifties*, by David Halberstam, copyright © 1993 by The Amateurs Limited. Used by permission of Villard Boooks, a division of Random House, Inc. **85:** By permission of Esquire magazine. © The Hearst Corporation. Also, Esquire is a trademark of The Hearst Corporation. All Rights Reserved. **88:** From *The Journal of Sex Research*. **89:** From *The Archives of Sexual Behavior*. **90:** From *Redbook* magazine. **93:** By permission of Indiana University Press. **95:** From *Look* magazine. **100:** From *Redbook* magazine. **105:** From *Life* magazine, "Nourishing," by Fannie Hurst, August 24, 1953. **110:** From *U.S. News & World Report*. **111:** "Too Darn Hot," Words and Music by Cole Porter, ©1949 by Cole Porter. Copyright renewed, assigned to John F. Wharton, Trustee of the Cole Porter Music & Literary Property Trusts. Publication and Allied Rights Assigned to CHAPPELL & CO. Lyrics Reprinted with the permission of Warner Bros. Publications, Miami, FL. All Rights Reserved including Public Performance for Profit. **116:** From the 1998 introduction by John Bancroft to *Sexual Behavior in the Human Female*, by Alfred C. Kinsey, Wardell B. Pomeroy, Clyde E. Martin, and Paul H. Gebhard. Reprinted by permission of KI. **125:** From *St. Paul, MN, Pioneer Press*. **130:** From *The Michigan Catholic*. **131:** From *Sacramento, CA, Union*. **132:** Cover story © 1953 TIME Inc. Reprinted by permission. **134:** From *St. Petersburg, FL, Independent*. **136:** From *Salina, Kansas, Journal*. **137:** From *Detroit, MI, News*. **137:** From *Detroit, MI, News*. **138:** From *St. Paul Minnesota Dispatch*. **138:** From *St. Paul Minnesota Dispatch*. **139:** From *Raleigh, NC, News and Observer*. **145:** Reprinted with the permission of The Free Press, a Division of Simon & Schuster Adult Publishing Group, from *Taking a Sex History: Interviewing and Recording*, by Wardell B. Pomeroy, Carol C. Flax, Connie Christine Wheeler. Copyright © 1987 by Wardell B. Pomeroy, Carol C. Flax, and Connie Christine Wheeler. All rights reserved. **155:** From *The Journal of Sex Research*, Volume 35, no. 2, May 1994. **156:** Reprinted with the permission of The Free Press. See credit for page 145 for details. **161:** From *Christine Jorgensen: A Personal Story*, by Christine Jorgensen © 2003. By permission of Cleis Press. **164:** Reprinted with the permission of The Free Press. See credit for page 145 for details. **166:** From *The New Yorker*, "Talk of the Town," March 27, 1948. **168:** Reprinted with the permission of The Free Press. See credit for page 145 for details. **171:** By permission of Albert Ellis. **175:** Reprinted with the permission of The Free Press. See credit for page 145 for details.

The publisher has made every effort to contact copyright holders; any errors or omissions are inadvertent and will be corrected upon notice in future reprintings.

For Further Reading

Allyn, David, *Make Love, Not War: The Sexual Revolution : An Unfettered History,* Boston, 2000

Boyle, T. Coraghessan, *The Inner Circle,* New York, 2004

Gathorne-Hardy, Jonathan, *Kinsey: Sex the Measure of All Things,* Bloomington, Indiana, 2000

Goulden, Joseph C., *The Best Years 1945-1950,* New York, 1976

Halberstam, David, *The Fifties,* New York, 1953

Jones, James H., *Alfred C. Kinsey: A Public/Private Life,* New York 1997

Kinsey, Alfred C., S*exual Behavior in the Human Male,* Philadelphia, 1948

Kinsey, Alfred C., *Sexual Behavior in the Human Female,* Philadelphia, 1953

Pomeroy, Wardell B., *Dr. Kinsey and the Institute for Sex Research,* New York, 1972

Trilling, Lionel, *"The Kinsey Report,"* in *The Liberal Imagination,* New York, 1953

Wolfe, Linda, *The Cosmo Report,* New York,1981

Wolfe, Linda, *"Take Two Aspirins and Masturbate,"* *Playboy* magazine, June, 1974